IN THE REALM OF TONES

IN THE REALM OF TONES

A COMPOSER'S MEMOIR

Allen Shawn

UNIVERSITY OF ROCHESTER PRESS

First published 2025

University of Rochester Press
668 Mt. Hope Avenue, Rochester, NY 14620, USA
www.urpress.com
and Boydell & Brewer Limited
PO Box 9, Woodbridge, Suffolk IP12 3DF, UK
www.boydellandbrewer.com

Our Authorised Representative for product safety in the EU is Easy Access System Europe - Mustamäe tee 50, 10621 Tallinn, Estonia, gpsr. requests@easproject.com

ISBN-13: 978-1-64825-117-7

Library of Congress Cataloging-in-Publication Data
Names: Shawn, Allen, author.
Title: In the realm of tones : a composer's memoir / Allen
  Shawn.
Description: Rochester, New York : University of Rochester
  Press, 2025. | Includes bibliographical references and index.
Identifiers: LCCN 2024051378 (print) | LCCN 2024051379
  (ebook) | ISBN 9781648251177 (hardback) | ISBN
  9781805436478 (pdf) | ISBN 9781805436485 (epub)
Subjects: LCSH: Shawn, Allen. | Composers—United States—
  Biography.
Classification: LCC ML410.S514 A3 2025 (print) |
  LCC ML410.S514 (ebook) | DDC 780.92 [B]—dc23/
  eng/20241029
LC record available at https://lccn.loc.gov/2024051378
LC ebook record available at https://lccn.loc.gov/2024051379

A catalogue record for this title is available from the British Library.

for NOA

CONTENTS

Preface   ix

PART I

1   New York: My father at the piano and other early musical
     experiences (1948–1962)   3

2   Vermont: Putney and Weston, Vermont (1962–1966)   18

3   Cambridge, Massachusetts (1962–1966)   32

4   Paris: Nadia Boulanger (1970–1972)   47

5   New York: Teaching, playing the piano, composing,
     studying (1972–1974)   58

6   Columbia (1974–1977)   65

PART II

7   A varied working life and a marriage (1977–1983)   81

8   More theater and personal music; Visit to Bennington
     (1983–1985)   106

9   Bennington (1985–1988)   118

10   Darker music (1989–1992)   137

11   Upheavals (1993–1994)   148

12   A changed campus, eclectic pieces, rupture (1994–2001)   153

PART III

13   New life (2001–2007)   169

14   Consolidation and gratitude (2007–2019)   176

Appendix: List of Works by Allen Shawn   183
Biographical Glossary   189
Index   207

PREFACE

T HIS IS A BOOK primarily about making things.
Since the "things" in question are pieces of music—ephemeral and intangible constructions of rhythm and tone—it may seem reasonable to put the word "composer" in the title. But I was hesitant do so, since "Composer" is a pretty lofty term, a designation which needs to be earned and which can mean so many things. The word suggests something achieved, whereas this is a book more about process more than achievement, about having an obsession with composing, and trying to get better at it. Even though I am seventy-five years old, I still think of composing as something aspirational, and of myself as an aspiring composer.

Rather than a summary of my public life, of how others responded to my work, this is an account of how my musical life looked to me from the inside, an account of trying to write music while constructing a life around it. To a large extent, it is also about education and teaching and includes accounts of working as a pianist and as a writer of four previous books. If I sometimes write at length about compositions that remained incomplete, and I neglect others that may have been among my better ones, it is because I am trying to tell a story, a story of searching, finding, losing, attempting, failing, at times reaching; a story of becoming.

Although I have taught at a college for most of my adult life, I would not describe this book as academic. It includes many musical references and a lot of musical detail but is still intended for the general reader. I revere music scholarship and study, but I believe in a music that breaks through academic categories and affects human beings emotionally and on the deepest level, whether they have a musical background or not. I have tried to write in this spirit. My hope is that anyone might be able to see themselves in this book. I hope for those who find the musical references daunting to realize that these are not the main point of the story.

The book balances an account of my musical evolution, ups and downs, and life choices with glimpses into family life, the many people with whom I have interacted (including Leon Kirchner,

Earl Kim, Nadia Boulanger, Pierre Petit, Jacques-Louis Monod, J.D. Salinger, John Updike, Benny Goodman, Louis Malle, Vivian Fine, and others), and reflections on social class, aging, loneliness, politics, music education, and other issues.

I began life in a literary milieu in New York City and experienced a childhood of privilege and cultural richness. My father, William Shawn, was editor of *The New Yorker* magazine and a gifted amateur jazz pianist who had once hoped to be a professional composer. My mother, Cecille Lyon Shawn, had been a journalist and remained obsessed with politics and current events her entire life. We lived in a comfortable, if scruffy, apartment on Fifth Avenue, overlooking Central Park. My parents could be described as "liberal democrats." Our family dinner table conversations were dominated by discussions about "the news" and the arts.

Since my brother, Wally, is five years older than me and was passionately interested in theater, literature, movies, and music from his earliest years, he was an intellectual and artistic influence on me as far back as I can remember. Today he is a playwright, essayist, and actor.

The impact of having a twin sister, Mary, who was intellectually disabled and autistic—sharing my life at first alongside her, and then suddenly, at age eight, being separated from her—is something I have written about and am still grappling with.

The financial privilege of my childhood was temporary. Today I live in Vermont, the product of a fortunate upbringing, but self-sustaining and unsupported by inheritance, except for the cultural kind. However, I carry my childhood privilege in my being—surely there is no erasing it—and my life as an adult would not be what it has been without all of the advantages I experienced in early life, including my education.

I started composing at the age of ten. But this precocity actually prolonged my days as a student. The book begins with five chapters devoted to what would be called "apprenticeship" years, were composition a true "trade": my childhood, my studies at boarding school, at Harvard, in Paris, and at Columbia, culminating in the moment when I started to finally compose music that I thought was worth keeping. (I was nearly thirty.)

Chapters follow describing the years in New York when I was first married, in which I started to teach, worked in the theater and dance worlds, and composed music of great variety. Then there are chapters devoted to my early years of being a parent and moving to Vermont, of teaching at Bennington College, including an account of the upheaval there in 1994 and its repercussions, and of reaching a point of greater stability in my life and in my composing.

The final two chapters outline the past twenty-four years succinctly. This has been a period in which I feel that I have pulled together the various aspects of my art together to make the best pieces I am capable of, at least in this life. This has also been the time in which I have written my previous books. It could be that at a later date someone other than me might consider this last period of my work particularly rewarding to write about, but it is still too fresh in my memory for me to do so. I feel that in terms of the tale I wished to tell in this book, a story of "becoming," and of finding my identity as a composer, my narrative is complete, even though, as I suggest at the end of the book, continued life and further adventures may lie ahead.

My two previous "personal" books, *Wish I Could Be There* and *Twin*, required considerable research, since they combined memoir with information. In each I focused on aspects of my life I had an urgent need to understand better: in the first book, my crippling phobias, and in the second, my sister, Mary. In those books I attempted to be candid but also abstract, to make use of my own life to shed light on universal aspects of being human.

In both books, I avoided using people's names for the most part, to distinguish them from standard memoirs and maintain their focus on subjects rather than known individuals. As self-portraits and reminiscences, they emphasize the darker aspects of life, at the expense of other sides, and they emphasize psychology. As one reviewer noted, I wrote them almost as if I were my own doctor describing myself both from within and as a case I was studying. A psychological self-portrait is surely embedded in this book as well.

In this memoir, I do use names, and in a Biographical Glossary at the end of the book I identify those mentioned in the text who may not be familiar to the reader, including those referred to only by their initials. (My intention is to be discreet, but not coy.) In the Appendix, I list my major compositions, current as of 2024.

I never had the intention of being a writer. This memoir and my previous two are simply attempts to articulate things that have preoccupied me. In this one, I have tried not to repeat what I wrote before, hoping it might fit like a puzzle piece with other two. Yet, it also doesn't presume any familiarity with the previous books. *Wish I Could Be There* contained a portrait of my father, as seen from the angle of his home life and in terms of his own psychological struggles. *Twin* in some ways did the same thing for my mother, as well as for my sister. In all three books, I hinted at Wally's multifaceted nature, but I leave it to him to give a firsthand account of his own experiences, which I hope he will do some day.

A reader of my two previous memoirs may be surprised by the joy in life I express at times in this one. I myself was surprised as I wrote it by how wonderful so many of the experiences seemed in hindsight, even those that had been painful or disappointing at the time. In looking back, my sense of having been extraordinarily lucky to toil in the field of music at all, even to have the chance to experience the disappointments I did, far outstripped any lingering feelings of sadness or regret. The sadness I feel as I get older and imagine saying goodbye to the world and everything in it is about leaving behind the memories themselves, the people I have known, and all of the music.

PART I

1

NEW YORK: MY FATHER AT THE PIANO, AND OTHER EARLY MUSICAL EXPERIENCES (1948–1962)

THE FIRST TIME YOU see a beautiful view of the countryside, or you hear the sound of a piano, or your lips touch someone else's, the experience plants a little flag in your brain, establishes itself with a marker. Likewise, when you see a dead person for the first time, or you are slapped by a parent, or are humiliated by a teacher. Childhood is a sequence of such first times, receding all the way back to the innumerable firsts you don't remember—your first breaths, your first sounds.

But who can say why some of these stay with you forever, why some flags keep fluttering throughout your life?

Not long ago I was listening to Bartók's *Divertimento* for String Orchestra played by the Sage City Symphony, a community orchestra that performs on the campus of Bennington College in Vermont, where I teach. It was a Sunday afternoon program on a beautiful early fall day when the leaves were just beginning to turn. When the mysterious, dark, and brooding slow movement began, music that plunges the listener into the deepest regions of the psyche within its first few notes and stays there, I was transported to a moment sixty years ago when I was thirteen years old, sitting between my parents at a concert at New York City's 92nd Street Y, listening to Bartók's Sixth String Quartet. That happens to be a quartet in which each of the four movements begins with a version of the same slow, doleful, folk-tinged melody. Like the Divertimento, it just takes as a given that listeners want to explore their innermost selves, some kind of deeper truth. While the first three movements eventually become animated, sometimes wild and raucously dissonant, and explore other melodies and ideas, the last movement sticks with the tone and tempo of the folk lament. The final word in Bartók's Quartet cycle, the movement finally realizes the potential of its sorrowful initial melody, reaching a conclusion that is a kind of dying away. The depth, beauty, and frankness of this music, and the fact that it was being performed in public, taught me that music was a place in which you could speak about anything, even death.

After the concert, I told my parents that I wanted to be a composer.

I have no idea if my first attempts at composing sounded like they were "speaking" of anything in particular. They were far too rudimentary. But they came from a private place, not from the impulse to imitate any particular music or "style." In fact, music's abstraction and the fact that it was nonverbal was an essential part of its appeal. I certainly couldn't articulate this at the time and can barely do so now. But it was as if there was a packaging over everything in the world that covered a deeper reality. Composing was a process of uncovering it. I did give my little pieces titles, though, and one of the first was called *The Dying Accordion Player*.

I had been making up music for several years when I heard the Bartók, and had in fact already played and listened to music of all kinds. But it was the direct expressive speech of the Bartók, along with the galvanizing intensity and power of Stravinsky's *Le Sacre du printemps* (a piece I had only heard on recordings), that most forcefully aligned with my own temperament, and made me feel that music could be my voice too.

I also had a role model in my father. Although I may not have modeled my earliest "compositions" on anything in particular, the fact that I gravitated to the piano around age nine had everything to do with his nightly playing and the extraordinary impact it had on me. I remember sitting underneath the piano while he played his key-of-C jazz improvisations by ear, engulfed by the joyful reverberations of the piano's wooden soundboard above me. I was, perhaps, five years old. As important as the music was the fact that my father seemed happiest and freest when he played, rescued by his musical talent from his extreme shyness and the burdens of his job as editor-in-chief of *The New Yorker* magazine, free to reconnect with his younger self and to remember his time writing music for dance and for musicals when he was in his twenties. He was such a careful speaker of English, and so emotionally reined in, and he appeared to be weighed down by a kind of global empathy that absorbed everyone's tragedies, along with his own. But in music he would spring to life, relishing his own physicality and unfettered imagination.

It was his rendition of *Rhapsody in Blue* that made me start going to the piano myself at around age nine and attempting to mimic his distilled Gershwin. The phrases and passages I worked out led me to explore the keyboard further (and what Ives called "the cracks between the keys"), and to mine it for ideas and fragments I had not yet heard. Even then, while one couldn't call the results "compositions," there was something serious going on (from my child's point of view), a process of excavation, as if there was music hidden in the piano strings that wanted to be let out, and I was tasked with releasing it.

None of this initially had to do with a social impulse, and in fact combined somewhat awkwardly with one. While my father enjoyed playing the songs of Rodgers, Gershwin, Kern, Cole Porter, and Harold Arlen for family guests, I felt ashamed when I was asked to publicly share what had felt like a private activity. I was torn between an impulse to play what I had made up, and embarrassment at what it revealed about me.

The most obvious and humiliating revelation, of course, was that I was a child, and that my "music" was intuitive and untutored. I knew this perfectly well. Like all children, I had emotions and seriousness and desires that were fully mature, however childishly expressed. And no matter how lighthearted or amusing the tone of my musical attempts may have seemed, there was a soberness behind them, a striving to build a meaningful sound-expression that was not amusing to me at all. And the imperfection of the results made me ashamed.

But there was another source of shame—something stemming from the non-social aspect of the art. Ephemeral, stirring, and provocative, music by its very nature seemed to undermine the civility and rationality that permeated my parents' household and my father's work at *The New Yorker*—which seemed to hold precision of thought and excellence of grammar as foundational. The domain of music seemed subversive of what I perceived to be the adult expectation that I "make sense" at all times, not be ruled by feelings, and uphold the agreed-upon myth that life itself made sense. And smitten as I was by the music I heard, I was equally in love with the vibrations and pulses that music harnessed and wanted to mold them to my own ends.

Anyone who has read my previous books knows that I grew up with an older brother, Wally, and a twin sister, Mary, who was first considered "slow," then "brain damaged," then "retarded," and eventually "intellectually disabled and autistic." At age eight, she was sent to a summer camp for disturbed children in Chatham, Massachusetts. This turned into a year-round institution in the fall, and she remained there. Perhaps the summer camp had always been planned as a trial run. Ten years later, she was moved to a large institution in Maryland where she still lives.

As her twin, and as a child myself, I was not prepared for her seeming banishment from our family, and the silence surrounding it was devastating and baffling. It is tempting to think that I eventually tried to fill the silence with music, but that sounds terribly simplistic.

Mary's femaleness, her mysteriousness, her ability to focus on small things for hours at a time, her volatility, her serenity, her beauty, her needs, her separateness, her singing, her screaming— the tenderness, concern, dread, and anguish she evoked in different ways in each of my parents—these and many other things were central to my first eight years. No matter what was done to make me feel that I was different from her, my own nature was formed in counterpoint to hers. Cut off as she seemed, unable as she was to adapt to normal schools or to conventional expectations, she still had some words with which to express herself, penetrating brown eyes that conveyed her feelings, and the ability to reach out or push you away. In her way, she communicated strongly, and she was an inseparable part of our family's life. However different she was from what was considered the norm, she was complete. She was a part of me, and originally quite literally all I knew. After age eight, her absence, which was barely acknowledged, did not change this, but covered it over. Since then, each time I think of our closeness, even now, I experience a shock.

Before age eight, along with my father's playing, are scattered other first impressions of music: excitement about drumming— Gene Krupa, Buddy Rich, and Joe Morello (whom we heard live); begging to be allowed to stay up late and hear Elvis perform "Blue

Suede Shoes" and "You Ain't Nothin' but a Hound Dog" on *The Ed Sullivan Show*; the glittering sounds of Stravinsky's *Petrushka* emanating from old 78s. But after age eight, I was hit by music in a new way. I had a sudden rush of illumination hearing the music of *Swan Lake* at the City Center. It wasn't just that the music "spoke" to me, it inhabited me.

Quite early, I had played along with my father on a child's tom-tom, gradually progressing to snare, hi-hat, and cymbal. I played recorder and later clarinet. School assemblies included folksongs sung by two hundred children, with Elizabeth Smith playing the piano. Eventually, I sang in the choir that marched up the aisle at Christmas pageants singing carols. But if there is such a thing as being "musical," I am not sure that my musicality manifested itself in these venues.

Even as I strove to learn to read music and repeatedly asked for piano lessons, I was already dimly aware that the orderly chord progressions and romantic associations of a Rodgers song resulted from an impulse somewhat distinct from what drew me to Bartók and Stravinsky and the modern music I had heard. I wanted to make things. For me, it was not so much a specific musical grammar that I needed to learn but rather more about musical materials, so that I could reshape them into structures, find out who I was and what I wanted to say by using them. This felt at odds with the idea of entertaining civilized people who were coming over for dinner.

Finally, at age twelve, I had a piano teacher. In my first meeting with Frances Dillon at the Mannes School of Music, she reassured me that learning to read music in two clefs would not take me long at all. (I was still writing note names on a pad when I composed, sometimes with exclamation marks when I found a combination of pitches particularly exciting.) Reading notation seemed a gigantic hurdle to be leapt over—something like the challenge of learning to swallow a pill without thinking about it. (My mother still mashed up aspirins in sweetened apple sauce for me when I had a fever.) I felt that the way forward in notation was barred by an obstruction.

But Miss Dillon was right. I don't even remember the process of learning. The hurdle simply vanished and reading became second nature. (The same thing happened eventually with swallowing a pill.) I had already figured out that when I was listening to the piano I always knew whether white keys or black keys were being struck, but Miss Dillon thought that I had perfect pitch. I was not convinced of this. I just thought that I was usually right. The notational fluency I gained by taking piano was supplemented by the music classes at Dalton, the progressive private school I attended from age three to thirteen, where we learned to identify intervals and basic triads, and even did a little dictation.

In my first years studying with her, I learned music by Beethoven, Bach, Chopin, and Bartók (the exceptional Three *Rondos*), along with Schoenberg's *Sechs Kleine Klavierstücke*, op. 19. Miss Dillon seemed to accept the fact that I wanted to learn piano not because I dreamt of becoming a pianist, but because I wanted to write music. She encouraged my improvising and listened to my pieces when I brought them to her. She was more focused on demonstrating legato playing, phrasing, and the depth of sound that comes all the way from your back through your arms when you play than she was on virtuosity. She had fleshy, rounded hands, and she would put my hands on her wrists as she played, to demonstrate how to achieve suppleness in phrasing and a weighty, deeper connection to the keyboard. I remember the freckles on her hand surface, and the cushiony pouch made by the muscles next to her thumb. Besides what happened through the arms and hands themselves, her motions at the instrument were minimal. She remained rooted and comfortable and calm, coaxing and enabling the richness of the piano sound to emerge, showing no visible effort. She achieved even the loudest forte in this way, and it was never harsh. I can still hear the deep singing tone of her A flat major slow movement from Beethoven's *Sonata Pathétique*, or the Bach Chorale Prelude, as transcribed by Busoni, that she demonstrated for me, which she had played to herself when the news of FDR's death came on the radio in April of 1945.

Although she never made suggestions about what I should write, and may have secretly hoped that I would someday focus seriously on becoming a pianist rather than a composer, Miss Dillon was my first composition teacher. It was she who explained in detail how the fugues I was playing were put together, who talked about how Bach, Beethoven, Bartók, and Schoenberg created such different-sounding music out of the same twelve pitches, who gave me the exercise of writing down as many ways of harmonizing one note as I could think of. Her assignments placed my fingers at the borderline between the tonal and non-tonal, and made me wonder what makes us know which territory we are in. The first six notes of Schoenberg's op. 19 contain the first five of Bach's *The Musical*

Offering. In his third "little piece," an A flat major melody in the left hand, marked *piano,* is pitted against dissonant chords entirely foreign to that key, played *forte,* in the right. Miss Dillon's handwriting over the left-hand in my copy drew attention to the tune's resemblance to the spiritual "Nobody Knows the Trouble I've Seen."

Her conception of teaching was holistic, uniting the visceral, emotional, and intellectual; it linked playing, improvising, and composing into a kind of circular whole. Left-leaning, an early feminist, and socially more bohemian than my parents were, she was an expert on composer-pianist Franz Liszt (she had edited a collection of his late experimental piano works) and collected and annotated concert pianist Amy Fay's writings about her European musical studies in the early nineteenth century. I was fortunate to have her in my life and on my side at this age. She mentioned knowing that there were days when I would lie on the bathroom floor suffering from stomachaches, and she was clearly aware that there was some pain in our lucky family, but she didn't dwell on it. She also did not exaggerate my talents.

From time to time, my mother worried out loud about Miss Dillon's influence. Her outspoken personality, her questioning of America's foreign policy at the outset of our involvement in Vietnam, her pride in me, and our long lessons—including some at her apartment, in which she walked dramatically around the living room dressed in her Chinese silk robe—stirred a bit of maternal suspicion and competition.

There were other undercurrents. Although, like Miss Dillon, my mother came from a humble Jewish background, she carried herself like an aristocrat. For my part, what I felt was Miss Dillon's unconditional support and faith in my musical instincts. This faith freed me from the kind of unhealthy focus on performance perfection that plagues many students of classical music and made it possible for me to play for her college pedagogy students without being crippled by anxiety. I remember with happiness our classroom performances at two pianos of the Bach D Minor Concerto, the Haydn D Major Concerto, and the Schumann A Minor Concerto, none of which I would have had any business performing in public, but which made these works a part of me at an early age. I performed the Chopin Prelude in B Minor, the Schoenberg and the Bartók and the beautiful Prokofiev Sonata no. 2 in D Minor, and, at the age of thirteen, the Sonata op. 1 by Alban Berg. I had heard this performed by one of Miss Dillon's older students and begged to be allowed to learn it. To her credit, she allowed it. I particularly related to the Berg and memorized it easily.

Now able to notate fluently, I composed much more music than I had previously, including a miniature "Piece for Miss Dillon," no more than twelve bars long, that suggested the aphoristic atonality of *Sechs Kleine Klavierstücke*. The next time my parents asked me to play for their friends, I performed it, eliciting a casual comment from my mother—"Very modern, dear"—that somehow stung. Not for the last time, I felt the tension between the private need to communicate something in sound and the public response. The idiom of the piece wasn't a choice, like a shirt or a tie. I hadn't chosen to sound modern. Style is involuntary, I thought, like a face.

Of course, it didn't occur to me at the time that it was the title that might have disturbed her.

My early musical attempts included many violin and piano pieces for Wally, who was already deeply immersed in short-story writing. Although his writing style was more ornate than it later became, somehow the tone and frankness of his mature plays were already there. "Loping Dogs and the Tiles of Time" was a favorite of mine. As I remember them, his characters were often solitary and tormented, living in squalor, just like the characters in his plays often are. There was a natural relationship between playing music for violin and piano and composing it, and my duets reflected the informality of the performance venue, which was our parents' living room.

While there was ambition in these pieces—I wrote a number of cyclical suites comprising multiple movements in a variety of moods and meters, with themes that would recur and outline a larger form—I don't remember ever thinking that these pieces would last or be played in the future. But they had a poetic quality, a sense of continuity and textural variety, with enough moments of counterpoint to maintain the flow. In hindsight, I would place their language within the world of mid-century modern tonality as exemplified by Ernest Bloch, Paul Hindemith, and American composers Walter Piston, William Schuman, and Vincent Persichetti. My melodies were often modal, and the harmonies favored fourths, fifths, sevenths, and ninths. Dominant to tonic cadences were outside of the style. Tonal home-base was more likely to be a minor seventh chord or an added sixth chord than a triad. Although lacking the tools to achieve anything comparable, except in perhaps one harmony or detail, I identified with the concentration and emotion achieved in the Bartók and Berg I so loved playing. Prokofiev was certainly in my thoughts, too, at least after hearing Sviatoslav Richter's stunning concerts at Carnegie Hall with my parents in 1960, one of which was an all-Prokofiev program. And jazz of various kinds was definitely in the picture.

In the summertime, my parents rented a house that belonged to Robert Saudek of the CBS network in Bronxville, New York. (We were apparently the first Jewish residents there.) CBS's connection to the Columbia Records of that era meant that Saudek's shelves were filled with extraordinary recordings of modern music. So it was in Bronxville that I first heard works by Carter and Barber, and Piston's Fourth Symphony, with its beautiful first theme. When I first heard Elliott Carter's *Elegy* for String Orchestra and Samuel Barber's Piano Concerto, I felt the electricity of encountering the idiom I aspired to in its mature form. I remember the opening of Ives's *Robert Browning Overture*, and Elliott Carter's First String Quartet. They seemed beyond simply exciting, or even beautiful, although they were that. It was as if they had captured some essence of how it felt to be alive and conveyed it in tones. In Bronxville, at age thirteen, I listened to *Le Sacre du printemps* with Miss Dillon, who was about to leave for Europe to pursue her studies of Amy Fay. She gave me the score of the piece as a present. Her inscription cautioned me that becoming a composer could take a long time:

To my dear pupil,
Allen
for his Birthday
This Thirteenth year will be
A most memorable one. I
shall be back, happily, to resume
teaching and learning with you.
(Remember this, Allen, dear,
Stravinsky wrote this score when
He was 31 years (an inverted interval
Of your age) much older than you. Nevertheless
a great inspiration for years to come.
Ever yours,
Affectionately,
Frances Dillon
Aug. 25, 1961

At a summer day camp, I wrote a composition for wind band that surprised my father, who couldn't believe that I knew how to write such tricky rhythms or to transpose all the wind instruments correctly.

As some readers will know from my previous books and elsewhere, our family led a protected existence, at least in part because of my father's romantic relationship with a *New Yorker* writer, Lillian Ross, who lived only ten blocks away. That his alternate family life could be kept secret from my brother and me until as late as 1979, when I was thirty-one years old and my brother over thirty-five, was due in part to a code of silence on the part of the restricted circle of my parents' friends who visited us regularly. These included Edith Oliver, Joan and Olivia Kahn, Philip and Edith Hamburger, Bruce and Naomi Bliven, Janet Flanner, Ved Mehta, and others—an extraordinarily eccentric literary group, all of whom were indebted to my father in one way or another and devoted equally to both of my parents.

It was for this group that my brother and I began performing our yearly puppet shows every Christmas night starting as early as 1958, when I was ten years old. This lent an unacknowledged tension to the performances, since already as a young teenager Wally saw writing as an opportunity to broach complex emotional subjects, undermine the complacency of privileged "bourgeois life," and expose hypocrisies. As the younger brother (at that point, there was a three-to-two ratio differential in our ages), I was Wally's "employee," enlisted to play my assigned roles, including most of the females, and, as I became more fluent as a composer, to provide the incidental music and music for songs.

The ten days before Christmas were always exciting periods of creative ferment, beginning with our collaboratively developing the concept behind the show, co-constructing the sets, and then pursuing our parallel duties as writer and composer. Along with his writing talent, Wally had a particular gift for design and lighting. As my skills improved, the music became increasingly notated, while always leaving room for improvisation and even lengthy extemporizing in the event of technical difficulties with sets and lights. I found a flair for setting his lyrics in an idiom that was tonal, tuneful, and sometimes jazzy—evocative of musical theatre, without exactly being that. The work was undertaken in all seriousness, yet it was not preserved. (As far as I know, none of the materials for these shows still exist.)

But however lighthearted, the puppet shows must have frequently touched a family nerve or two, particularly since they were performed for an audience of people who knew things about our parents we did not. For example, the plot of *Fins and Feet* concerned a psychiatrist who had a secret life in the ocean consorting with dolphins and whose brother was a career criminal.

Our first puppet show was based on the fairy tale, Rapunzel, but the plots and settings evolved as Wally's interests did, eventually embracing subjects as arcane and abstract as Horace's *Odes*. We produced a four-hour version of Milton's *Paradise Lost* in a rare summer presentation, and I can still recall the thrill of enacting the part of Satan and reciting the narrator's lines describing Hell ("yet from those flames, no light, but rather darkness visible"). I remember some rather Handelian phrases from the music I wrote to accompany Adam and Eve's expulsion from the Garden of Eden. In one of many nonmusicalized ventures, Wally also had me learn the role of Clov in Samuel Beckett's *Endgame*, which we rehearsed earnestly and in costume, without the intention of performing it for an audience.

My improvisational and theatre sides also flourished at school and during the summers. In between classes, I tended to play spontaneously and at length on any available piano, and I was not self-conscious or even particularly aware if peers sat down to listen. In the summers, I studied with an innovative piano teacher named Emilie Harris at her house in New Rochelle, New York. Her lessons have left memories of warm sunshine and greenery viewed through the screened windows next to her piano in the living room; of her husband's chocolate milkshakes; of her particular affinity for teaching Bach (or "Mr. Bach," as she called him); and most of all of her allowing me to record my half-notated, half-improvised pieces, some including singing, on her tape recorder. She also gave me lessons in species counterpoint.

I remember both the uplift and the disorientation of first performing some of my short piano pieces in a Dalton School assembly, around the age of twelve. Psychologists speak of "self-states." If I close my eyes, I can almost reenter the self-state of that first performing experience—the sense of being there at the piano, but also being separate, of becoming somehow larger than just a person.

Music only exists when it is being played. Performing has something of a séance about it. When your hands are at the keyboard and your fingers make contact, you lose any sense that there is a distinction between your inner self, the will that causes your hands to move, the elaborate chain of mechanisms that connect the keys to the strings, and the sounds that ring out from them. You become a listener to the music that is happening as a result of your own actions, music which you must also shape. On the one hand, you are addressing those in the room, and you mean what you are saying. On the other hand, you are playing to wherever sounds go—beyond the room, simply outward and upward. Music locates you where you are, but also questions where you are. There is awe in being at the center of it.

There was no denying the thrill of the applause. When I imagined some of the girls in the audience who might be clapping for me, my entire body seemed to tingle with ecstasy and the promise of bliss. Yet, I also felt painfully self-conscious. A part of me was proud. Another part found the applause unearned. After all, these were only musical fragments I had tinkered with on my parents' piano.

Dalton in those years was a heady environment presided over by a cross-section of idealistic, left-leaning New York intellectuals and artists who needed work, among them musicians Channing Robbins, his sister Rena Robbins, LaNoue Davenport (of the New York Pro Musica), conductor Harold Aks, John Seeger (son of modern music theorist Charles Seeger, stepson of Ruth Crawford Seeger, and brother of Pete Seeger), Peter Buttenwieser, Gus Trowbridge (who later founded Manhattan Country School), abstract expressionist Gwen Davies, and the unforgettable Emily Alford ("Alfie"). Alfie's brilliance and crusty candor simultaneously cut through our childhood prevarications and inspired us to intellectual heights.

It was Alfie who asked me to perform the role of Ariel in *The Tempest* in seventh grade, as well as to compose incidental music for it that I could sing and play myself. Her casting of my childhood friend Jay Hamburger as Caliban, and of tall and studious Jonathan Levi as Prospero, was inspired. Setting the Shakespeare songs to music, and writing recorder tunes and short piano interludes, proved a shrewd composition assignment for me.

In 2020, my friend Hank (Henry) Chapin could still remember the melody to my setting of "Full Fathom Five" from start to finish, and he sang it for me. Hank's musical memory astonished me. I was also surprised that the prosody of the song was respectable, and the tune was credibly Elizabethan in sound, straddling major and minor in a poignant way.

By the end of my middle school years, I had already heard pieces by Varèse, Ives, Cowell, Cage, Schoenberg, Berg, Webern, and the then brand-new "late" works of Stravinsky, along with music by any number of lesser-known contemporary composers. I soaked it all up avidly, with minimal awareness of the fierce battles being fought between various musical factions at the time.

Occasionally, some of the musical issues of the day would break through. I remember Schuyler Chapin, Hank's father, pronouncing that with his adoption of "serialism" Stravinsky had "gone from being one of the most important living composers to being one of the least important." I also remember my shock when Uncle Mike—a saxophonist and composer of advertising jingles—said that music had ended when composers stopped writing tonally, that the newer composers were insincere and mocking their audience: "After Prokofiev, all of the later composers are just pulling your leg."

In eighth grade, Channing Robbins suggested I compose a piece for the school orchestra. I produced sketches exploring spiky rhythms, extreme dissonance, and some free atonality. He seemed very excited by these ideas, but he had to advise me to write to the abilities and skills of the performers at hand, none of whom were over thirteen years old.

I decided to refashion a set of piano variations I had written called *Older Brother* into a miniature piano concerto. This put a teasing theme initially played by two clarinets (as in the opening of Prokofiev's Piano Concerto no. 3) through various moods and tempi, from lyrical to tempestuous, and included a variation in which I played on the inside of the piano on the lower strings using timpani mallets, evoking a jazz bass solo.

At around this age, I became aware that my parents were more supportive of my musical abstractions than they were of what Wally was expressing in words. In fact, I bristled at their wonderment at what I was writing, as if it had something miraculous about it, rather than that it took hard work, and was in that respect no different from what Wally was doing. I dimly perceived that the "miracle" of my composing might seem to them to be some kind of compensation for the misfortune that had descended so inexplicably on my sister Mary. In my peripheral vision, I also glimpsed that considerations of musical "style" carried social, political, and psychological implications, and I wondered if my "abstractions" would meet with approval if they went in the direction of the wild atonality I had showed to Channing Robbins.

Once when I was listening to Berg's *Wozzeck* in the living room, my father became visibly upset by the music and quickly left the room.

While he continued his nightly piano playing, and even took us to jazz clubs to hear such giants as Thelonious Monk, Charlie Mingus, and Duke Ellington, there was tension at home around my interest in jazz. Miss Dillon herself encouraged me to listen to Art Tatum to appreciate his pianism and hear how he approached Chopin. Yet, jazz performance and theory were not taught at Mannes. I adored big-band jazz, and I played Ray Charles's recording of "Let the Good Times Roll" at top volume, much to my mother's chagrin. She eventually made it a rule that jazz should only constitute one fifth of my listening. This was echoed later by the rules at the Putney School, which I attended between 1963 and 1966, where jazz or rock music could only be listened to in the "jazz room," a humble shack, not in the classy, newly built music wing.

It was only fifty years later that I began to understand the full implications of the "otherizing" of jazz in American music education.

The impact of sitting near Monk in a smoke-filled club (either the Five Spot or the Half Note) was indelible. Every note was so interesting, and lyrical in a hard-edged way. While his left hand hinted at a conventional bass line, his right jabbed at interval combinations and melodic fragments that had an angular poignancy. Monk's eccentric fingering generated arpeggios I had never heard before.

On the night we heard Charlie Mingus's beautiful compositions, he interrupted his playing to rail against society and those of us in the audience. I don't remember the content of what he said apart from hearing him scornfully refer to "white people."

My mini-piano concerto, *Older Brother*, was followed by further forays into orchestral writing during the four summers I attended Kinhaven Music Camp in Weston, Vermont. In my first orchestral piece for Kinhaven, perhaps influenced by Leonard Bernstein's inaugural recording of Ives's Second Symphony, which we had listened to as a family, I felt emboldened to be humorous and raucous, use musical quotations, and create a tone poem drawn from my own experience.

Overture to a Ball Game, which I conducted myself, charted the course of a baseball game. Baseball was my favorite sport, and the only one I could actually play decently. (I kept a scrapbook devoted entirely to Willie Mays, whom I continued to follow even after the Giants moved to San Francisco.) I remember the fun of using fragments of the song "Take Me Out to the Ball Game" as musical motives, deploying the wood block to evoke the sound of a bat, creating orchestral textures suggestive of a ball ascending into the sky, with a crowd murmuring in anticipation and then roaring in excitement when the ball was caught. I also tried to evoke the moments of waiting and beautiful boredom when there are men on base and the manager comes out of the dugout to talk to the pitcher and catcher.

But the trick was to do these things within a convincing musical structure, and it was structure and harmony that fascinated me perhaps most of all about music.

2

VERMONT: PUTNEY AND WESTON, VERMONT (1962–1966)

FOLLOWING AN UNHAPPY YEAR at the Friends Seminary School on 14th Street, I followed my brother's path to the progressive and artistically minded Putney School in Putney, Vermont. In a sense, I had already been influenced by their remarkable music teacher, Norwood Hinkle, through Wally. He had introduced me to Bach's B Minor Mass, *Christmas Oratorio*, *St Matthew Passion*, and several cantatas, along with the late quartets of Beethoven, works which we regularly listened to while following the scores. These pieces—particularly the *St Matthew Passion* and the Beethoven quartets—became personal touchstones for me, and their beauties have never faded.

At Putney, all of the students learned to read music and sang together on Friday nights, and everyone took Music I, in which traditional classical forms were studied and a standard history of Western classical music was outlined. The excellent, enthusiastic, and plain-spoken form summaries of Donald Tovey were read by every Putney student. Norwood was a great musician who poured the intensity and depth of a Szell or Klemperer into conducting his teenage orchestra and chorus, sometimes achieving astonishing results.

With my questionable clarinet playing, I participated in Beethoven's eighth Symphony, Haydn's "The Clock" and Symphony no. 104, Mozart's 40th Symphony, and pieces by Ralph Vaughan Williams, among many other things. I also got to play the piano part in the delightful Concerto Grosso by Ernest Bloch.

In the chorus, we performed music by Vittoria, Byrd, Randall Thompson, much of the B Minor Mass, Handel's *Messiah*, parts of the Mozart Requiem, Brahms's *Schicksalslied*, "How Lovely Is Thy Dwelling Place" from the German Requiem, and *Liebeslieder-Walzer*.

Norwood was a moody and sometimes irascible musical mentor with a sly sense of humor, who moved with grace and sported a wardrobe of sweaters, crisply pressed slacks, and comfortable shoes that had real style. A youthful accident had left him blind in one eye. The mystery of this impairment, however well concealed by its glass replacement, somehow suggested a deeper injury. Sometimes his frustration would boil over. He would chastise us for our tardiness, lack of practice and commitment, or for not bringing our full teenage energies to our playing and singing. Once, he bitterly paraphrased a line from *Moby Dick*: "The older I get, the less I want to have to do with anything that looks like death."

Every student at Putney sang madrigals by Gibbons, Morley, Weelkes, and other Renaissance composers, and we all knew Wilbye's "Adieu, Sweet Amaryllis," and Gibbons's "The Silver Swan." Purcell's "In These Delightful Pleasant Groves" was practically the school anthem. A healthy respect for American and European folk music was in the air, too, and the music history course valuably underscored the connections between folk traditions and those of the concert hall.

For Norwood, music was a religion and the highest thing in life, and his devotion to Bach and the symphonies of Brahms rubbed off on most of us. He communicated the power and joy of the music with all sincerity and humility. We did a lot of listening in class. I remember the way he threw his hat in the air during the ecstatic coda of the finale of Beethoven's *Eroica*, beaming and shouting, "Hooray for heroes!"

Norwood was suspicious of showing off or stardom of any kind. He had been in Walter Piston's harmony class alongside a young Leonard Bernstein. "Lennie used to play jazz at the piano until he heard Piston coming down the hall," he told me, "and then he would quickly run to his seat."

Bernstein was not his favorite type of person. He was even somewhat skeptical of the idea that new music needed to be written at all, that there was anything to add to the storehouse of works left to us by the great composers of the past. The music history course went past Debussy and reached *Petrushka* but became sketchy after that. In orchestra, we played Holst, Hindemith, and Copland's *An Outdoor Overture*, but when the Juilliard String Quartet was planning to come and to include Webern's *Six Bagatelles*, op. 9 in its program, Norwood introduced the piece to us in class uneasily.

Nevertheless, like my piano teachers, he encouraged me. Despite his skepticism about new music, he allowed me to compose a piano sonata as a winter project in December 1963. It was just a month after President Kennedy had been assassinated, and like many of my friends I was still shaken and shocked. I wrote music that sounded like tolling bells. I knew that it was not a good piece.

Norwood tolerated my clarinet playing to the extent that he let me play both the Mozart and Brahms clarinet quintets with fellow students in special weekend camping trips during which we pursued projects of interest. It would be difficult to think of more beautiful pieces than either of these. It was fascinating to switch from "B flat" to "A" clarinet—with its darker, more covered sound. He applauded when I performed Mozart's B flat major Piano Sonata at a Sunday night meeting in which silence after music was expected. Most surprisingly, he asked me to perform the Mozart C Minor Concerto, k. 491, with the school orchestra, despite his belief that music is communal and should not draw attention to anyone.

Preparing the Mozart meant practicing four hours a day, making extra trips to New York to work with Miss Dillon, choosing a cadenza (Hummel?), and memorizing the music. I bonded with the modernity of this work. As those who know the piece are aware, the outer movements are stark and fatalistic sounding. The last movement is a stern march with variations that ends on a note of harried distress. There, and from the outset, Mozart's themes emphasize the notes and harmonies in the key that are most in tension with it. In the opening movement, the piano's first entrance is extraordinarily spare and expressive; a sensitive operatic right hand is accompanied by a few minimal harmonic pulsations in the left. Having stayed within a vocal ambit in the first phrase, the second statement in the piano includes unvocal leaps of a 12th, a diminished 14th, and a minor 13th, creating a sense of vast space that the strings then fill in. Playing the serene E flat major slow movement, in which the piano part sings like a clarinet or mezzo soprano in dialogue with exquisite wind writing, was a lesson in cantabile piano playing and tone.

Being at the center of the orchestral sound, knowing the entire score by heart—and not just the piano part—changed my understanding of what music is and what music-making is. It was a composition lesson.

Unexpectedly, I received a very kind note the day after the performance from Felix Lederer, a teacher who, like Norwood, praised very rarely. He wrote simply, "The Mozart was <u>beautiful</u>." Felix was an excellent, strict but benevolent Latin teacher. German-born, although actually, it turns out, part-Czech in ancestry, he was as precise in his expectations of his students as he was in his dress and in his ornate, even handwriting. He was so orderly that he even announced when he was about to make a joke.

Although he frequently mentioned that "Felix" means "happy," his good mood struck me as buttressed by will. I don't remember ever seeing him relaxed. Like Norwood, he had something haunted about him. I knew that he seemed very knowledgeable about music, but only learned after his death that he in fact had a doctorate in musicology and extensive acquaintance with contemporary music, including with the music of the Second Viennese School that eventually came to interest me so much. Apparently, he kept his musical erudition a secret at least in part because his views of music differed from Norwood's, and he didn't want to intrude on his colleague's territory. I know now that Felix's father was a distinguished Jewish conductor who only narrowly escaped being taken to Auschwitz through the intervention of Wilhelm Furtwängler. His brother, a book designer and professor of art, survived the camps. Felix and his Italian wife Marissa were in a way permanently in hiding in Vermont, still devastated by the war years. Marissa's terror of airplanes also contributed to their isolation.

Around this same time, I wrote a piece for clarinet, viola, and cello that was choreographed and performed by my beautiful and gracious friend Karen Roeper. It was such fun to perform it offstage with Frank Morris and Steve Hinkle (Norwood's son), as Karen moved through space. I can still remember the opening measure, but not the rest. After hearing it, Felix came up to me to say, "It reminds me of David Diamond or so."

In Summers at Kinhaven, my musical world continued to expand. We performed a new Bach cantata every summer under the direction of Dorothy Dushkin, wife of David. I got to sing in

Hindemith's *In Praise of Music*, to play clarinet in woodwind quintets by Persichetti, Irving Fine, and Darius Milhaud (*La Cheminée du Roi René*), to play piano in Trios by Beethoven and in the Horn Trio by Brahms, and to have a lesson in conducting the orchestra in Beethoven's "Egmont" Overture.

In his tent, on a little portable phonograph, my camp-mate Jonathan Fast introduced me to Schoenberg's moody *Begleitungsmusik zu einer Lichtspielszene* (*Accompaniment to a Film Scene*) and explained something of its method. Jonathan's own composition, *Variations on a Hexachord*, which he conducted, was probably the first piece by a fellow young composer that I had ever heard, further piquing my interest in the twelve-tone method.

He also orchestrated some of Stravinsky's delightful "Easy Pieces" for piano duet. I knew nothing then of the factions that had divided the contemporary music scene between adherents of Stravinsky and Schoenberg in the early part of the century. One day, I excitedly glimpsed Samuel Dushkin, David's brother, coming to visit—Stravinsky's partner in concert tours, and the first performer of the Violin Concerto in D, and the *Duo Concertant*!

Overture to a Ball Game was followed in successive summers by Rondo, Fantasy, and Essay for Orchestra, all of them, like *Overture*, pieces that compressed multimovement symphonic structures (or impressions thereof) into one movement. I remember the feeling of carrying these structures around in my head, and the satisfaction of thinking of them as totalities that contained and reconciled contradictory moods and states of mind.

The pieces always had an essentially songful lyricism and emotionality at their core, but I particularly exulted in moments of modal counterpoint—sometimes at slow tempos, sometimes at a faster tempo conveying tension and excitement. I had fallen in love with the fast-tempo anguish so characteristic of Mozart in the 40th Symphony and other works, as well as at the end of Bartók's Concerto for Orchestra, and, of course, in *Le Sacre*. Although I had started by making up my pieces at the piano, I now often sketched them out away from the instrument, or, in the summertime, outside, sitting under a tree. Sometimes this led to mistakes in hearing or transposition, errors which Mr. Dushkin, director of the camp, called "crudities."

As I have written elsewhere, I was not a comfortable performer, at least not when conducting my own pieces. The journey of taking the music from the inside to the outside was mimicked by an annual cycle of illness and recovery, my succumbing to a feverish flu after completing a piece and recuperating just in time to mount the podium to rehearse and conduct it. It was as if I didn't want to be there when the piece was played.

As in my earliest performances, I both basked in the excitement of being applauded and recoiled from it. On the occasions when my parents were present, their pride and emotion about my music disturbed me. Although of course I savored it, too, there was something about being made to feel special and loved to that degree that felt false and even alarming.

A visitor at several of these occasions was the writer J.D. Salinger, who lived in a Vermont town not too far away from Weston, where Kinhaven was. At that time, "Jerry" and my father were close friends, probably as close as they ever got to be. Having published *Seymour: An Introduction* in 1959, Salinger was working on what turned out to be his last published story, "Hapworth 16, 1924," which appeared in *The New Yorker* of June 19, 1965.

One of my father's ways of communicating regularly with me when I was away was to send me the current issue of the magazine, and to write me a few words on 5 x 7 red *New Yorker* note paper clipped to the front cover. When this particular issue arrived, with its beautiful William Steig cover of a young couple kissing in a verdant setting, it made a huge impression, and I read the story immediately. I also took the cover personally, because my girlfriend, L., whom I had met at Kinhaven but visited during the year as well, looked like the girl in Steig's painting.

Since he lived in Vermont, Salinger was a particular presence in my brother's and my life during the years I spent summers at Kinhaven, and when we both attended Putney.

From my teenage perspective, Jerry was warm, joyful, direct, and funny in a way no one else was. Tall, and with a long face that reminded me of Jason Robards or a portrait by El Greco, his lanky frame was hard to miss even seen from a great distance. For some reason I remember our moments of encounter, when his face would brighten and his arm shoot up in a wave. Being with his calm yet vibrating energy, you felt that nothing bad could happen to you.

Naturally, I see now that given the preciosity of his Glass family children, he must have been particularly amused and intrigued by my youthful musical efforts. My father sent him a recording of

Overture to a Ball Game, and he wrote me a letter playfully saying that in it I "comported [myself] like an old master," and that, like many artists, I had "outgrown [my] theme" (presumably "Take Me Out to the Ball Game") by the end of the piece. Somehow he acknowledged my young age but also accorded my "work" an adult seriousness. There was perhaps a hint of his belief in reincarnation embedded in his observations.

This belief was quite literal. He once told me that he and my father had been friends long before this life, and that he had once seen him sitting under a tree in ancient China. He also sent me presents: a recording of Wanda Landowska playing Mozart Sonatas, and a picture book devoted to paintings, drawings, photographs, and letters documenting Beethoven's life. In *Seymour: An Introduction*, I read his reference to Beethoven's late quartets, written "after he ceased being encumbered with the sense of hearing."[1]

While I was busy becoming acquainted with Stravinsky's Concerto for Piano and Wind Instruments or Berg's *Lulu*, some of the most immortal music of the 1960s passed me by. Unfortunately, I associated the combined timbres of miked voices, electric guitars, and drums with the loneliness of being at dance parties on the sidelines, only grudgingly allowing a dance or two with girls who were inevitably taller and more mature than I was.

This outsider status spread to my listening habits. Although I loved the Beatles, Bob Dylan, Otis Redding, Ray Charles, Carole King, and Aretha Franklin, I missed out on much great music. I didn't even hear the Beach Boys, let alone Jimi Hendrix, Frank Zappa, the Grateful Dead, Pink Floyd, Jefferson Airplane, Captain Beefheart, or Led Zeppelin, all music I would have liked, until years later.

But at the age of sixteen, my musical efforts began to add up to something. My Sextet for Piano and Winds had a kind of clarity and specificity and sounded strong when the Kinhaven Wind Counsellors played the piece with me (and there were no crudities!); a cycle of pieces for piano included a respectable fugue and harmonically interesting blues; and a set for violin and piano, *Evening Songs*, explored the poetic and songful realm I favored when writing for Wally, with newfound assurance.

---

[1] J.D. Salinger, *Seymour, An Introduction*, 110.

My Fantasy for Orchestra was good enough to be played by the Vermont Philharmonic. My conducting teacher at Kinhaven, Jon Borowicz, was musical director of the Vermont group, and he invited me to come lead my piece in a concert in Montpelier over winter vacation. Wally took the long bus ride with me from New York to play violin in the orchestra.

We arrived in the late afternoon, and I remember facing the informally dressed adults in the orchestra in the evening rehearsal, and leading the second section of the piece at a tempo that was faster than the one in which Jon had rehearsed it, much to his chagrin. In a letter he wrote me later, he said that when he listened back to the tape he realized I was right, adding that I had led the orchestra with "authority but kindness" and that my conducting was "clear and commanding."

It was twenty below zero and extraordinarily dark when we left the hall after the concert. Wally and I stayed at the home of a very nice family. I don't recall the parents, but I still remember the pajamas and fluffy slippers worn by their daughter. The reviewer in the *Barre-Montpelier Times Argus* wrote kindly that the piece had "a contemporary sound and, at times, a mystical quality."

I remember shaping the key relationships of the four sections of the Fantasy and building the overall form, the slowly unfolding D minor melody that started the piece in the cellos, the way the harmonies expanded and became more chromatic, eventually breaking out into the energetic Allegro that followed. I remember the sense that there was something urgent that had to be said that couldn't be said any other way, something much bigger than me. Even the first tones already had a presence behind them, already containing the rest of the piece within them.

If I was extraordinarily nervous conducting my pieces, it was at least in part because I did not understand where they came from, and yet they spoke for me. In the realm of tones, my horizons expanded; time and space changed; it was as if the notes remembered everything that had ever happened to me; I could say whatever I wanted to.

Composing was like pulling on a thread that kept getting longer, bringing with it sounds that were full of passion and expression, revealing a much more emotional self than the reasonable one I was used to showing. Sharing this larger, more emotional self was almost unbearable.

At a summer program at Emilie Harris's house in New Rochelle, I had an extraordinary experience hearing a performance of Ives's Sonata no. 2 (*Concord*) by pianist Hadassah Sahr, who later recorded the work. The music seemed to instantly lodge in the spirit and in the reptilian brain. With its dense chords like huge granite boulders, whole-tone scales, pentatonic clusters, tonal melodies pitted against complex figurations, triadic hymns, Scottish airs, and jagged ragtime rhythms, it captured a different world and sensibility than any I had encountered. Its very lack of conventional "clarity" and playability pointed to a truth independent of the tradition it alluded to in its quotations of the motto from Beethoven's Fifth Symphony. I sensed a connection to the deliberate stridency of Thelonious Monk's playing, in which piquant seconds and sevenths and angular intervals were layered above conventional chord progressions. Although transcendent in impact, its modernity also had a humble, home-grown quality to it, its use of quotations suggesting a connection to daily life, and an aspiration to reach the listener directly.

Visits to Salinger's home both in my senior year with Wally and with my friend Leonard Rieser, who lived not far from Jerry, made a big impression on me. I visited the cabin in which he wrote, saw some of the many texts on Eastern religion he was studying and the vast collection of herbal medicines he kept in a very large cabinet. He would talk about his macrobiotic diet and other approaches to eating that were extraordinarily original at the time. At home, one could sense that social outings cost him, and that the high spirits I had seen at Putney and Kinhaven were balanced by darker moods.

Long before there were VCRs, not to mention DVDs and DVD players, he had a library of old films—Hitchcock, the Marx brothers, W.C. Fields—which he would project for himself or friends. A kind of humble religiosity seemed to attach to these popular entertainments, as to actors and acting. Eccentric as he was, and immersed as he was in Zen Buddhism, Hinduism, and other spiritual traditions, he had an almost bottomless belief in the kind of everyday normality that Hollywood movies from the '40s and '50s exemplified, and he was most at ease with working people, attending a football game or cookout. He wanted to do his own studying in his own way. He was suspicious of the word "artist," uncomfortable with intellectuals, professors, literary analysts, and even with the idea of ambition and fame. He was critical of Picasso, Stravinsky, and other public greats of the era for being photographed and interviewed and courting (or curating) attention. Renegade that he was, and critic of the commercialism and phoniness of American life, he was loyal to the soldiers with whom he had fought in the Second World War, and looked askance at the hippies and privileged draft resistors of my generation, finding phoniness there too.

For Jerry, the Glass family characters were real. He told me that he knew enough about them to fuel his writing for the rest of his life. He spoke not of creating their pasts, but of remembering them and recording them. He spoke about his work with love, but also with a sense of urgency.

He was as frank as if we were adult friends when talking to us about his children, Peggy and Matthew, or his wife, Claire. At times, he expressed his sense of isolation. Once he shocked me by saying, "I wish I had someone to talk to" when Claire was right there in the room. There was an extraordinary intelligence and gentleness about Claire, not to mention beauty. I couldn't imagine being lonely with her as a companion. At another time, he told Wally and me, "I have become a monster."

Perhaps by knowing him, we soaked up a hint of the Zen Buddhism he embodied. Even just being in his presence one could feel objects and people beginning to take on a vividness and colorfulness that was in fact coming from his sensitivity to them. Possessing his expanded, heightened awareness must have also been a burden.

Salinger was simply one of my favorite people.

There are composers who become themselves at an early age, whose music fuses craft and intuition and a sense of urgency with an internal musical logic that makes considerations of age irrelevant. I played the work of one just the other day when I was teaching a class on composer Vivian Fine. Her Carl Sandburg settings, called *Suite for Voice and Piano*, were written when she was just seventeen. They already had her stamp, and a musical technique—her version of Ruth Crawford Seeger's dissonant counterpoint—to support it.

My music at the age of seventeen was utterly natural, with every note and rhythm intentional, heard, and felt. But it was too intuitive and uninformed—both by life experience and by technical understanding—to be mature. And no one had yet looked at it very closely or with a critical eye. My pieces were personal and attractive but fundamentally sketchy, not painstakingly crafted. I already thought of myself as a composer, but knew that I was not one yet.

It was around this time that my parents began to talk with me about where I might go to college, and began to wonder out loud what a young composer needed to study. Composer and writer Alec Wilder was an acquaintance of my father's. He lived at the Algonquin Hotel where my father had lunch almost every day, eating either corn flakes or toasted pound cake. (Given how sparse this diet sounds, it seems likely that he also ate an additional lunch with Lillian.)

Wilder visited us one weekend to take a look at my scores and advise me on my future. He struck me as a complex man with a lot of emotion in him, and as someone who would always speak his mind. In his flannel shirt with a striped blazer, he looked both dressed up and casual, both old and young, both irascible and playful, both certain and uncertain. In common with my father, E.B. White, Salinger, and other luminaries I encountered, he seemed self-made, an expert through hands-on experience rather than professional pedigree. Wilder took his time looking at my scores, some of which, like my Fantasy and Essay for Orchestra, were on a big scale. Later, my father sent him a recording of one of the orchestra pieces.

After listening, he wrote a long letter to me that I wish I still had. He cautioned me to be more modest in the tasks I assigned myself, to work on writing smaller pieces that were carefully made rather than larger ones that were looser and which had details that were not finely worked out.

What I do have is a second letter he addressed to my father:

November 19, 1964

Dear Mr. Shawn,

I've written your boy a letter concerning the record you so kindly sent me.

I have very clear ideas about it and what I believe would be a sensible course to pursue.

I have been composing (or trying to compose) for, God help me, forty years. Many musicians whom I admire respect my work.

However, to The Establishment I am an ancient tinpan-alley upstart. I am usually negatively reviewed and my name does not appear in Grove's Dictionary.

To make it worse, but for counterpoint, I am self taught.

All of this naturally causes me to be fearful of offering opinions and suggestions to your son.

If he keeps in mind that I am unauthoritatively submitting these notions to him, he will permit me to feel less presumptuous.

Most Sincerely,

Alec Wilder[2]

Needless to say, Wilder is in Grove's Dictionary today.

I had a second encounter with a real composer during a family trip to visit Mary in Delaware. On the way, we dropped in on Vincent Persichetti and his wife at their house near Princeton, where he taught at that time. Persichetti and I retired to his studio on the second floor. He listened to me play some of my piano pieces, and then charged to the piano and started improvising on my themes as if they were his own. "You could do this… or this," he shouted, ranging over the entire keyboard with energy and passion, expressing my harmonies more contrapuntally, sometimes abandoning any key center, and exploring rhythms that I would have had a great deal of difficulty writing down. His dynamism at the instrument was exciting, and he made a tremendous racket.

The implication was that my music was too hemmed in in every dimension, perhaps most of all rhythmically. He was particularly critical of the frequency with which I used accompaniments that were steady eighth notes. He also pointed to my over-reliance on tenths on the bass to support the harmonies—a trait, however transformed, traceable to my father's stride piano left-hand.

The visit was stimulating. My mother was at her most gracious and flirtatious with Mr. Persichetti, and my father was clearly very taken with Mrs. Persichetti, a superb pianist who premiered many of her husband's Piano Sonatas. Romance was in the air—the romance of life as an artist.

It would be hard to overestimate the educational impact that our ability to attend concerts, ballets, and operas had on me. Without knowing it, I was soaking up what people call music "theory" (which is actually practice), orchestration and an entire repertoire at the 92nd Street Y, Carnegie Hall, the (old) Met, and City Center, where the New York City Ballet performed, and from the many small clubs our father took us to.

From a cultural, educational and artistic point of view, I was as fortunate as a child could be. We knew we were privileged in a

---

[2] Letter to William Shawn from Alec Wilder, November 19, 1964.

world in which so many were not, but we had the luxury of thinking about this only as much as we wished to. We had the luxury of
not discussing money. Our parents were not extravagant, and they
dressed and fed us simply, but they could hire people to cook, clean,
and drive for us and for them. We knew that we were surrounded
by violence, but we mostly did not have to fear it. We knew that
we were surrounded by racism, but we were white. Well, we were
Jewish, but in an environment mostly free of antisemitism.

Although, unbeknownst to us, our father had no savings and was
struggling financially to hold together the life he was supporting,
which included an extra unseen family as well as our unseen sister,
this life—as experienced by Wally and me—was extraordinarily
privileged and comfortable, and, for the most part, extraordinarily
shielded from worry.

In 1962, at the newly built Lincoln Center, we saw Stravinsky
conduct his Symphony of Psalms in an eightieth birthday celebra-
tion that included Symphony in Three Movements and *The Flood*.
In those days before the computer and when television fare was
limited, we listened to records in the living room as a family, taking
in such music as the Mendelssohn Octet, Liszt's monumental Piano
Sonata (played by Rubinstein), Stravinsky's Concerto for Piano and
Winds (Bernstein's recording with Seymour Lipkin), *Ragtime for
Eleven Instruments*, and *Apollo*, and even Messiaen's *Le Merle Noir*.
Since Wally was at Harvard, where composer Leon Kirchner was
chair of the Music Department, we all listened to Kirchner's Piano
Concerto together when Wally was home for the holidays.

I had already played and loved Kirchner's *Little Suite* (1949). His
music had an electricity to it. It was romantic, but also steely; dramatic, but also precise and transparent; non-tonal, but thrillingly
resonant; virtuosic, but without dross or decoration. The music
could express in-extremis states in a concise, tightly coiled way,
from Bergian anguish, even despair, to dream-states conjured in a
way I hadn't heard in music before. I was eager to study with him,
and I sent him the score of a Prokofiev-inspired String Quartet first
movement I had finished. (Unfortunately, it was my only copy, and
I never saw the piece again.)

Not long after this, I applied to Princeton, Harvard, Yale, and a few
other colleges, and I somehow got into all of them. Despite only

modest abilities in math, apparently my verbal side was at least decent enough to qualify me to be accepted.

I had always been amazed by Wally's literary gifts and grasp of history and philosophy, and I was surprised. I had never considered myself particularly verbal or intellectual. People in groups carve out their roles and niches. Somehow mine had become music. In fact, Wally was very musical too (he even wrote a few songs for our puppet shows).

In the same way, my mother's talents as a writer, reader, and thinker were hidden behind her chosen role as a support for our father. She had in fact been a reporter for the *Chicago Daily News* when she was in her late teens and early twenties. It was thanks to these credentials that she had been able to secure a job as a reporter at *The New Yorker*, a position she deliberately sought so that she could introduce her husband to the Editors. Just as she had hoped, he was allowed to carry out his own reporting assignments, and was soon on the staff, while she withdrew. In other words, she had played a crucial role in my father's obtaining his first job at *The New Yorker*, the one from which he rose to become Managing Editor, and eventually Editor.

I was not a stranger to Harvard, as I had visited Wally there and had even been to hear the Harvard-Radcliffe Orchestra in which he played violin. Particularly memorable was their performance of Frank Martin's *Le Mystère de la Nativité*. I had also sat in on a rehearsal of the Bach Society Orchestra conducted by Greg Biss and Isaiah Jackson, where I heard pianist Ursula Oppens, a classmate of Wally's, playing Beethoven's First Piano Concerto, an exciting piece by a composer about five years older than my brother, John Harbison, and *Three Little Pieces* by Mark DeVoto (whom I was to encounter fifty years later). The DeVoto work included a loud first chord that made the young composer jump with glee in his seat, and it closed with the entire orchestra humming quietly.

More in the spirit of following in Wally's well-trodden path than for any other reason, I accepted the invitation to attend Harvard in the fall. Thus ended a certain stage of life.

3

CAMBRIDGE, MASSACHUSETTS
(1962–1966)

A T HARVARD, IT TOOK me until junior year to be accepted into Earl Kim's composition class, and until senior year to be accepted into Kirchner's. But already in my first year, I was plunged into a world of study far from the personalized tutelage of Miss Dillon and Emilie Harris, the mini-paradise of Kinhaven, or the joyful hands-on music making at Putney. Classes included heady dissections of Brahms by theorist David Lewin, somber musicological discourses on Monteverdi given by pale and nervous graduate-scholars, a challenging course in traditional forms taught by composer John MacIvor Perkins, in which we composed sonatas, minuets, and rondos in the idiom of Haydn, and realizations of Baroque figured bass at the keyboard with the vivacious and brilliant pianist Luise Vosgerchian, who had studied with Nadia Boulanger in Paris.

Rather quickly, I met a number of composers my own age whose histories were similar to mine. These included my roommate Danny Troob, who eventually became a noted movie and Broadway orchestrator and composer. Danny had written orchestral pieces at an early age, too, and was a fine pianist. He performed the Mozart A Major Concerto with the Bach Society Orchestra. Others included Bob Telson—today a successful song writer and composer for film and dance—and Leonard Lehrman, a fiercely driven and prolific composer who wrote music reviews for *The Harvard Crimson* and later studied with Boulanger in Paris alongside me. All three were more adept and comfortable with theoretical analysis than I was, but even they could not approach the level of brilliant young Robert Levin, today perhaps the foremost scholar associated with Mozart, who has completed his own version of the Requiem, and has recorded the complete Piano Concertos with his own cadenzas, improvised on the spot, in the Mozart idiom and manner.

Genial as he was, Robert seemed to intimidate even the professors with his erudition. Soon I encountered John Adams, one year my senior, who, as I learned later, had started composing early, much as I had. John struck me even then as someone with such a strong identity and creative spark that he could quickly shuck off what he did not need from his studies, and see his way to being himself. It wasn't long before he was conducting the Bach Society Orchestra and in charge of a production of *The Marriage of Figaro* for which I played rehearsal piano.

Then there were the two graduate school composers roughly my brother's age: Michael Riesman (later closely associated with Philip Glass) and Tison Street, both of whom were already crafting mature works (the latter in a modernist idiom he eventually abandoned).

Among the younger faculty were Ivan Tcherepnin, a superb electronic composer, and David Del Tredici, later an eminent and historically significant composer and Pulitzer prize winner with whom I had the good fortune to study counterpoint.

It is difficult for me, even today, to think back on these years without feeling a slight rise in my blood pressure and anxiety level. I was overwhelmed by all of the information coming my way, by all I didn't know about the art form at the heart of my identity. I also had to adjust to a shift in the way I was treated and the way I viewed myself. Much as I had bridled at the wonderment with which my music had been received when I was a child, and had even been irked by it, I had also been protected by it from criticism and close scrutiny. It was stunning to awaken and realize that the magic had worn off. Now, there was nothing particularly special about the fact that I loved to compose music. I was just a music student, one of many.

Some people finally start to discover who they are at college. For me, it was rather the opposite. I began to shut down, the way I had at parties in eighth grade when I stood by myself, feeling immature and lonely. There was a competitiveness and sense of entitlement in the air that I found stifling. The competitiveness—or comparativeness—included my own. Inspiring as the experience could be, it was also painful to listen to works by classmates that were written with a level of sophistication and maturity I did not yet possess. Many of my peers seemed to feel that they belonged at Harvard. I wasn't sure that I would be able to last there.

Since I didn't have a composition teacher, my father decided to write to Walter Piston to see if he was still taking on private students, even in his retirement from Harvard. In his courteous reply, Piston said that at his stage of life he needed to devote his attention to his own music. (He was 72 years old at the time, and lived another decade.)

I began weekly lessons in Lexington, Massachusetts, with Francis Judd Cooke, the father of Wally's old roommate and friend, Brian Cooke, a composer who taught at the New England Conservatory. I loved taking the bus from Cambridge out to Lexington, and I felt a sense of relief and safety at Mr. Cooke's house. He was a gentle mentor who gave me a sense of the contours of the contemporary music world by showing me scores, introducing me to new concepts, and sharing his own current musical experiences with me.

Much as Boulanger would later do, Mr. Cooke made observations about my music, but rarely suggested changes in it. In our very first lessons, I brought in "Evening Songs" for violin and piano. He pointed out that there was something poetic in the fact that the theme of the first movement did not appear in its complete form until the end of the piece.

We spent a great deal of time listening to music and following scores. I devoured every piece he introduced me to, particularly Bartók's *Bluebeard's Castle* and many works by Stravinsky, including the Concerto in E flat (*Dumbarton Oaks*) and *The Rake's Progress*. He introduced me to *Themes and Episodes*, the latest Stravinsky book written in collaboration with Robert Craft, and I was instantly smitten with its extraordinary wit and vitality and became a life-long devotee of Craft's writing, eventually reading every word of it.

We listened to works by Gunther Schuller, director of the New England Conservatory, and he told me about Schuller's new jazz program there, and that he had hired Alec Wilder to serve on the faculty. The notion of "third stream" music fascinated me. Later, I had the chance to attend a performance of Schuller's opera based on Kafka, *The Visitation*, in which a small onstage jazz band plays an important musical role. I already loved the moments in Berg's operas where such juxtapositions of idiom occurred. I could play the marching band music from Act I of *Wozzeck* by heart, as well as the out-of-tune honky-tonk piano music from its Act 3 tavern scene, and had copied out the offstage "jazz band" music from *Lulu* in my own handwriting.

Mr Cooke introduced me to Schoenberg's *Moses und Aron*, in which he himself was singing in the chorus, and explained aspects of twelve-tone music to me. (This was the first time that I understood the ideas of inversion and retrograde, and their connection to mediaeval and Renaissance music, not to mention the music of Bach.) I was mesmerized by the production, conducted by the extraordinary Sarah Caldwell. The chorus is essentially the star of the opera. (A year later, Mr. Cooke told me that in spite of having memorized his part, he could no longer remember any of it.) I also became fascinated by Webern's music, and spent a magical four hours with Mr. Cooke's gifted son Nym (today a conductor and scholar of shape-note music) listening to Webern's entire output, as recorded by Robert Craft.

Soon after, I saw Schuller conduct Stravinsky's *Oedipus Rex* and *Le Rossignol* in a stunning double bill. I started going to the top floor of Hilles Library where there was a beautiful music library with scores and listening stations that overlooked Radcliffe Yard. There, ears encased in cushioned headphones, I listened, transported, to the complete works of Stravinsky, everything from the early songs and pre-Firebird Symphony to *Requiem Canticles* and *The Owl and the Pussycat.*

In my dorm room, I tuned in to a television broadcast of the Boston Symphony performing his Huxley Variations for the first time. I can still remember the nose-thumbing effect of the flutter-tongued high E in the trumpet in measure 67 coming from the television set, and my amazement that someone in their eighties could write music that sounded so fresh and full of energy.

Not long after, with my parents in New York, I watched a program on public television that featured a performance of Pierre Boulez's brand new *Éclat* for fifteen instruments. Its orchestration of mixed winds and strings along with tubular bells, celeste, vibraphone, glockenspiel, piano, harp, and cimbalom created a scintillating sound world encompassing every means of percussively sounding pitch. Innocent as to its technical underpinnings, I heard in its brilliant concision a fusion of Webern with recent Stravinsky. I was surprised that my parents did not share my enthusiasm for it.

I was bowled over by Stravinsky's music in all its phases, identified with him temperamentally, almost metabolically, and with his attitude towards making. Although I wrote a paper about *Agon* and studied the use of a twelve-tone row in its later sections, I did not truly understand the relationship between the twelve-tone approach and the way the music sounded and felt. What I looked at most closely on my own was the harmonic language and voice leading in his middle-period works, starting with *Pulcinella*. Although the word "neoclassical" has stuck to this long phase in his output, I have never felt that the term begins to capture the originality and variety of approaches in these works, and it has never seemed to me that the intricate rules and the logic behind the mysterious sense of unity achieved by pieces like *Jeu de Cartes* or *Orpheus* have been fully grasped.

I was trying to find a contemporary language in which I could feel satisfied by every note and in which changing one pitch would truly matter. I was far from being able to manage complexity of the kind I heard in the current music of Carter or Stockhausen or Boulez. In middle-period Stravinsky, every single note seemed to be placed exactly where it should be and to ring out freshly. I became obsessed with it. I played through the score of the *The Rake's Progress* repeatedly. Further encounters only added to this almost unhealthy affinity: Kirchner's conducting of the Mass and *Movements* at Sanders Theatre; John Adams leading the Bach Society Orchestra at Paine Hall in the Capriccio, with Luise Vosgerchian as soloist, as well as the lovely *Danses Concertantes*, which I attended with my friend Jonathan Schell (my brother's old roommate, an oboist, former counselor at Camp Kinhaven, and a soon-to-be important political writer at *The New Yorker*). After the performance, we talked about *Danses Concertantes*, completed in 1942, as an oblique commentary on the Second World War, poignant in its lyricism and playful high spirits.

Home for the holidays, I composed a piece for two pianos, *Marsch*, which awkwardly merged the style of Berg's *Wozzeck* marching band with ideas recalling the finale of Stravinsky's Symphony in Three Movements. I performed it for my parents and a few friends, playing the first piano part live along with a tape recording I had made of the second piano part. With its acerbic harmonic vocabulary, hints of cabaret melody, and shifting meters, it was an exciting, intricate failure, a demonstration that a piece can be carefully crafted from moment to moment but superficial overall.

I contributed a set of pieces called *Three Animals* to a concert of music by students who were not yet admitted into composition courses. The piece was for an ensemble of seven wind and brass instruments. Shy so much of the time in those days, I at least had the chutzpah to conduct it myself in Paine Hall. It had much more of my own music in it than *Marsch* had. Jonathan Schell played the oboe solo in the lyrical slow movement (with its accompaniment often in tenths). I had asked John Adams if he would play E-flat clarinet and he did a great job on the part, despite the fact that I barely gave him a second to breathe in the lively finale. The tone of the piece was lighthearted, a cross-pollination of *Dumbarton Oaks* with my earlier idiom, complete with repeated eighth-note accompaniments. The first movement contained an amusing fugue, initiated by the trombone.

I knew I was going through a transition. In this dense forest of contemporary music, it seemed as if there were so many paths that one could take. I had left most of my own instincts behind somewhere in the underbrush. Perhaps I had a good ear and some insights into all the music I was absorbing, but my understanding was more intuitive and impressionistic than technical. Lacking any one clear language, I was left with a jumble of sound impressions from twentieth-century music, assorted bodies of information about techniques that this or that composer had used, and, underneath it all, a pianist's deep familiarity with eighteenth- and nineteenth-century tonality. For better or worse, aspects of Stravinsky became my dominant voice, for a time crowding out others, and my own.

Miss Dillon died in Vienna on New Year's Eve of 1968. She was there to continue her research into Amy Fay's life and studies. I had not known of her heart problems, and like most nineteen-year-olds I had no understanding of what it was like to be a teacher, or a parent, or fifty-nine years old, or in fragile health. Her body was returned to the States for burial, and I went to New York to see her husband Charles Haywood at the funeral home standing by her casket. He looked as distraught as I had ever seen an adult look. At her funeral, her colleague Carl Schachter, the distinguished theorist and teacher, talked eloquently of her piano tone.

In subsequent years, I never bonded with piano teachers, despite trying to. It continues to haunt me that I never properly thanked Emilie Harris or Frances Dillon for what they gave me: along with such valuable instruction, a kind of love and support that was human-sized and grounded in reality.

I was unhappy enough at Harvard to consider transferring to the New England Conservatory. I applied and was accepted there, and for a few weeks I hovered on the threshold between the two schools. But eventually, I stepped back to where I had been. Perhaps I knew deep down that no change of school could cure me of what I was going through. Besides, my unhappiness was perhaps most acute in music classes. At Harvard, I had the amazing opportunity to study biology with George Wald, literature with Stanley Cavell, psychology with Robert White, to take a course in Renaissance art, and to study German with the lovely Donna Baker, with whom I could talk about Berg's *Lulu*.

On Mr. Cooke's recommendation, I attended a summer music program in Ipswich, Massachusetts, where I was able to sing in the chorus of Monteverdi's opera *The Coronation of Poppea*, performed outside on several nights in the lush garden on the Castle Hill estate, with original instruments playing the bewitching score. This introduced me to a tonal sound world quite different from the later Baroque one I was used to, a world in which the vocal lines are wedded to the text in a particularly expressive way, and can be embellished according to the dramatic choices of the singers. Pungent appoggiaturas and suspensions sting the ear and sound like they have just been invented, since they have.

I made friends with a young Craig Smith, who later became the conductor of many Peter Sellars operatic productions, as well as a Bach expert and director of Emmanuel Music in Boston. At meals, Craig would regale me with his encyclopedic musical knowledge; he gave a wonderful performance of Beethoven's op. 111 Sonata, mystical in its closing pages, which was the first time I had ever heard the work.

The summer was also notable for introducing me to John Updike, whose home was nearby. A devotee of Renaissance recorder music, and a participant in an amateur ensemble himself, he attended the performance of the Monteverdi and was having a drink at the reception afterwards when I spotted him. I had read *The Centaur*, *Rabbit, Run*, *Pigeon Feathers*, and *The Same Door*, and felt a special connection to him, even imagining that I looked as if I could be his son. I responded to his exquisite use of language, his nostalgia for childhood and comprehension of the uneasiness and turbulence of adolescence, and I related to the combination of sexuality and religious feeling in his fiction. Needless to say, I was also in awe of the spectacular beauty and virtuosity of the writing itself.

For whatever reason, and quite uncharacteristically, I introduced myself, saying, "Hello. I am Allen Shawn, William Shawn's son," to which he replied, "Well, what do you know? I am John Updike," and invited me to lunch.

At his home, we played volleyball with his teenaged children, and he seemed to enjoy both the game and being a figure of fun, falling all over himself attempting to return the ball. He was high-spirited at lunch, too, but with serious asides, as when he recommended the writings of Unamuno and Ortega y Gasset, or responded to my comment about fearing death with the statement that "most people who are afraid of death are very cheerful." I took this to be about himself. I had a number of further encounters with Updike over the years, and received several kind letters from him later in life; I also became friends with his son, the writer David Updike.

Despite the way in which I had introduced myself, I was terribly naïve about how those who worked for *The New Yorker*, or hoped to, might view me. I was surprised when my father told me that Updike had written him about our visit, and equally so that he had described me as sunny and contented.

In my junior year, I was admitted to Earl Kim's composition seminar. Kim's settings of Beckett, *Exercises en Route*, was performed in Sanders Theatre around that time. Like Kirchner, Kim had been a student of both Arnold Schoenberg and Roger Sessions, but his work suggested an even stronger affinity with Webern's.

Exercises, sung hauntingly by Bethany Beardslee, was exquisite and spare, with potent silences; each detail was telling, crucial to the structure, and pierced the heart. Kim was clearly a master.

At his home, on a blackboard in his music studio, I remember seeing a fragment of only a few notes writ large on a staff (perhaps the seed of an entire composition)—expression pared down to one essential element. He surprised us all by saying that every composer has their touchstone, and his was Mozart, whose music represented an internal world, without which this one would be intolerable.

Kim was deeply political. He told us about his sympathy for students who were marching against the Vietnam War, and about how those recently arrested were held overnight and only given water. He mentioned a childhood memory of being at a political parade holding a little flag in his teeth, falling on it, and having it pierce the roof of his mouth. One sensed a current pain in Kim, too, a man of such elegance, with deep emotion powerfully restrained.

Not all of us were mature enough to rise to the level of Kim's high standards at this stage of life. I brought a rather threadbare jazz sketch to the first class, a page which Kim returned held between two fingers, as one might a used piece of Kleenex. Throughout the fall, my subsequent attempts were criticized in minute detail, reducing my pieces to useless scraps.

Perhaps in reaction, I was becoming rebellious and unpredictable. Over Christmas break, when Wally, already twenty-five, was preparing for our traditional puppet show, I balked, saying that I couldn't participate anymore, that it was too confusing to combine such creative casualness with the serious study I was doing at Harvard. In the end, we negotiated a compromise, with the understanding that the show would be our last one.

We made a puppet show about Mr. Kim himself, with young "Earl" taking composition lessons, bringing a waltz to his teacher, and having it systematically dismantled and altered. The show had an austerity and rigor that Kim himself might have admired. Convincing in its first appearance, the waltz was then dissected and revised in the lessons, reappearing transformed, although not necessarily improved, at the end of the show. I remember the warmth with which the initial playing of the waltz was applauded by guests Janet Flanner and her companion Natalia Murray, and their sympathetic groans when the teacher, played by Wally, ripped it to shreds.

An ironic aspect of the show, *Kim's Waltz*, was that it contained nice music, in two versions, written without self-consciousness. It also offered a metaphor for our father's profession, perhaps even a metaphor for our family life.

By the end of the year in Kim's seminar, I finally eked out an acceptable Stravinskian song in C major, suggestive of the idiom of Anne Trulove's arias in *The Rake's Progress*, that even went so far afield from my own life as to be the setting in translation of an antiquated nineteenth-century Russian verse called *The Kiss Refused*. I performed the piece with student soprano Greta Gribble at Kim's end-of-the-year concert. Afterwards, Luise Vosgerchian, who had been present, passed me in the hallway and shouted, "Igor!" with a big smile.

In my final year, I studied with Kirchner, whose seminar was a heady workshop environment that remained fluid from week to week. Sometimes, students would bring in their music-in-progress and sit at the piano playing it, but just as often, Kirchner would play recorded examples of music he wanted us to hear, write a fragment on the board for our consideration, or play the piano himself.

Kirchner was an unlikely department chair. I once overheard the harried music department secretary say, in a tone of affectionate exasperation, that he was "on another planet."

Like his music, he was volatile, subject to sudden shifts of mood, seemingly propelled from within, like a weather system. His nature, in contrast to Kim's intense introspectiveness, was dynamic and passionate, projecting an animal restlessness. His was not an orderly soul.

What I remember best is not his composition teaching itself but his conducting and the expressivity of his piano playing in class, the tone and concentration he brought to Brahms op. 119, or playing the wind solos that began his own, brand new *Music for Orchestra*.

In class, we listened to the first movement of Schoenberg's Suite op. 29, for instrumental septet, and the then-recent Penderecki Capriccio for Violin and Orchestra, a work Kirchner seemed to particularly admire for its risky juxtaposition of stylistic elements, and courting of outright vulgarity. Kirchner spoke about music in cosmic terms, likening the creation of a composition to capturing the structure of the universe, about how one tiny detail could be the key to an entire work and to how the world is put together.

There was a momentousness in the air. He spoke philosophically about how a trill or decoration in Mozart or in his own music, or a short cadenza in a Beethoven sonata, could fleetingly convey an "idea of elegance or refinement." He made careful distinctions between approaches, drawing attention to Carter's almost maniacal attention to detail in recent works, like the Piano Concerto, which clearly touched him, or to the seriousness and importance of composers such as Milhaud or Hindemith, even mentioning the genius of Jimi Hendrix, while dismissing Cage with the remark that "every art form needs its clown." (Like Kirchner, Cage had passed through Schoenberg's tutelage.)

This was the first time that I fully grasped the degree to which the world of contemporary music was riven by divergent views. Kirchner felt embattled, writing in his brief, famous credo about avoiding the twin excesses of seeking a false simplicity on the one hand, or of "making a fetish of complexity" on the other. Kirchner had known both Stravinsky and Schoenberg during a period when the two men would not meet, despite living within ten miles of each other in Los Angeles. Kirchner told of having played the same two-movement piece for each composer in turn. Stravinsky advised him to keep one movement, Schoenberg the other.

The so-called "neoclassicism" I was moved by had been considered anathema in Schoenberg's circles. Kirchner's attitude towards Stravinsky's middle period was evolving. He considered him a genius, conducted pieces like *Movements, Mass*, or *Dumbarton Oaks* with precision, refinement, and enormous depth, but was also sarcastic about *The Rake's Progress*, or at least that is how I interpreted his remark about my little *Kiss Refused*. When I showed him my song from Kim's seminar, he said with a laugh that it could have been added unnoticed into the Stravinsky opera.

Among the issues Kirchner wrestled with was the relationship between academia and the world of performance. He was deeply troubled by Stravinsky's admonition to composers that teaching in an academic institution was not a good way to spend one's non-composing time. This was a period in which private contemporary music performing groups had started to proliferate, and the rift between what notating composers were up to and what larger audiences responded to had widened to the point of an almost complete estrangement. Universities gave contemporary composers a home, and a place to develop their ideas and their work. But they risked creating a closed system in which new ideas and music were generated and then shared only with others in the field.

Over the centuries, many of the greatest composers produced more outgoing works alongside those whose intricacies tended to appeal to specialists, but the artform itself had not risked this degree of insularity. Mozart famously expressed the need to combine both the universally accessible and the learned in each work, passages that everyone could enjoy alongside those only connoisseurs could fully appreciate.

But perhaps for the first time in history, composers were raising the question of whether music required an audience at all, or even needed to be legible as an experience in sound. While some composers had systematized their work to the point that almost every element was separated out and subjected to mathematical control before even a note was written, Kirchner's methodology appeared to come from within his ideas. His music resembled the twelve-tone school in its sound palette, but was defiantly human in its rhapsodic unfolding, with rhythms, pitches, orchestral colors, and manners of playing molded as an integrated language, not as discrete, atomized elements.

When his former teacher Roger Sessions came to deliver the Norton Lectures at Harvard, Kirchner appeared to be uncharacteristically nervous introducing him. While understanding the need of composers to support themselves by teaching, as he himself did, in his talks Sessions decried the current rage for music analysis and the academicism of the music being written by many, describing art as a "chemical reaction" between all of its components, not a collection of them. Significantly, Sessions included the listener in his thinking about music. In an interview, Sessions said that he found nothing more boring than reading a theoretical analysis of his own music.

Kirchner had his pulse on the times, as Schoenberg had in his day, and unlike many of his contemporaries maintained a presence in the concert hall as both pianist and conductor. Among the Kirchner works I saw him conduct at Sanders Theatre was his thrilling Second Piano Concerto, with Luise Vosgerchian as soloist. To my amazement, my classmate Leonard Lehrman was critical of the performance in the *Crimson*.

Kirchner had been a serious biology student in his younger days, and his friends were artists, scientists, philosophers, linguists, novelists and poets. Despite its complexity, his music seemed to want to reach out to a broader public from this intellectual base, much as the novels of Norman Mailer and Saul Bellow did. In fact, in the early 1970s he would create an opera based on Bellow's *Henderson the Rain King*. It was impossible to hear his String Quartet no. 3, new in 1967, with its rich electronic component, without feeling the presence of the Vietnam War and questions about human survival in the nuclear age looming behind it.

My friend Jonathan Schell quit Harvard graduate school and traveled to Vietnam as a freelance journalist in the same year Kirchner wrote this work, returning with the manuscript of *The Village of Ben Suc*, a devastating portrait of the war in microcosm, that appeared in *The New Yorker* in July 1967. I was able to go with Jonathan to the Washington march against the war in October 1969. By the spring, with the American invasion of Cambodia, campuses across the country erupted in protests and sit-ins, objecting both to the war and to the entire structure of society, which shut colleges and universities down. Harvard was no exception. I participated in the sit-ins and protests. But in the turbulence I also witnessed jaw-dropping hypocrisy, as when well-heeled students chanting "power to the people" set fires in the streets and then pelted with rocks and bricks the firemen who came to put them out.

In my final term, the threat of the draft loomed over us. I applied to be a conscientious objector, but was spared from even a hearing by drawing a high lottery number.

Some of the music my peers brought in during this time was frightening in its intensity, seeming to express in cruder form the struggles that Kirchner's music distilled with such precision and transparency.

I remember a moment when John Adams had started to explore Cage's work and said to me, almost in passing, after class, "You know, music can also be up here," gesturing upward with his right hand to a higher, lighter, transcendent clime.

A happier, freer spirit was also expressed by a young David Del Tredici in his counterpoint classes. His intense and atonal *Syzygy* for soprano, horn, and orchestra, settings of poems by James Joyce, was performed while I was student, and he was still some years from the huge stylistic shift to tonality that occurred in his work when he began setting the words of Lewis Carroll.

But even then he spoke with delight about being spontaneous in one's composing, about the importance of allowing one's instinctive intelligence to come to the surface, an intelligence keener than any conscious design. These were words I needed to hear, and they were particularly striking in the context of this course, in which we were schooled in the strict rules of counterpoint.

Once, when my homework was late and I was struggling with it, he had me write out a missing exercise on the blackboard, as if daring me to forget myself and just write. I was taken aback by how well I did, adding three upper lines over the assigned bass, as if improvising. Del Tredici's comment was typical of his love of innuendo: "You see, you like to be watched."

Even so, by the end of the course I still owed him several assignments.

I encountered another surprising view of current music from a young pianist, Bill Epstein, whom I met at Hilles Library, where I was continuing my listening sessions. He told me that his favorite living composer was Dmitri Shostakovich. When I asked him why, he said, "Because he has a complete language that has the same depth as Beethoven's."

At the time I was working in Kirchner's class on a setting of the Latin "Gloria" section of the Mass for chorus and piano-four hands that was to be performed at the end of term, and I asked Bill Epstein if he would play the piano part with me. He agreed.

I was, of course, a nonbeliever and a nonpracticing Jew, but was so familiar with the Mass text from music that it came naturally to me to set it. Beyond this, I had a devotional bent, a bit like the character of young Antoine Doinel, whose little altar to Balzac catches fire in *The 400 Blows*. ("I was honoring Balzac!" he says, in tears, to his angry mother.)

Along with my almost religious reverence for certain composers, I had a naïve nostalgia for the Catholic services I had frequented as a thirteen-year-old at a Spanish church down the street from my parents' apartment house. I knew Latin well from my studies with Felix at Putney. I had prints of sacred paintings by Fra Angelico hanging in my dorm room.

Kirchner never interfered with a student's style. My "Gloria" was in some ways a patchwork without a through-line, yet it came close to cohering. Although I now no longer recall his input, he must have guided me to shape and prune it, because in the final version the tonality had an arc, beginning and ending in a kind of pandiatonic C major (the first chord was a resonant C major 9th chord), with digressions to a French-sounding melody in B flat minor, among other key areas. Heterogeneous as its materials were—some resembling Poulenc, others the Stravinsky of his Mass—each moment was focused and clear, had a radiant sound, and interesting piano writing. It couldn't have been farther from Kirchner's own music, or as alien to our own time period; but it was sincere. After the performance, I ran into Earl Kim, who said something like, "I hear that you are getting closer to composing what you would like to be composing."

Beset with student unrest, Harvard was shuttered for the month of May. Students were sent home, only to return in June to a graduation that was interrupted by a group protesting its housing policies. Protesters seized the microphones; Harvard's crimes as a landlord were recited; officials of the college were spat upon.

I knew that I needed to continue studying, if at all possible. I had sent examples of my music to Goffredo Petrassi at the Conservatorio Santa Cecilia in Rome, with an application to continue my studies there. In his letter rejecting me, Petrassi said that I did not have sufficient "tecnica pratica" to be admitted. Hearing this, Kirchner generously offered to take me along with him on his sabbatical year teaching at the University of Southern California. At the same time, Luise Vosgerchian wrote on my behalf to her old teacher Nadia Boulanger in Paris. She included no examples of my work, only her endorsement. The result was an invitation to study in Paris. Out of one rejection emerged two tantalizing offers. Much as I admired Kirchner, my instinct was to go to Paris.

Many years later, I heard that Kirchner had said of me during that time that I had talent and that the only thing I needed was "a kick in the ass."

4

PARIS: NADIA BOULANGER (1970-1972)

A FTER MY MOTHER'S DEATH in 2005, when we were clearing out her apartment, I found in her dresser five light-blue international envelopes held together by a thick rubber band. They were addressed to my parents in my handwriting. Here are the contents of the first one:

Oct. 3, 1970

Dear Ma, Dad, and Wall,

My address: 5 rue Audran, Paris 18ème. Please send Wall's letter! I hope you are well, all of you. I have moved in, my piano has arrived, and I've had my first lesson with Mademoiselle Boulanger.

I don't know if it is a good thing to recount something so important to me as meeting Boulanger right away, but if I don't, you will be annoyed. But my heart is still thumping from this wonderful occasion.

I waited in a white-walled room with sofas, an ornate ceiling, religious etchings and paintings covering the walls, and a large grandfather clock with Atlas carrying the world on top. Then she asked me in, while the student before me went out. I entered the adjacent room and shook hands with a small, terribly thin, and terribly friendly-looking woman with beautiful silver blue eyes (almost sightless, as you know). She sat me down at the piano (on which were photographs of herself as a child, and one of Stravinsky wearing a beret with his back turned) and, looking closely at me, asked me what I wanted to do. I told her I wanted to work on composition. She asked me what my background was, and I explained as best I could. But already she was making a strong dent in me just by the power of her face and the warmth and honesty of her way of speaking.

She made me feel that there was no need to be other than the way one was, and that one was free to write music. She tested my ear as we talked by plinking various chords very fast, whose members I named correctly, except for one Bb instead of B natural. When I halted at one point, she said, "Continue your confession," and, in fact, much of her talk was sprinkled with religious terms—"the devil of piano technique" (may urge one on to practice properly), or referring to blindness as a "gift of the Lord, a trial." She is a devout Catholic, as you know—and there is a picture of Pope Paul in the study of the house.

She said so many wonderful things that I would like to mention, but you may be more concerned with her reaction to your son and brother. She expects to hear as many of my things as possible over the weeks, but for the first time she wanted me to play, so I played and sang (atrociously!) the "Gloria." She said when I was done: "There is no doubt that you are a composer," and, "There are passages that I am indifferent to"—the very ones that I am also indifferent to—"but there are some passages of very high quality. The beginning and end are very good. And you will see when you get to know me that I am not very nice—nice enough—but not very nice. I think that you are very gifted."

This sounded good!

She got a great deal said in the rest of the hour about music— Haydn, Bach, Beethoven, Mozart, Stravinsky, Poulenc, Strauss, Chopin, Scarlatti—and also played many examples in the treble half of the keyboard. Her enormous seriousness and courage were a joy to see. After one chord she asked me what it was, and I said, "It was..." and she stopped me. "It is," she said. "What was, is. One's sins are never forgotten, even if you atone for them. Now I can forgive everything, but I cannot forget."

We talked about the Requiem Canticles, which you must listen to—it is under S., I think in Mary's room, or just sitting on the pho-nograph. She called the Postlude "a vacation for bells; how wonderful not to end with voices." Then she talked about the "polar opposite" Requiem, Fauré's.

"When you think of the incredible privilege to have... a hand," she said, holding up her own, "and what you can make it do, you must not let it become useless. Twenty minutes a day of technique practice everyone can do. There are things I cannot play; I would like to play the Chopin Étude in thirds or the Stravinsky Capriccio—but I cannot. I can hear those thirds, I love them, but I cannot play them."

"Are you religious? No, I will never ask you such a question again. One mustn't."

"Haydn forgot each Symphony after he wrote it, otherwise there wouldn't be one hundred and four. He would have died of meningitis if he had carried them all in his head at once. But now all one hundred and four exist."

"I went to a concert the other night. Just tricks. They offer me samples—a bazaar. Will you have some of this stuff or some of this?—like pieces of cloth at a market. But you know what a very different thing it is to pick a sample piece of velvet and make an entire curtain out of it, and how different the curtain looks from the sample. The amazing thing is that one must have a sense of the whole before one has any idea of its parts."

"What I wrote when I was young was useless, and I had the intelligence not to show it to anybody. It was well done, but—no, not boring—simply without personality."

"Poulenc was always Poulenc. Sometimes he did what was too easy, but he was always himself, and you knew whom to blame when you heard his music."

It appears that we will be doing some counterpoint to begin with—very strictly—while I continue to write as I please. She feels that I am very young and it is important to write a lot and freely.

Needless to say, I was thrilled at the honor of coming in contact with her and made joyous just at the prospect of being able to continue what I'm already doing. I hope you get some idea of the lesson from this letter.

Please write. I loved your letters, Ma, and was delighted with the cake (still fresh). I hope you are enjoying your work and travels, Wall, and feel good. M. sends her love.

Love, Allen

Keep the presses rolling, Dad.

Remembering my two years in Paris now, I wonder if I dreamed them. I was living with my girlfriend, Marina, I was feeling independent, yet supported by my parents, paying rent to Monsieur and Madame Force, our landlords at 5 Rue Audran, where we had two rooms, one of which contained a kitchen area and a rented upright piano, the other a large bed and a bureau. I was under the spell of young love, under the spell of the city, still under the spell of Stravinsky, awestruck by my teacher.

I knew I was lucky: lucky to have had the extraordinarily nice life I had; to have loving and sympathetic parents, no matter their complexities; lucky to have such a wonderful brother with whom to share artistic interests, outlooks, and confidences; lucky in all of the schools I had been permitted to attend; lucky to be in Paris studying with an extraordinary teacher.

But I was also inexplicably lonely, and this was the first time in which the full force of my fears took hold—my extreme dread of subways, elevators, tunnels, open spaces, windowless buildings, trips to strange or faraway places—and it was when I first began to imagine the challenges ahead, even if I was still cushioned from them for the time being, as I had been cushioned from so many things throughout life so far.

Even now Boulanger and her teachings are with me. Rereading this letter, I am struck once again by the power of her mind, the essential correctness of her way of approaching the student, her intimacy, humor, and depth. She taught the whole student, and she taught us about an entire life spent in music. There was no division between her teaching of music and her teaching of how to live. Put another way, everything she did and exemplified was part of her teaching.

In our very first lesson, she already spoke to the older person I am today—about dealing with failing faculties, about adapting to what you still can do and to what you can no longer do. And there she is, still providing fundamental support for the legitimacy of my efforts to be a musician and to compose music, no matter my failings, limitations, and ignorance.

She instilled a musical conscience about doing the best we possibly could, and about the way we treated the elements of music. But hovering above us all was an acceptance that we could not change who we were, what level we were capable of achieving, or what was authentic for us. This was of a piece with her religiosity. She quoted Leviticus: "Eat your bread, and be satisfied."

The goal was for us to have the tools to become whatever we could be. We were to be patient: "It takes ten years to make a musician," she would say. She did not impose a way of composing. In fact, she assumed that, being young, most of what we were writing would be imitative and not yet fully developed. Instead of teaching contemporary techniques, she assumed that with work and the development of our ears, familiarity with the repertoire, and building of our musical muscles, our personalities, and the techniques with which to express them, would emerge. And she was the first to recognize that a composer's music needs personality most of all. I can still hear the way she pronounced that word—"personality." But whose personality? "In the end there is only you—one little man," she said holding up a finger. "One little person, alone."

She gave her students a grounding in musical verities so fundamental that they could be applied to anything new we tried: principles of voice leading, of tension and release, of balance between different types of textures, of repetition and change, of the long line of a piece from beginning to end. One could find analogues for any of these in electronic music, or music using microtones, or in which there were only unpitched vocal sounds and uncoordinated rhythms.

Boulanger's emphasis on the long line of a piece started in her linear approach to harmony exercises. These were written out on four staves in four different clefs: soprano, alto, tenor, and bass. We used the same soprano or bass lines again and again, pasting multiple versions one over another. She would have us sing one line—the tenor, say—and play the other three. Chords were not simply things in and of themselves—they were the result of independent voices converging and moving through them. Chords in Chopin or in Debussy were to be heard contrapuntally. The past and future of a piece existed in each of its moments. Yet in our pieces, she could pounce on an individual note in a chord or a specific voicing with laser-sharp precision ("That note is unnecessary—it was in the previous harmony." "Those thirds in the right hand are very good".)

Boulanger was eighty-three years old and her vision was almost gone, consisting of lights and shadows, vague forms. She taught all day, sometimes even eating a bowl of soup rather than stopping for lunch. In the weekly lessons, she would sit to our right, sometimes reaching out and grabbing our arm ("A hand from the grave!") or groaning when one of the voices went awry ("Oh, the poor tenor!").

Every Wednesday, we convened as a group to work through designated repertoire with her—playing, singing, and discussing it. In the first year, we studied a series of piano and vocal pieces, including the Liszt Sonata, the Schubert *Wanderer Fantasy*, the Schumann Fantasie, song cycles of Debussy and Moussorgsky.

In the second year, Wednesdays were devoted to four Masses: the *Pange Lingua* by Josquin, the Bach B Minor, the Beethoven *Missa solemnis*, and the Stravinsky Mass. However well we thought we knew these works before going through them in class, our understanding and perceptions were quite altered afterwards. She also had us internalize the past through copying works by Bach and others by hand, having the music flow through our minds and hand as if it were our own invention—a matchless way to notice absolutely every detail. In a way, this was like what Miss Dillon had me do in piano lessons, the compositional equivalent of resting our own hand on Bach's as he composed.

Being with her opened us to dimensions and depths in music that would have otherwise remained closed to us. There is no denying it: whatever Boulanger's blind spots or limitations were, she was transformative. She left it up to each of us to find our own specific techniques and language, but she made us hear and feel music, and be grounded in its essentials, in a way that no one else could.

Lessons and group classes were supplemented by weekly ear-training and solfège with Annette Dieudonné, Boulanger's seventy-five-year-old assistant, whose home was in Montmartre, only a mile from Rue Audran. I would walk there on the cobblestones, with the domes of the famous Sacré Coeur cathedral looming ever larger as I approached her house. There we did score reading, sight singing, clef reading, ear-training, dictation, and exercises in rhythm. The latter included being given a melodic line to be played by the right hand, a tricky rhythm to tap with the left, while counting off the beats ("1, 2, 3") at the same time. Then one reversed hands.

To my parents, I described the "mischievous twinkle" in her eye, the way this diminutive woman called me "my dear" before playing a seven-note dissonant cluster in which all of the pitches needed to be identified, or a passage in three-part atonal counterpoint to take down as dictation.

My letters also contain alerts about my deficiencies in theory, or at least in theoretical terminology ("she says repeatedly that my problem is not my ear or my musicianship"), and my requests that my parents share my "alarming stupidity" with their friends, so that they temper their "grandiose" expectations of me. I felt the pressure of having grown up surrounded by geniuses and their extraordinary accomplishments, with little evidence of the learning process behind them.

As for the lacunae in my understanding, I don't believe I ever completely filled them. After the experience of studying with such masters of harmony and counterpoint as Boulanger, Dieudonné, and later Carl Schachter and Jacques-Louis Monod, I have never considered myself capable of teaching these skills myself. Much as I love tonal music, I was never fully rooted in it, having first sprouted from the soil of early twentieth-century music.

Missing from my letters was any mention of my struggles with the claustrophobia and agoraphobia that also plagued my father, and that eventually caused me to curtail my French studies. Neither does my loneliness come through.

Despite my fears, I walked endlessly around the city, going to museums and attending countless concerts and plays during my Paris stay, including some that were quintessentially French—an opera by Ambroise Thomas, *Le Sacre*, conducted by Igor Markevitch, along with *Hymne* by Olivier Messiaen, with the composer in attendance, and a performance of the play *Mon Faust* by Paul Valery.

If I needed any reminders of the essential aloneness of each person, such reminders came along soon enough.

News of my father's mild heart attack in December 1970 cast a shadow over my life in Paris. He was hospitalized but soon considered out of danger. In fact, he was back at work before too long. However, he was psychologically fragile, and he clearly carried the sense of a threat from within for the rest of his life, never knowing whether his symptoms of acute anxiety were heart-related or not, never being quite sure whether or not to take the protective medication he carried with him in a small oval pill case. My mother didn't want me to frighten him by returning home, and the feeling of distance from family and security that this created affected my own state of mind.

In April, word came of Stravinsky's death. I came down with a kind of flu for several days. Boulanger seemed altered at our next group class meeting, tired and slightly remote, deep in her own thoughts, speaking of how a work like *Apollo* was already "in eternity." The entire class listened together to the Symphonies of Wind Instruments. Written in memory of Debussy, the concise piece felt so huge, with its lively passages as if carved in marble, the solemn chorale like a monument to the phenomenon of breathing. The final chords hung in the air for a long time, after which she said, "Immortal, impersonal art."

While learning priceless lessons in harmony, counterpoint, and musical understanding from Boulanger and Dieudonné, I was floundering in my own composing, so drawn into the sound-worlds of other music that I was becoming cut off from my own identity.

I wrote to the Dushkins of Camp Kinhaven, asking them if I could visit and record a new orchestral piece with the camp orchestra that summer, and they generously agreed. This gave me a goal to work towards, and by June when M. and I returned together to the States, I had completed a sizeable piece, *Prelude*, in my old sectional, one-movement form. (I have no idea why I chose such a meaningless title for this work.)

Before going to Kinhaven, M. and I took a short bus trip to Montreal, where we stayed at a hotel and had the romantic experience of signing in as a married couple. As I was scrambling to complete the orchestral parts in time, instead of coming down with the fever as I had done as a teenager, I developed a painful case of shingles. We arrived in Weston, Vermont, with many parts left to copy, and with a large supply of calamine lotion. At Kinhaven, I was introduced to a younger composer named Bruce Adolphe (today a most distinguished one), who kindly assisted me in my last-minute copying.

Conducting the piece felt strange. Although Dorothy Dushkin thought the score had some very interesting orchestral colors in it, I knew immediately that it was mostly derivative, essentially a choppy collection of passages recalling pieces I particularly liked. In my quest to equal what had made a deep impression on me, I had become a mimic.

The reader may have already rightly deduced that the early adulation I received for my music left me not swell-headed but in fact painfully self-conscious about my inadequacies. It is also possible that having vaulted over most rudimentary studies I had become simply unteachable. For whatever reason, my summer experiences left me seeking a more prosaic form of study to complement the atmosphere of greatness surrounding Boulanger. The next fall when I returned to Paris, I paid a call on Pierre Petit, director of the École Normale de Musique, to see if I could go to him for supplementary weekly lessons.

We met at the conservatory in a room with a high white ceiling, ornate molding on the walls, and a framed portrait of Stravinsky on the wall. Monsieur Petit was a fifty-year-old composer who had once won the prestigious Prix de Rome. Bespectacled, dark-haired, rather nattily dressed in a bow tie and jacket, there was something crisp and humorous about him that put me at my ease. He had studied with Boulanger when he was in his twenties and knew her well. He seemed to understand why I could use his help.

I went to the piano and played through my *Prelude*. Gesturing with mock grandeur to the portrait on the wall, he said: "We admire Stravinsky, and we salute him." He paused. "But we do not write like him." Then he asked me what else I had to play for him, and I took out a blue spiral music notebook containing some of the piano pieces I had written at seventeen in my parents' living room.

I played him pieces with quaint titles, among them *Five A.M. Blues*, *Spring Breeze*, and *Bells*, and he quickly said that he preferred those to my orchestral piece. Speaking in French, he said, "These pieces are very natural, with references to jazz, and in which one note leads to the next one."

He recommended that I also study piano with his colleague at the conservatory, Jules Gentil. I now added weekly lessons with "Mr. Small" and "Mr. Nice" to my schedule. In his piano lessons, Monsieur Gentil emphasized developing supple arm and wrist motions, and discovering just the right fingerings to make a given passage happen with the greatest relaxation and naturalness.

While continuing my lessons and classes with Boulanger and Dieudonné, and working with Jules Gentil at the École Normale on Chopin Études, Debussy's *Estampes*, and Ravel's *Le Tombeau de Couperin*, I went weekly to Monsieur Petit's apartment to show him my latest pieces, orchestration assignments (such as the opening of the first movement of Beethoven's C Major Sonata, op. 2, no. 3) and fugue writing.

I felt guilty not telling Boulanger about this additional study, but I found that it complemented what I was learning from her. Petit could scrutinize my work visually. My scores benefited from his notational suggestions, and as a result became more precise. Being with him was also a comfort.

Like every newspaper, every teacher has her biases and assumptions. Boulanger leaned towards transparency, clarity, pandiatonicism, and an ideal of objectivity, and away from heavy textures, dense chromaticism, and hyper-emotionalism. She recognized Wagner's genius, but she did not often refer to his music; she veered away from Strauss, Mahler, Reger, and Schoenberg. There were rumors that she disliked Milhaud and Messiaen. Given her devotion to Monteverdi, I assume that she was not attracted to Gesualdo.

She respected Penderecki, Xenakis, and Boulez. There were a few composers she spoke of almost with pity, including Leoncavallo and Menotti. For those students who regarded her as an oracle, these judgments could be destabilizing. I was already trying to pry myself loose from my musical heros, as well as from the perfectionism I had grown up with—embodied in the impeccable *New Yorker* typeface and prose and in the notion of the "greatness" of the artistic giants discussed at the family dinner table. I adored Boulanger, but I also recognized the danger in worshipping her. Paradoxically, her confidence in me helped me to not be intimidated by her views.

Having now made the conscious decision to suppress any Stravinsky influence, I embarked on a series of pieces that had less discernible reference points in other music. The first of these, a dissonant fanfare, was a response to Petit's shrewd assignment to compose "an angry piece." This was followed by a theme and variations in which I subjected a brooding atonal melody to a series of transformations of equal length, in various tempi and characters. I identified with its dark mood.

When I played it for Boulanger, she said that it "sounded like Schoenberg," adding, "You are more direct than that." I told her that I felt connected to it. Then she made an astonishing observation: "But in almost every piece there is something beautiful. The moment near the end where you have the slow tenths descending in the bass is such a place." She had recognized my father's voice in the left hand. Later, she asked me to perform the piece at one of her public concerts.

I felt a rush of joy when Monsieur Petit told me that he would arrange to have these two piano pieces published, but the joy fizzled when nothing came of this idea. Perhaps I had misunderstood a French colloquialism. I wrote to my parents that composing was not coming easily and that the new piano pieces "leave me uncertain... The real truth is that I haven't yet found my style or a real technical foothold. Both pieces are atonal."

In the spring, I completed three short pieces for piano four hands, and I was again able to perform them publicly at one of Boulanger's programs, sharing the piano with my friend, Greg Vitercik. Although more tonal (and French) in sound than the theme and variations, the middle movement, perhaps the most original, again had a darkly brooding tone. It was a viable piece; I understood the four-hand medium.

Boulanger's romantic life was a subject of much curiosity to us. Some speculated that she had had romances with women, some that her past attachments were with men. Somehow, it never occurred to us that she might still be in a romantic relationship. Scholars now believe that the older composer Raoul Pugno was her lover during the time in which they collaborated on their opera, *La Ville Morte*, an intense, romantic symbolist work to a libretto by Gabriele D'Annunzio that deals explicitly with illicit sexual desire and with incest between brother and sister.[1] Once she said to me: "Of course sex is important. But it is not the only thing for which we live." Fortunately, this didn't seem to call for a response on my part, and I didn't make one.

It was not easy telling "Mademoiselle" that I would not be returning to France in the fall. Two years with her was a fraction of the time some of her students stayed within her orbit, and she made it clear that she took a dim view of my interrupting my progress so soon. However, she kindly wrote me a general recommendation that I could use later, if I wished, and gave me two inscribed scores as a gift.

I also felt sad leaving Monsieur Petit. Twenty years later, I was able to see him again and to thank him for all the good he had done me during that period.

And in 1983 I heard from Mademoiselle Dieudonné, when she wrote to thank me for accurately and truthfully describing Boulanger in an article I had written. In it, I depicted the unforgettable experience of sitting at the piano next to her, and her celestial playing in the upper register: "Music students always know their teacher's hands, and Boulanger's were exceptionally beautiful... as silky and elegant as Dietrich's legs. These hands produced, at the drop of a hat, musical examples spanning five centuries—Lasso, Monteverdi, Victoria, Fauré, Chabrier, Stravinsky—always bringing out the voice leading."[2]

---

[1] Nadia Boulanger's diaries have recently revealed that she was in a romantic relationship with the pianist Raoul Pugno (1852–1914). He died in Nadia's arms while on a tour (Nadia Boulanger, 1914 Diary, unpublished, Bibliothèque nationale de France, Music Department, Rés Vmf ms 152). On this topic, see Alexandra Laederich and Rémy Stricker, "Les trois vies de Nadia Boulanger. Extraits inédits de la valise protégée", *Revue de la BNF*, 2014/1, no. 46, p. 77–78, online at <http://www.cairn.info/revue-de-la-biblio-theque-nationale-de-france-2014-1-page-77.htm>.

[2] "Nadia Boulanger's Lessons," *The Atlantic*, March 1983. Her aim was to reveal the life present in the basic materials of music.

5

NEW YORK: TEACHING, PLAYING THE PIANO, COMPOSING, STUDYING (1972-1974)

BACK IN NEW YORK, I searched for an apartment where I could live with M., who luckily had decided to join me in the fall. She would be looking for work, and was considering embarking on a graduate study program in the city.

For me, life was about to change dramatically. My parents told me that they could no longer support me. After all, I was turning twenty-three. With the exception of their assistance paying for a therapist to help me deal with the fears that had started to have such an impact on my life in France, I was on my own.

I was able to find a job working as a pianist at the Lenox Arts Center that summer, performing songs and piano music by Charles Ives in a music theatre production by Brendan Gill based on the composer's life, and conducted by veteran new music expert Richard Dufallo. It introduced me to many Ives songs I had not known, including the extraordinary piece *On the Antipodes*, which was so densely written it required a second pianist. I remember my excitement when I realized that the pitches constituting the chords in the initial beats became the source for the entire rest of the piece.

In the following year, on the recommendation of Emilie Harris, I started teaching in the preparatory department of Mannes School of Music. I was also playing for dance classes at the Finis Jhung dance studio on West 79th Street, at the rate of nine dollars for each hour-and-a-half class. While I improvised tonal passages in regular meters, and chopped up Chopin Études and Schubert *Moments*

Musicaux into four-bar units, I gazed at the attractive leotard-clad women doing their pliés and fouettés.

When my shift ended, I would be succeeded at the piano by a young song writer named Alan Menken, for whom improvisation was second nature. He was a very nice guy and we would chat about what we were composing. He seemed wistfully admiring of my efforts to write chamber music. In fact, enormous success and fame awaited him as the composer of world-renowned scores for Disney films and Broadway.

It was also obvious to me that I had not completed my studies. I resumed piano lessons with Emilie Harris, and I started taking composition lessons with Peter Pindar Stearns at Mannes and counterpoint with Carl Schachter at his home, with a plan to apply to Juilliard that spring.

Emilie Harris submitted my Theme and Variations to a Music Teachers National Association contest, and it won the Eastern Division college-level prize, though it didn't win at the national level. An anonymous judge left this perceptive comment:

> This is actually a work of a gifted composer with a good ear for chromatic harmony. I wish the ear would be more astute in making textural decisions, because it seems as if one is playing the same "thick" music at times slow, at other times fast. The fast harmonic rhythms and starchy harmonies are not an asset in this piece [and] would have been relieved by some variations of lighter and cleaner polyphonic writing. The composer has much talent and... should concentrate more on the melodic gestures, which are too hidden in the maze of notes.

Peter Stearns intuited that what I needed most was to produce music, and he interfered very little in my process. He introduced me to the tri-chords used by composer Carl Ruggles in the "Lilacs" movement of *Men and Mountains*, *Portals* for string orchestra, *Evocations* for piano, and the muted brass ensemble piece, *Angels*, all of which I loved. These still strike me as among the most beautiful and perfect pieces by an American composer, and their use of intervals as building blocks became a part of my language.

After writing a three-movement violin and piano piece, with a boisterous finale Stearns called "a humdinger," I wrote a libretto for a one-act opera called *Desire*, a dark fairy tale about a princess who marries an owl. Although without any prospect of a performance except an awareness of Mannes's opera program, I worked happily on the piece for the rest of the academic year, completing the piano score and orchestration for full orchestra late that summer.

In the story, the princess's mother has died and she is raised by her maid, and courted by three suitors—a lawyer, a poet, and a playboy—who represent three different lifestyles. She has a romantic dream of a mysterious owl, and it is the owl who arrives in a "wedding suit" to kiss her and carry her away at the end of the story, much to the consternation of the king, the chorus of courtiers, and the maid. The arias of the suitors, as well as the music of the king, the maid, and the courtiers, are all indebted to *The Rake's Progress* (including some of that score's eccentric prosody).

The music of the princess has a more Bartókian sound. I could sing all of the tricky vocal lines myself, but they are difficult. Since the piece was never performed, its practical challenges, including the balance of voices and orchestra, and the orchestration itself, were never tested. The piano-vocal score is convincing, but chances are good that the orchestration would need to be revised were the piece ever played. The half-hour tale is a mixture of surrealism, innocence, and humor, and it has believable characters. The text has an antiquated feel and is entirely rhymed. In the last lines of the libretto, the king accepts the princess's choice to marry the owl, and he asks the couriers to bow before the strange couple:

> Allow your king a final word:
> Dismay I will not deny at such a thing as marriage to a bird.
> Nor do I claim to be delighted
> At seeing loveliness thus plighted.
> Yet a poor king would I be
> If a wedding day I scorned
> And felled our family tree.
> Let those who judge be warned:
> A wedding is this, if any be.
> And while as host I still hold sway over guest,
> Let me pronounce a last request,
> That since acts can be the best persuasion,
> By kneeling, you rise to the occasion.

In a way, I had written my own "puppet show" libretto, set to music as a through-composed opera.

When I applied to Juilliard in the spring, I brought a sketch of the piece with me to show to Elliott Carter, who had agreed to see me alone for fifteen minutes in his office. I was struck by Carter's kindly blue eyes and his air of contentment. He perused the score for at least five of the fifteen minutes, listening intently in his inner ear while clutching his fist close to his mouth, as if he could hear better that way. After this, he said, "Not many people are writing this way anymore, but it is decent music." He then added, "Sometimes the harmony does not support the vocal line." I have taken this last observation to heart in every vocal composition since.

In my application statement, I wrote:

> In general my music has been fairly tonal, and instinctive rather than highly mathematical in its organization. Craft has not come easily to me because of the amount of time that passed before my compositions were really examined or criticized, but I feel that I am beginning to gain control over what I do and therefore to write music that is closer to what I would like it to be.

My interview with Carter, Persichetti, Diamond, and Babbitt was brief, but indelible. It included some questions about music history, a few tests of the ear, and one that combined the two, when Babbitt asked me to identify the half-diminished chord in the first phrase of *Tristan*.

I was devastated by the rejection letter that arrived a few weeks later. It marked a shift in my sense of myself and my possibilities. I went over to Juilliard to inquire if I could find out more about what had derailed my application. I was told that there were very few composition positions available in the master's program and that, at age twenty-three, I was already considered too old to be applying.

Although I was not permitted to see the notes taken about me, a few excerpts were read to me. I have forgotten, or blocked out, most of what I heard. The comments were discouraging. The only one I remember is: "Good ear; little used."

Though disconsolate, I decided to reapply the following spring.

That summer, I again worked at the Lenox Arts Center, this time playing in *Dr. Selavy's Magic Theatre*, a surreal play written and directed by Richard Foreman, with music by Stanley Silverman, a superb guitarist who had been a student of both Kirchner and Darius Milhaud. The score was an intriguing mixture of idioms ranging from popular ballad, to jazz, to atonality, all composed with crystal clarity for a mixed ensemble that included new-music veteran cellist Fred Sherry and the electronic composer and vocalist Joan La Barbara.

In the fall, the show moved to a theatre in Greenwich Village, where it ran for many weeks, giving me another steady paycheck. Among Stanley's guests in the audience was Babbitt himself, an ebullient, small man, bald, with flyaway gray hair, who afterwards commented on the music with lighting speed in his inimitable basso profundo voice. I remember him speaking to Stanley and referring to a song as "one of your hit tunes."

Stanley also invited me to come to a rehearsal at Lincoln Center of a new piece by Pierre Boulez, which he was coaching (the first version of *...explosante-fixe...*, written in Stravinsky's memory). The performers included Paula Robison and Walter Trampler. The work was extraordinarily challenging and the rehearsal was filled with tension, as well as intoxicating sounds.

Shortly after that, Stanley invited me to tag along for a dinner at a Greenwich Village café with the composer. Boulez had become music director of the Philharmonic in September of 1971. Enormously charming and energetic, he talked animatedly about the plans he had made with President Pompidou to erect a giant new center for contemporary music and research in Paris. He was impressed with Pompidou's willingness to take such a risk and support his vision, which would result in the creation of IRCAM and the Ensemble Intercontemporain. I believe that Stanley mentioned that I wrote music, but I was too dazzled by Boulez's eminence and dynamic personality to have much to say.

I started a new job in the fall, teaching at a small progressive high school on West 12th Street. The school was created by former Dalton teachers, including Emily Alford, and named for Elizabeth Seeger, teacher and writer, sister of modern music theorist Charles Seeger, sister-in-law of Ruth Crawford Seeger, and aunt to Pete Seeger.

Given the Seeger family's involvement in folk music, the school's founder Carole Losey was understandably disappointed that this was not a deep interest of mine. However, it turned out that I did do some good at the school, by directing a chorus, offering music history and theory, and teaching my first-ever composition student, sixteen-year-old Linda Catlin Smith.

I had met Linda when I visited the previous spring and was already aware of her composing. I was only nine years older than her, and still a student myself. In "teaching" her, I probably felt a bit of the caution and sense of responsibility that Miss Dillon and Emilie Harris had felt towards me. She was unmistakably a composer, in touch with her own sound world. As a person, she had a patient, unusually self-contained quality, and a playful sense of humor. When she was listening, either to her own playing or to music I played in the history class, she was as still and attentive as a cat. She was fond of Baroque music and Irish music and went on her own to hear the Gil Evans Orchestra rehearse, drawn to their painstaking artistry and beautifully orchestrated chord voicings.

The sonorities and some of the rhythms in her own piano pieces were distantly reminiscent of jazz, but without the "jazziness." Her aesthetic gravitated more towards stillness, at that early time in her work, in the vein of Satie. But she was herself, not an imitator; she had something to say, and I did my best to inform her about all kinds of modern music and the history behind it, and to stay out of her way.

Once, when she was sick, I sent her a recording of the complete Bartók String Quartets. At my recommendation, she went to the Lincoln Center Library to check out a compendious and inspiring exhibit about Elliott Carter, full of scores, manuscripts, sketches, photographs, and music playing from speakers.

Not long afterwards, I was able to take the entire music history class to a rehearsal of the American Composers Orchestra playing Carter's Variations for Orchestra, one of his most eloquent early works.

There was a term when I was teaching at three schools at once, the third being an all-girls Catholic high school. I have almost no memory of how I got there or whether I left after one term because the job didn't suit me (it didn't) or because I didn't suit them. I had to direct a choir from the piano, and the repertoire was assigned to me. My most vivid memory is of being introduced to a group of at least fifty girls in uniform, almost all of whom were taller than me, by a nun who said: "Now, girls, Mr. Shawn is married. So hands off." Somehow, this was as absurd and embarrassing an introduction as I could have been given. (And, of course, I was not married.)

Meanwhile, I worked on the first two movements of a String Quartet with Peter Stearns and continued studying with Schachter, while planning to reapply to Juilliard in the spring. My String Quartet again explored my "brooding" side, its language at times evoking Bartók and reaching back to people like William Schuman and Quincy Porter, as well as alluding to Carter's first quartet and Berg's *Lyric Suite*. The opening theme in the viola grew out of a major-minor third motive that sounded bluesy, but the piece never veered in the direction of jazz.

My spring application to Juilliard was again unsuccessful. This time, my interview committee consisted of Carter, Sessions, Babbitt, and Persichetti. Thanks to letters from Schuyler Chapin, father of my old friend Hank, I had a chance to talk with both Babbitt and Carter on the phone later, and to meet Roger Sessions for a chat at a restaurant near the Empire Hotel, across from Lincoln Center.

My brief meeting with Sessions left me with an impression of his warmth and directness, starting even with the way he shook my hand. He spoke to me as if to a friend, first about looking forward to hearing Wagner's *Götterdämmerung* at the Met, and then, for some reason, about Leonard Bernstein's music.

He mentioned his disappointment that Bernstein had taken the path to "success" rather than to "accomplishment" after producing such a marvelous and authentic First Symphony (*Jeremiah*). We must have talked about Kirchner and about his visit to Harvard when I was there, but I don't recall it. My sole memory of phoning Babbitt was of the delightful way Sylvia Babbitt introduced her husband, as if on a TV talk show: "Here is Milton Babbitt!"

My call to Carter put me on the phone with sculptor Helen Carter, who told me that her husband had advocated for me and thought I was talented. Her main point, though, was to question why I needed to go to graduate school anyway: "You should just keep composing your music, and you can do that anywhere, and no matter what. You don't need to study!"

She was perhaps entirely right, but I did not yet have the confidence to believe her.

6

COLUMBIA (1974–1977)

A LOT OF EXCELLENT COMPOSERS were essentially self-taught, Poulenc, Schoenberg, and Takemitsu among them. Bernstein was highly schooled in piano, conducting, and orchestration, but apart from receiving personal critiques from Copland ("This passage isn't you"), he evolved as a composer without interference. In fact, he mainly used his counterpoint classes with Arthur Tillman Merritt at Harvard as a stimulus to write his own spiky, dissonant, and rather Coplandesque piano pieces.

On one occasion, when Merritt pointed out that what Bernstein was playing did not fulfill the assignment, he pounded his fist on the piano and said, "Well, I like it!"

As someone who has now tried to "teach" composition for roughly fifty years, I would say that composers need information and practice most of all: information, practice, and support. Much of the information they need comes from hearing what they write. No teacher can tell them more than their own ears can. And if their ears learn nothing from hearing their own work, then no teacher can help them. But aside from information and practice and support, composers mainly need respect (including respectful listening on the part of the teacher) and to be left alone.

Erudition in music is a good thing, but music itself is not academic. It is actual.

Study that is beneficial tends to be at an angle to original work: playing, listening, score study, analysis of other (mainly older) music, ear training, counterpoint and harmony study, and many other kinds of practice and immersion in the substance of the art. Listening as broadly as possible is a good idea. You never know where the tentacles of a mind will stick: it could be in the Middle Ages, or in Indonesia, or in the West Indies, or Appalachia.

But then the composing mind and ear need to be free, need to find their own way of doing things. Composing takes place on a different plane from that of the classroom or the concert hall. For it to happen, both the teacher, and even the composer him or herself, need to get out of the way. The composer should be informed and have a sense of musical language as it was previously used. There has to be discipline behind their work, but the craft must correspond to the nature of the mind doing the inventing, not to a preexisting template.

The goal, the piece itself, is like the still point that dancers stare at in the distance while they spin.

For composers, sometimes that still point is something behind or beyond the music, like childhood, or a feeling, or a concept. Maybe this is what Ives meant by saying about music that "what it sounds like may not be what it is."

Fearing a second rejection from Juilliard, I had applied to the master's program at Columbia, and I soon found myself in the office of composer Jack Beeson, being interviewed and playing him the first two movements of my String Quartet. He seemed respectful of the music, but more taken with my piano playing, which he thought was "terrific."

He expressed his dismay that I was applying for student loans and a scholarship from Columbia, and seemed to assume that my father had the means to continue supporting my education but was opposed to my having a musical career. I am not sure I convinced him otherwise. Fortunately, I was accepted into the program, which I would enter in the fall.

That summer I was hired yet again by the Lenox Arts Center, this time to perform the spiky and athletic piano part in a work called *Arabia Felix* in a concert devoted to music by the contemporary composer Charles Wuorinen. Charles had written the score for a performance group comprised of former students, including Erik Lundborg, Peter Lieberson, Alison Nowak, David Olan, and Stephen Dydo.

In May, I received my copy reprinted from the composer's original manuscript. When I showed it to Carl Schachter at one of my counterpoint lessons, he said that you could tell from the handwriting that the composer "doesn't love what he is doing." He could see that I was intrigued by the music, so he added, "At my age, you start to make choices about what you care about and what you don't; you know that you can't take an interest in everything."

At Lenox that summer, my roommate was the remarkable flutist, composer, and conductor Harvey Sollberger. With his dark eyes, beard, and moustache, Harvey looked like a magician in a circus—someone who might ask a woman to enter a wooden crate to be sawn in half—and his playing was magical too: theatrical, sensuous, and extraordinarily precise. Every morning, I had the pleasure of hearing him practice Wuorinen's intricate Flute Variations. His playing was so rhythmically and tonally accurate that you could take dictation from it (if you had the ears of a Boulez), but also vibrantly alive and dramatic.

Likewise, *Arabia Felix* was electric; in fact, Harvey described the opening unison octave F's as "like putting your finger in a light socket." Wuorinen wrote serial chamber music with tremendous rhythmic verve, colorful doublings, and sudden bursts of ensemble chords that were fresh and resonant.

Wuorinen reminded me somehow of Donald Barthelme. Like his music, he was learned, articulate, mischievous, crusty, and opinionated. I did not know then about his somewhat reactionary and off-putting social views. I was more struck by the contrast between the disciplined dynamism of his music and the looseness with which he ambled and crawled through the set of Richard Foreman's latest theatrical work when he had been smoking pot.

The evening also included his brilliant instrumentation of pieces from the fifteenth-century *Glogauer Liederbuch*, the first of many arrangements of early music I heard of his, including music by Machaut, Josquin, and John Blow. Later, I also heard his wonderful sacred music. He was an important composer, with his own complete musical language.

After the concert, I met two of the original performers and dedicatees of the music I had played, violinist-composer Alison Nowak and clarinetist-composer David Olan, both of whom were already at Columbia. It was nice to know that I would be seeing them again in the fall.

In my first-year composition seminar, my professor was Dennis Riley, a young composer who had studied with George Crumb, and who at that time wrote atonal music that was as compressed and meticulously detailed in its performance instructions as Webern's.

I still remember the striking final chord from his String Trio, an F major triad superimposed over an E-flat major triad.

Later, his style changed considerably. He was a gifted composer and a kind teacher whose life was cut short by AIDS in 1999.

My fellow composers were a talented group, all slightly younger than me, including James Lauth, Mark Birnbaum, David Macbride, who became an important friend, and Donald Sosin, a natural improvisor who wrote pieces exploiting new music techniques, but who also had a flair for theatre and for musical humor. Classmate Joe Hudson asked me to perform an exciting Berioesque work for piano and electronics, which I thoroughly enjoyed.

I brought Dennis the first two movements of my String Quartet, and we worked on the third. He encouraged me to explore more extended techniques in the finale—arguably not the best guidance for me at this point, when I had actually finally found a consistent language.

Nonetheless, he helped me compose an animated final movement that integrated counterpoint and peppery rhythms, and effectively used materials from the previous two movements. The complete piece was performed at a Columbia Composers Concert in McMillan Theatre.

The Quartet was twenty-five minutes long, ambitious and austere, with no sociability whatsoever. Picking up the chromaticism of the little Theme and Variations, it was doggedly un-Stravinskian in its dark sound world: introspective, unified, contrapuntal, and—making use of sonata and ternary forms—structurally convincing. The major-minor third and other aspects of the opening theme were the main seeds of all three movements. The slow movement had a compact, somber expressivity.

The night of the performance was an exciting one. M. and my parents were there, along with several friends, and even my student Linda Smith.

It strikes me now that my little opera *Desire* had derived largely from the language of the three movements for piano four hands I had composed in Paris, while the Quartet stemmed more from the more introverted side that Boulanger had thought "sounded like Schoenberg."

David Olan and Alison Nowak and I met regularly to rehearse music for violin, clarinet, and piano, including Stravinsky's arrangement of pieces from *L'Histoire du Soldat*, Donald Martino's Trio, and the Ives *Largo*. I also became a regular in the audience of performances by their group, the Composers Ensemble.

Although all of its members had studied composition with Wuorinen, and their music was serial and had a kinship with his, they were clearly developing their own voices. Peter Lieberson often conducted, and his own music was commanding and full of character. Alison's work was angular and uncompromising, with a mathematical severity in its rhythms—a kind of abstract expressionism in music that didn't hearken back to a previous era.

I was attracted to the way it was simply itself—so different from my work in that it did not seem to be reconciling opposing tendencies. It was already completely realized, mature music. The concerts occasionally included classic early-twentieth-century pieces. For example, David performed Berg's intense, compressed *Vier Stücke* for clarinet and piano, op. 5.

Despite benefiting from Beeson's support, I felt a persistent sense of alienation at Columbia, even a sense that I was in the wrong field. It was a feeling I had never had before. Miss Dillon had urged me to always "compose from the heart." Boulanger had quoted Valery: "Do not enter without desire". At Columbia, I learned that my desires were probably mistaken. As for the heart: it was never mentioned.

As part of the application process, I had met with Professor Chou Wen-chung, an important Chinese-born composer who had moved to the US in his twenties and was originally a protégé of Edgard Varèse. Of course, I knew nothing of his struggles as a composer, or of how he had carved out his own idiom from an array of both Western and Chinese sources. All I knew was that he was in charge of my fate at Columbia and that, after examining the score to my opera, he told me, "The sooner you break out of this, the better." Later, I took his music analysis class, too much of which, it seemed to me, was devoted to musical method. But to my surprise, he had photos of Stravinsky on the walls of his office.

I started to think about Helen Carter's words and Stravinsky's advice to Kirchner, to wonder what becoming a musician or artist of any kind had to do with going to school. My father had not graduated from college; neither had E.B. White or Salinger. The fact is that Columbia obscured from view many of the contemporary composers I might have been able to learn most directly from. In classes, the prevalent theory of creativity seemed to be a kind of "trickle-down systematics"—as if composers were first and fore-most theorists. Design, logic, and control were everything.

Some of my peers chose a system for composing before starting to create the music itself. I had peers who brought "pre-compositional sketches" to class, full of plans for the structure that their musical ideas would eventually populate. This approach was intellectually "top down," or so it seemed to me. Instead of deriving their sound world and structures out of their own ideas and out of the way their minds worked, many young composers were imposing newly learned methods on their music-making, stamping out any possibil-ity of real discovery. The systems dictated musical ideas from above, and through an overarching logic were assumed to guarantee the compositions their order and meaning.

And no wonder, given that many of the prominent composers of the day spoke primarily in technical jargon about their work. Our classes did not balance analysis with listening, playing, focusing on how to write idiomatically for instruments, or discussions of the music from an aesthetic point of view. Music was abstract: discon-nected from the ear and the body as well as from society, history, politics, and the other arts.

Our teachers did not play the piano for us, and we did not sing in class. Even when speaking about Edgard Varèse's vision of unbounded space, and of sound "as living matter," we did not play gongs, tubular bells, or bass drums, or open the piano lids to make the strings resonate. We turned away as if in embarrassment from Webern's exquisite ear for vibrations and for silences, and instead counted the notes. We did not sing or play the beautiful row from Stockhausen's *Mantra* (as he himself does in the lecture he filmed on the piece in 1973). And the contemporary composers we studied were a very restricted group.

While Boulanger's classes had been filled with sound, here music was quite literally "theoretical," since it was primarily presented on the blackboard and on paper.

Paradoxically, it was the electronic music that needed to be heard to be evaluated, since no score could properly represent it. I always appreciated hearing this colorful work in Beeson's semi-nar. I remember his reactions of "handsome piece" and his specific suggestions after hearing these. Despite his own musical language—Beeson was highly skilled, pragmatic, and a rather traditional opera composer—he had the ability to enjoy any kind of music and to comment usefully on it.

Another dominant figure in the department at the time was the composer-conductor-pianist-theorist Jacques-Louis Monod. Monod was known for his conducting of Schoenberg and Webern and for his fierce advocacy of their music during a period when their work was new to listeners in this country. It was impossible not to be impressed by his brilliance and knowledge. In class, he produced long scrolls displaying meticulous analyses of entire movements by Mahler, in which every harmony and every pitch were accounted for. He did similar feats of exegesis about Varèse's *Ionisation* and many other works.

Rumor had it that he had been working for many years on a sur-real opera in which, instead of an orchestra in the pit, there was a chorus. I do not know if this tantalizing rumor was true. He must have thought I was a reliable pianist, because he asked me to play one of his Cantus Contra Cantum works for a class. I was astounded by his erudition and shocked by his negative views of some of my idols. He said that Stravinsky was "a juxtaposer, not a composer," and said of Kirchner's music that it created "a muddle in the mind."

Monod had once been married to Bethany Beardslee. His rela-tives included two Nobel prize-winning scientists and the filmmaker Jean-Luc Godard. I admired him and his convictions. In some ways, I wished that I could be like him, but I was not.

In the university environment, what the great composers of the day had actually accomplished—a wild, personal expression of an aspect of human life that had never before been expressed—had now become dogma, and had been reduced to a catalogue of techniques.

But the techniques had come from what they needed to say.

I couldn't articulate this at the time, and it isn't easy to do so today: Much as I was excited by the music of Boulez, Stockhausen, Berio, Babbitt, and Carter, I didn't identify with them. My mindset was different. Their iconoclasm and originality were inspiring, but there was an aura of the mathematician-scientist about them that was alienating. Looking into the faces of Mozart, or Beethoven, I felt that they were brothers. I could identify with the nervous, wounded bookishness of a Shostakovich, or the immersive, accomplished, joyous musicianship of Duke Ellington.

But were the Columbia role-model composers the future, or an ending?

I appreciated their music in an impressionistic manner, and could often be thrilled by it, but I rarely became attached to every detail and every note, the way I did with Stravinsky's or Bartók's music, or Bach's or Schoenberg's. Their work remained a dazzling impression. It carried a powerful human charge, leaving as residue the desire to hear it again and investigate it further. It did, in fact, express who they were, and I loved the state of beautiful bewilderment their music created. But I also felt that my ears and outlook were different.

During this period, I heard many student pieces vaguely resembling theirs that I never wanted to hear again, not because they were youthful efforts, but because the processes behind them were artificial. At Columbia, I heard enough "gestural" pieces, saturated with detail and seemingly all twelve pitches, all of the time, to last me a lifetime.

In Paris, I had attended a concert of Boulez's three Piano Sonatas played in a single evening, and the effect was energizing and genuine. But I sometimes wondered if some of my peers even enjoyed what they were writing. Some of them happily played in bands on the weekends, music that left no trace on what they composed for class. Apparently, their education had crushed this physical and recreational side of music out of them, separating it from their "serious" sides. But isn't that part of the greatness of Bach—that playing and singing his work is healing and actually feels good to perform?

There was, of course, no actual "tyranny" dictating that one needed to write such intellectually conceived music, only a tsunami wave of peer pressure. I attended a composition master class at Juilliard, presided over by Boulez, in which a student presented his brass quintet. Referring to the influence of William Schuman and Aaron Copland on his work, he mentioned a "foot-tapping" rhythm in a fast section apologetically, almost as if it were a sin.

I know now that many composers simply rejected the cerebral music of the post-serialists altogether, as if it had been a mistake. I never rejected them at all. It just wasn't my way. For me, music is first and foremost an organization of pitches and rhythms that contain and convey emotions. The pressure to think of pitches and rhythms as merely two out of many "parameters" was cutting me off from my roots, my memory, my instincts, indeed from whatever talent I had, and whatever I could contribute to music. It was as if a cook was told not to taste his food.

This did not mean that I was not interested in timbre and sound and issues of architecture and musical language, or that I did not see creating music as in some sense a "science" as well as an "art." It meant that I had to find my own way of wedding intellect to instinct.

Not even Columbia was a closed world. I remember discussing a shared enthusiasm for Poulenc with fellow composer Mark Birnbaum, almost in the spirit of the young Soviet-era composers who exchanged clandestine copies of scores by Webern and Cage. Clearly, Jack Beeson himself was feeling no pressure to work against the grain of his own predilections. In 1975, he was at work on his comic opera, *Captain Jinks of the Horse Marines*. I was in his seminar, having completed and performed my Trio with Alison and David the previous spring. My first contribution to class was a three-movement Piano Sonatina, my second twelve-tone piece. (It is best left forgotten, and has been.)

Soon I was working on my master's thesis, a two-character, twelve-tone, one-act opera to my brother's libretto, and receiving Beeson's expert advice on prosody. Lyn Austin of the Lenox Arts Center had agreed to present it the following summer in the Berkshires. I had lunch with Francis Thorne, a composer with an eclectic musical background who was also executive director of both the Arts Center and the newly formed American Composers Orchestra. When I told him that our opera was twelve-tone (albeit based on a row that suggested G minor), his reaction stuck with me: "Well, I hope you don't waste this opportunity trying to impress Milton Babbitt and composers of his type. You have to ask yourself: 'Do I admire these composers because of the way they compose, or because they are being themselves?'"

Not long after this, I heard several thrilling Duke Ellington orchestral compositions, the George Antheil "Jazz Symphony," and John Harbison's Piano Concerto, a work with which I immediately identified, performed live. I felt emboldened.

Two of the other composers in our seminar, Don Sosin and Jim Lauth, had attended the University of Michigan and brought with them tales of studying with a virtuosic composer, William Bolcom, for whom any style was fair game. An accomplished pianist, whose improvisational accompaniments could be heard on his wife's recordings of jazz standards and popular songs from the turn of the century, Bolcom alternated composing complex non-tonal works and finely crafted tonal Ragtimes. I bought the sheet music for his haunting *Graceful Ghost Rag*, composed in memory of his father, and learned to play it.

Another Columbia composer whose work I thoroughly enjoyed was Wendy Chambers. She was creating mosaics of tuneful folk-like melodies, ostinatos, and colorful shifts in key areas, which seemed to breathe a different air. A few years later, I had the delightful experience of performing in her piece for multiple pianos, *Ten Grand*, in the plaza of Lincoln Center, alongside Ursula Oppens, Aleck Karis, and seven other pianists.

Twelve-tone or not, presenting our little opera, *In the Dark*, at Lenox that bicentennial summer was a joy. Howard Hensel and Barbara Ann Martin sang the two solo parts, and I conducted an ensemble of seven players: clarinet, bassoon, violin, viola, double bass, percussion, piano. The thirty-five-minute theatre piece was preceded by Stravinsky's *Duo Concertant*, played by violinist Sandy Strenger and pianist David Holzman. Because of the interests of the musicians and singers, there was a "new music" atmosphere in between rehearsals of the show. I remember hearing David practicing Wolpe's *Battle Piece*.

Wally's text was a playlet in speech that was partly colloquial, partly poetic. The two characters are a couple who know each other from their office, on an awkward date. Like our puppet shows and our later collaboration *The Music Teacher*, *In the Dark* combines an almost banal realism with a strangeness that makes an audience laugh uneasily. It culminates in the pair going to bed together while the lights descend on restrained, pulsing music, suggesting sex as a suspension of time, accompanied by groans and a few words from the woman. It ends with breakfast the next morning, in an atmosphere of profound alienation.

The angular vocal lines suggest a connection to Schoenberg's *Von Heute auf Morgen*, but there is a hint of Kurt Weill in the final duet, the first time since the opening that the couple sings together. The spare orchestration gives each instrument a moment to shine. A local reviewer found that my music didn't quite take the bait offered by the text.

We had written to Salinger hoping he might be able to come hear *In the Dark*, and he had written back saying that he was charmed by the notion of a "chamber opera" but was too busy working to attend.

However, he proposed meeting soon for dinner in New York, and Wally and his companion Deborah Eisenberg, M., and I joined him at Gaylord's, a restaurant we thought he would like. It was a very festive evening, but also the last time any of us saw him. I wrote him several times in later years, hoping to go visit him again, but he had apparently withdrawn from most social contacts. That night, he seemed particularly enchanted by our romantic attachments and curious about our lives. He had read Wally's plays, and he was struck by their explicit and often tortured sexuality. He asked him, "Do you really think that sex is so important?"

In the fall of 1976, Wally and Debbie took me along to the Metropolitan Opera House to attend *Einstein on the Beach*. It was breath of fresh air to hear Philip Glass's ecstatic score, and to be thrown into Robert Wilson's time-suspended dream world. While I didn't personally bond with Glass's musical idiom, I was delighted by it; it expanded my horizons and sense of what music could be.

In April, I attended the rehearsals and premiere of Leon Kirchner's long-awaited opera *Lily* at the New York City Opera. Kirchner had written his own libretto based on Bellow's *Henderson the Rain King*, and it had taken him eighteen years to compose it, during which time he had found the character of Henderson increasingly akin to President Johnson, and the novel symbolic of America's tragic destructiveness of other cultures. He had always been highly self-critical, and he had often postponed scheduled premieres of his pieces because he wasn't satisfied with them, and the gestation period for this one had been constantly interrupted by his teaching schedule.

I was so taken with many of the extraordinary musical passages in the opera, including the overture (related to *Music for Orchestra*), the tribal choruses, the bewitching "jazz song" for the title character—music that couldn't have been written by anyone but Kirchner—that I did not worry about any weaknesses the work might have had, including those in the libretto and the production itself.

While some critics had warm words about the music, the daily *Times* issued a devastating, unnuanced pronouncement of the work's failure, and there was a second dive into its defects in the Sunday paper. The complete opera remains unrecorded to this day. Kirchner apparently himself felt that the work needed revision, but its negative reception took a toll on his health (he had suffered from a heart condition since the early '70s) and on his spirits. He was also wrestling with his own complex reactions to the musical polemics

of the day, with its emphasis on methodology and technical innova-
tion over human expression. It took some years after *Lily* for him to
recover his creative stride and produce such wonderful later pieces
as the *Music for Twelve, Of Things Exactly as They Are, Music for
Cello and Orchestra, Music for Orchestra II,* and *The Forbidden.*

Meanwhile, matrix at the ready, I worked on a Fantasy for flute
and piano, my fourth twelve-tone effort, which I was fortunate to be
able to perform later that year with Harvey Sollberger at a Columbia
concert.

Now officially a doctoral candidate, I was studying one-on-one
with Vladimir Ussachevsky. Young students are often quite unaware
of the paths traveled by their teachers. As had been the case when I
studied with Professor Chou, I was ignorant of Ussachevsky's journey from his birth in Inner Mongolia, the child of a Russian army
officer and pianist mother, to his life in the United States. I knew
nothing of his early Russian-sounding music, his path-breaking
electronic works, his wonderful piano playing, or his intersection
with Otto Luening and Bennington College, where I have now spent
much of my adult life.

We did not become close in lessons, despite frequently meeting
in his Upper West Side apartment. He often seemed weary and
unwell, with an alarming, persistent cough. But I now wonder if he
understood me better than I realized at the time. He once asked me
casually if I had heard Britten's *Peter Grimes,* commenting on how
"beautifully done" it was. I almost jumped. No Britten, Shostakovich,
Barber, or even Messiaen works had ever been mentioned in class.
Neither had jazz, rock, American folk music, or ancient musical
traditions from India, Japan, Indonesia, or Ghana.

After completing the Fantasy, I started on a large chamber work,
again filtering my music through a serial grid. The piece stalled. I felt
stuck and disembodied. Composing was like being in a nightmare
in which I was manipulating puppets on strings who were putting
down notes on my behalf.

In the margins of the score, I started writing nostalgic jazz fragments, with big-band chords redolent of Duke Ellington or Count
Basie, and wistful melodies hearkening back to the Rodgers songs I
had heard my father play in the family living room. The fragments
turned into complete pieces, and additional pieces started to almost
write themselves. Eventually, I had seven of them, which I called

Jazz Suite, and I played through them for Ussachevsky in a class-room at school.

Although he dismissed the most romantic one, calling it "something I might have written for my first girlfriend, but not after that," Ussachevsky also seemed to get a kick out of them. When he saw Jacques-Louis Monod passing in the hall, he called out to him to come hear the Suite. Monod listened with attention, afterwards commenting that, "There are things one may enjoy that one shouldn't learn from. Dixieland jazz, for example. "

That spring, my relationship with M. came to an end, and I went through a morose and lonely spell, giving my brother excellent material for his portrayal of a divorced man in the film *Starting Over*. I then briefly dated a delightful, intelligent, and lovely woman who worked at the New York Shakespeare Festival.

I felt that my relationship to Columbia had come to an end as well, and I sent in my withdrawal from the doctoral program.

In the early summer, while continuing to rehearse trios for clarinet, violin, and piano with Alison Nowak and David Olan, I composed a set of six violin and piano pieces I could play with Alison. Building on the more spontaneous way of composing I had discovered when writing my Jazz Suite, but in a tighter style, and without overt jazz references, these pieces felt both authentic and interesting. Each movement had its own texture, meter, and character. A reprise of the melody and harmonies from the pensive first movement in the fifth gave the set some unity. Perhaps with their hints of Ives, Bartók, Stravinsky, and even Bernstein, they were too varied in language, but they were expressive and well written.

The main thing was that, after becoming so alienated from composing, I had gone back to square one, to a way of writing in which I enjoyed each and every note I put down.

Boulanger was certainly right that no matter our influences, we are eventually left face to face with ourselves. Looking back on my long "apprenticeship," I see the validity in all of the many critiques I received. I also see a broken line of progress, and what could at least merit being called "juvenilia" in those pieces where "one note leads to another" (to quote Pierre Petit), and where a musical through-line is not splintered into bits by blatant imitation or paralyzing self-consciousness. I also see where my teachers succeeded and where they failed. Those whose guidance still reverberates in me never lost track of what music is, nor of the need to stay rooted in sound and in joy. The Psalm says: "Make a joyful noise."

One activity at Columbia that truly taught me—and that also showed me a way I could be useful—was serving as an ear training instructor, playing and singing intervals and rhythms in their purest forms, the same ones used by William Byrd, Duke Ellington, and Karlheinz Stockhausen. We are but small leaves on a gigantic tree that is the long story of music itself.

When I was lying on the floor underneath the piano at the age of five, listening to the vibrations, I was already a composer. Whenever I kept truly listening to what I wrote, I was making progress. Those who tried to impose their own history onto mine were wrong. Music is much bigger than that, and time is much more complex than that. There are many paths through the present. No one can tell me what contemporary music should be.

Like the sun peeking through dark clouds, what I started to write in 1977 shed a warming light. In my own humble way, I was re-emerging, not by finding a radically new way of doing things, but by returning to where I had started.

PART II

7

A VARIED WORKING LIFE AND A MARRIAGE (1977–1983)

L OOKING BACK NOW TO the early summer of 1977, I see a very young person, only twenty-nine years old. At the time, I felt that I had already been through a lot. Yet in terms of composing, I knew that I was just starting out.

In July, I received a request from the Composers Ensemble to perform the piano part in some songs by Poulenc in a concert of lighter music that they were presenting at Carnegie Recital Hall the following February. The singer would be Joyce Suskind. They also asked me to compose a piece that I could perform with them on the program.

This was an amazing opportunity, and I set to work on what would become an eight-minute piece in three movements for clarinet, violin, cello, and piano, called *Cabaret Music*. I wrote this in a new way. My first idea simply came to me at the piano: a quiet melody in the low register of the clarinet with a jaunty, march-like accompaniment in B flat minor, vaguely suggestive of Berlin Cabaret.

Instead of ignoring or censoring this idea, I built the first movement out of it. I introduced the tune with harshly dissonant syncopated chords and figures that related to it, embedding it in a chamber-music context, then continued with juxtapositions of both ideas. The language was compressed and full of interest, and combined two seemingly contradictory idioms—the neoclassic and the expressionistic. There was a brief piano outburst that almost recalled Kirchner.

The second movement was slow and again rooted in B flat and derived from the *Cabaret* tune, but it had a feeling of suspended time, as contrapuntal ideas in different configurations floated over drone-like accompaniments. It exploited the invertible counterpoint that I had learned about in David Del Tredici's counterpoint class. The buoyant, at times waltz-like last movement was again full of counterpoint (sometimes in five parts) and of developments of previous materials. I relished a moment where there was a canon in two voices, with a simultaneous retrograde in a third.

The harsh chords from the opening of the first movement returned, combining with the waltz idea. The opening of the first movement was alluded to, as if in a memory. The piece ended with the first note of the original clarinet tune held as a long tone, as the other instruments quietly played fragments from the first measures of the piece.

This was a breakthrough. The piece was derived from an idea that had simply come to me. I had gotten out of my way and allowed my memory, musicianship, and whatever intelligence I had to emerge.

It seems to me that mature work reconciles our contradictions. On the one hand, we hope to make something that is "together," that has craft. On the other hand, meaning comes from allowing our broken places to speak through our music. Even when we are at our most accomplished, we are still human. So-called "mastery" is only interesting when it comes from the whole person. When I heard the Bartók Quartets—I was hearing Bartók himself.

I knew that *Cabaret Music* would be perceived as "light," but I was aware of the contradiction between the seemingly "light" flavor of the work and something tragic way beneath it. While composing it, I had been thinking of my Jewish ancestry and unknown distant kin, dead in the Holocaust. I could feel my sister speaking through me. I could feel the place music had occupied in our fractured family life.

But lest the reader find this pretentious, I should say that my intention was only to compose a piece. It was the music itself, as it evolved, which brought with it sad and tragic thoughts about the past. It was one of countless times that the intense concentration and self-forgetfulness of composing has stirred intimations of being rooted in the long chain of being, even if the actual music I am writing is light and transparent. Like falling in love, composing brings with it a strange sadness.

As if to echo this counterpoint of emotions, after the premiere, I was in a foul mood. But the piece had gone well. David Olan had played the clarinet, Curt Macomber the violin, Myron Lutzke the cello, and I had played the piano. Perhaps I simply felt the inevitable disillusionment that comes with every performance. While you are composing, you are in a heightened state, and fundamentally content. There is a moment in Hitchcock's psychological thriller *Marnie* that illustrates this state perfectly: the moment when all of the doors open in her imagination, and suddenly her life makes sense. When composing, you feel justified; you are in continuity with the natural world, in touch with your past, and optimistic about the future. You feel in communication with your fellow humans—as if you are embracing them. You feel you can transcend your problems. However, when the piece is played and shared, along with the pleasure of hearing it, you realize that it is finite; it is in fact just a piece of music; it is, inevitably, an imperfect creation, just as you are an imperfect creature; the moment of composing it is past; perhaps the performance as heard was not ideal; perhaps the piece will never be played again; perhaps you will not be able to compose again.

In any event, I considered this my "opus one." Even though my education as a musician would never end, even though I might never feel truly qualified to call myself a "composer," this was the first piece that made me feel that I didn't give a damn, that my ignorance didn't matter, and that I had a right to put my music in front of an audience.

Peter G. Davis in the New York Times wrote that *Cabaret Music* "lived up to its title, a deftly written, tangy divertimento with a nice sleazy Cabaret flavor."[1] This was a more than decent response, comparing quite favorably to the *Harvard Crimson* reviewer's description of *The Kiss Refused* as "poor" and "tawdry." After the performance, I was approached by a young conductor who asked me if I would consider composing a piece for his chamber orchestra. My foul mood went away. I was overjoyed.

This new phase in my music coincided not just with my departure from Columbia, but also with the beginning of my relationship with Jamaica, an accomplished staff writer at *The New Yorker* who wrote for the Talk of the Town. I first met her at a friend's house in the spring of 1997. J. was nearly six feet tall, West Indian by birth, an extraordinarily gifted person who could have been a photographer, a designer, a performer, a botanist, or many other things, had she not chosen the more solitary road of becoming a writer.

She was instantly memorable. She could hold a large room of party guests enthralled with stories of her childhood, travels to this

---

[1]   Peter G. Davis, *"Concert offers 4 premieres,"* New York Times, Feb. 4, 1978.

country as a teenager, work as an au pair, attempts to conform to student life at Franconia College, and her wild life as a freelance writer in New York. I, too, was enthralled when I met her at a friend's party, and even more so when I was playing some pieces from my *Jazz Suite* at the piano and she came and sat next to me on the piano bench.

I soon invited her over to dinner at my house, and a relationship began that led to our moving in together on Hudson Street in the Village in the fall of 1977. We were married two years later and eventually had two children. Our marriage lasted for twenty-three years, until the spring of 2001.

Although few people might have anticipated our becoming a couple, Wally apparently had, since—ever optimistic about my romantic prospects—he had mentioned J.'s name to me as among the women my age who were currently available.

J.'s flamboyant, original outfits (which included hot pants) and her party-going, dancing, and outspokenness were counterbalanced by her quiet, beautiful, English-accented speaking voice, as well as an inner vulnerability, complexity, and brilliance that began to fully emerge in her imaginative fiction during the time we were first together. Seeing her developing voice as an author as it materialized was a profound experience and a powerful spur to my own creativity, and her boldness as a person gave me strength too.

Both Wally and I were raised in an atmosphere of extraordinary civility and politeness. But somehow Wally never suffered from an inability to express himself, even while remaining unusually kind and unusually courteous. He had rebelled against our parents when he needed to, and had staked out a territory in his writing that was at odds with *The New Yorker* and with society, was ferociously frank, and, in his own words, chronicled his "inner life as a raging beast."

As Mary's twin, my situation was different. Mary had been sent away to an institution precisely because she was unruly and could not adapt to normal life. (The fact that she was autistic and vulnerable and that this was probably better for her was surely lost on me at age eight.) At least in part as a result, I emulated my father's reticence and held my own inner "raging beast" in check. I instinctively tried to appear normal and logical, and kept my deeper feelings inside, even as I was struggling with crippling anxieties. Just as I took courage from Wally's expansive temperament, I was inspired by J.'s fearlessness. At the same time as I embarked on this relationship and marriage, I had not even begun to realize the extent to which being Mary's twin brother had affected me or my relationships with women.

I am a short Jew—five feet two on a good day. When J. and I held hands on the street, I was suddenly aware of us as an atypical couple. This was a period in which there were far fewer interracial couples than there are today, and if any were visible in mainstream media, they were presented as curiosities. But I don't think that either of us quite thought in those terms. J. was a brilliant and unique personality who did not meet her biological father until she was thirty. In her daily life, she was surrounded by Americans, most of whom were white. I had my mysterious twin, an occluded connection to Judaism, and a recent long-term relationship with a French girlfriend, suggesting, perhaps, a leaning towards those with a history and country of origin different from my own. At any rate, the differences in our backgrounds and heights were sometimes noted out loud by passersby. (I remember someone saying to his companion, "Get a load of this!")

I was already self-conscious about my height. J. couldn't have cared less; she barely seemed to notice that I was short. My father had commented on the issue when I first went to see him to tell him that I was going out with a *New Yorker* writer. "When the woman is a bit taller than the man," he had said, "you notice it. But when she is a great deal taller, well, then it just becomes a whole other thing." When I mentioned that we must "look unusual" to my old teacher Emily Alford at the Seeger School, she looked at me crossly and said, "Allen! Grow up!"

J. introduced me to an entire world of popular music I didn't know. I didn't know Motown, and I had never even heard the Beach Boys. We had noisy dance parties in our New York apartment, two inexpensive floors above an Italian restaurant on the edge of what is now Soho, but which at that time was practically deserted. The living room was still painted orange from the time that tantric Buddhists had occupied the space. J. started her first garden on the balcony that faced the back of the building, off the kitchen. There were gates on the windows there, but even so we experienced a break-in in the middle of the night, watching from the stairway above as two men carried off our stereo and television set from the living room. There was also a serious fire in the restaurant below that came close to engulfing the entire building and left it scarred. But the most persistent problem was the mice population. We had dinners with friends during which these many little uninvited guests raced along the walls as if they were the primary tenants of the house. (From their perspective, they were.)

Extraordinarily different as J. and I were in temperament and personality—certainly, my extreme phobias clashed with her love of travel—we also had many interests in common, and we were always talking: about politics, books, movies, and art. Yet, perhaps even more essentially, we could also be very domestic and quiet with each other, something she particularly needed. And we were fascinated with each other's work. I read every word she wrote, and I played her all of my new pieces, sometimes asking her which version she preferred when I was unsure of something. She liked it when I played *Graceful Ghost Rag* and the immortal works in the Dover "Scott Joplin" collection. We went to many classical concerts together, which deeply affected her. The vitality of the pop music she introduced me to had an impact on what I was writing as well.

I actually had two premieres back to back at Carnegie Recital Hall in the early spring of 1978. The second was a brief, highly chromatic acapella choral piece, *Music, When Soft Voices Die*, a setting of the Shelley poem. It was performed by The New Calliope Singers, a group formed at Columbia and conducted by Peter Schubert, a musician-friend I had known first when he was a Putney student, then later with Boulanger, and then again at Columbia, where he worked closely with Jacques-Louis Monod.

I remember the lovely sound of the choir wafting through the hall, and the pleasurable sense that the quiet piece, while not earth-shaking, was at least a sincere effort, organically exploring its own materials and not an attempt to ape someone else's style and methods. (This was, incidentally, the exact opposite of what the *New York Times* reviewer thought.) Peter told me that my piece was "all about half-steps."

Having put Columbia behind me, I was now in a position to take on more work in the theatre alongside my teaching. In one rash moment, and with my brother's encouragement, I even tried auditioning to be an actor in a comedy. (I was simply terrible.)

Back in the summer I had been hired to work with talented composer Margaret Pine on the instrumental arrangements for a musical based on Molière's *The Misanthrope* at the Public Theater, for which I would also be the music director. Margaret and I did the arrangements over the summer, and rehearsals began in the fall. The band was placed in a kind of treehouse above and behind the main set, and I conducted from the keyboard.

Among the talented cast were two actors with whom I became good friends: John Bottoms and the delightful Deborah Rush. But the production ended up in great difficulty, and Joe Papp decided that the entire concept behind it should be scrapped and the original creative team removed. The intensely serious director Leo Shapiro, a passionate socialist, was replaced by a new director with a lighter touch, the set being gradually transformed, and much of the Brechtian score gradually supplanted by new music more in a Broadway vein.

Margaret was banned from the set, and I was left in the position of defending her music not only from being reorchestrated, but from being rewritten. I felt guilty that I had not served the music well enough, and I knew that being disconnected from the project must have been a terrible blow to Margaret.

There was one dreadful but comic moment in one of the transitional shows when actor John Bottoms came onto the set by himself for his usual solo number, not knowing it had just been cut. He waited for a full minute, but the music never started. When the reason for the silence finally dawned on him, he said, "Oh my God" to the audience and walked off.

Wally was rehearsing one of his plays down the hall at the Public Theater, and he used to drop by during rehearsals of the changes. I could sometimes see him in the last row in his raincoat, looking like Columbo, trying to analyze exactly what had gone wrong with the show.

As happens so often in the theater, nerves became frayed and tempers barely contained, and when the new director told me to change the harmonies in one of Margaret's songs, and that she only cared about getting her weekly paycheck, I lashed out at him, saying, "Go fuck yourself," hardly my usual style. Later that day, Joe Papp called me over to him and told me that I was fired as music director. However, he said I could stay on as pianist if I wished. And I did stay. Not only did I need the money: I loved being in the theater. The more upbeat *Misanthrope* opened in November, only to immediately close.

Another theater project came along in early 1978 that allowed me to try out my more spontaneous puppet show-composing skills in a professional setting for the first time. Writer-director James Lapine was doing a workshop staging of his new play, *Twelve Dreams*, at the Theatre of the Open Eye.

Both the subject and James's aesthetic approach resonated with me. *Twelve Dreams* was based on a case history recounted by Carl Jung, in which a psychoanalyst's daughter, Emma, gave her father a homemade book as a present in which she had written down her strange and disturbing dreams. Jung looked at them and thought that they resembled the troubled dreams of an elderly person nearing death. Shortly afterwards, Emma became ill and died. I bonded with the character of the young girl and the notion of dreams as unbidden expressions of her troubled psyche.

The score was collaborative. My work on acoustic instruments (piano and toy piano) was complemented by Pril Smiley's evocative electronic music, some of which reused and modified my ideas, putting them in another sonic context and dimension. Our score accompanied non-verbal dream sequences of various lengths that were beautifully staged and choreographed.

James had originally been a designer. His incomparable gift for theatrical concepts and for the visual and scenic aspects of a production would later bear fruit in his many collaborations with Stephen Sondheim, including *Sunday in the Park with George*. Although at times I had to swallow having my pieces reduced to fragments or cut altogether, the dream sequences allowed me to compose real music in my own style, and they stretched my emotional range.

But playing the acoustic parts of the score live for the performances was a magical experience. I felt like I was back in the family living room working with Wally. James became a friend for life, and many years later in Vermont I renewed contact with Pril Smiley and got to know much more about her extraordinary electronic compositions.

I was soon hard at work on the chamber orchestra piece. I had spoken to the conductor on the phone, and he had agreed with the idea that I make it a miniature piano concerto I could play with the group. I could feel my teenage ambitions and chutzpah returning.

I was also taking pains not to let my Stravinsky obsession overtake my newfound fluency. I had determined that Stravinsky's influence on my composing was most constructive when it was not apparent, that whenever the music started to sound like his, it became technically and emotionally diffuse. As the work took shape, it became clear that it would be an eclectic one, consisting of four heterogeneous movements which I called *Nocturnes*. I see now that here and in *Cabaret Music* I was aided by impressions gleaned working with Francis Judd Cooke and Stanley Silverman, both of whom had, in different ways, allowed elements of vernacular idioms into their music.

Nocturnes was twenty minutes long and evoked nighttime in four different ways. The Ivesian first movement pitted an improvisatory, sometimes choleric piano part against impassive strings and winds, with a liberal use of whole-tone chords and scales. The second evoked a nightclub in two raucous, jazzy sections interrupted by a brief quiet recall of the first movement. This was a throwback to my childhood piano and orchestra piece *Older Brother* from fifteen years earlier, when I had included a jazz variation, playing with mallets on the piano strings.

This was followed by a heartfelt, lyrical Nocturne for piano and strings, beginning and ending in E flat minor. The finale was a kind of swirling dreamscape that made references to the opening movement and included a surreal quotation of "Old MacDonald Had a Farm," ending in quizzical quietude. I thought of the movement as a child's stream of consciousness.

Even if the big-band sonorities of the second movement were those of a previous generation, and the tonal slow movement was reminiscent of Samuel Barber, I was excited about the work, and felt it spoke for me. I finished it over the summer, and I thought I had succeeded with the orchestration too. A chamber orchestra of one wind and brass to a part fosters a healthy spareness, protecting one from unnecessary doublings.

Unfortunately, my conductor wrote me in the fall to let me know that his chamber orchestra had folded, and no performance would take place.

To recover from my disappointment, I began another piece, again for violin and piano. I had been performing some recitals with a remarkable violinist, Marilyn Dubow. We played extraordinary repertoire, including Ives's Second and Fourth Sonatas, the Schoenberg Phantasy, and Cage's *Six Melodies for Violin and Piano* (1950). Although I hated traveling anywhere new, it was exciting to play the "In the Barn" movement from Ives's Second Sonata with Marilyn for a huge audience in a high school gymnasium in Ives's home town of Danbury, CT. We also presented programs in New Jersey and at a church in New York, and at the McMillan Theatre.

Another musical encounter that made a big impression was hearing Tobias Picker play his Violin and Piano Rhapsody at a Group for Contemporary Music concert in 1978. Here was a composer who was using serial procedures to make music that had its own kind of lyricism, rich harmonic vocabulary, and eccentric musical syntax, full of surprising shifts in direction. It wasn't the technique that struck the listener; it was Picker's poetic vision, and a frame of reference that included many of my favorite composers, even Gershwin. I called Picker and asked him for a copy of the score so that Marilyn and I could learn it.

Despite its Stravinskian title, it was the spirit of Ives that hovered over my *Movements for Violin and Piano*. The first and last movements, "Hymn" and "Epilogue," were fervent, flowing, and turbulent, with a confident independence between the two instruments. The middle movement was the most tonal of the three: a theme and variations, in many tempi and sentiments, on a good-humored, folk-like melody in B flat major.

In the first movement, a lyrical theme sounding like the transcription of a pre-existing song intruded on the prevailing intensity. This melody returned at the close of the epilogue of the third movement, preceded by a fiercely discordant climax. I was proud of the quiet last measure, which seemed to summarize the entire piece.

I finished this shortly after the first of the year in 1979, just in time to present it on a program I had arranged to give at the Mannes School of Music with one of my friends from composition seminar at Columbia, James Lauth. James's expertly written music featured percussion instruments, and it contrasted nicely with my more traditional chamber music ensembles. My contributions to the concert consisted of Fantasy for Flute and Piano, *Cabaret Music*, four pieces from my *Jazz Suite*, and the premiere of *Movements*.

Cellist Myron Lutzke was unable to make the date and had recommended his friend Maxine Neuman to take his place in *Cabaret Music*. Thus began my lifelong friendship with Maxine, the most nourishing musical collaboration I have ever had.

Veteran new music clarinetist Laura Flax stood in for David Olan. Curt Macomber again played violin in the piece, and in the premiere of *Movements*. I even managed to get Harvey Sollberger to perform the Fantasy again.

My parents not only attended but also gave a nice party for all of the performers and their guests afterwards, which was notable for several reasons. To begin with, Harvey made a comment for which I will be forever grateful: He said that although he liked the Fantasy very much, he thought my new pieces embedding jazzy and tonal materials within more dissonant contexts were much stronger. "I would just lay into the dissonance still more," he said.

He was particularly taken with *Movements*, which he said "evoked Ives" but "in a personal way." Apparently, my nostalgia didn't represent a step backward. In fact, he proposed that *Movements* be performed at a Group for Contemporary Music concert the next fall, and it was.

Another kind of corroboration came from my parents. My mother particularly liked *Cabaret Music*, which, she said, "really swings." I later dedicated the piece to her. My father was excited about the *Jazz Suite*, but I felt that I could do better in this vein. Taking advantage of his editorial instincts, I asked him if he preferred the entire set of seven pieces, or just the four I had excerpted at Mannes. He preferred the piece in its entirety.

I felt honored when the marvelous violinist Linda Quan and pianist Robert Miller performed my *Movements* at a Group for Contemporary Music concert. The event was followed by a party at which Ursula Oppens, who was also on the program that night, told me she had listened from backstage and really liked the piece. I had already heard her play numerous times in New York, and I could also tell her that I remembered her rehearsing Beethoven with the Bach Society Orchestra at Harvard years ago, when she was an undergraduate.

Not long after this, I bought her recording of Rzewski's monumental *The People United Will Never Be Defeated!* and was completely bowled over both by the work and by her playing of it. I hoped that someday she might play something of mine.

I began to wonder if I had something in common with the work of the generation of American composers born ten years before me, in 1938, a generation that included Rzewski, Harbison, Del Tredici, Bolcom, and Joan Tower.

According to Boulanger, Stravinsky described going from one piece to the next as climbing a rope ladder. "If you don't grab onto the next knot... you fall!" In the next few years, I tried to climb my rope ladder as a composer, reaching for the next knot, and sometimes falling. I accepted assignments from the outside, testing different ways of composing and new grips on the rope. Many of the artists I admired were clearly single-minded hedgehogs, but I seemed to have many sides. How can one know if one is a hedgehog or a fox, or even some other creature entirely, without experimenting?

Having experienced a "breakthrough," I began to realize that in adult life, no less than in childhood, there is no smooth narrative; our expectations of having achieved stability are continuously thwarted.

In the fall of 1979, I gave a concert at Greenwich House Music School during which I performed the Berg Sonata, Schoenberg's *Sechs Kleine Klavierstücke*, some piano pieces by Jelly Roll Morton, and, with Rebecca LaBrecque playing my orchestral reduction on a second piano, a new Piano Concerto in one movement. The Concerto was an ambitious and exciting piece, with a convincing form. But somehow it felt empty, like a shell with no turtle in it. After the concert I put it aside, and never orchestrated it.

Seven years later, I was able to fulfill my vision of a true Piano Concerto, and Ursula Oppens would be the soloist.

In the summer of 1980, I began working as rehearsal pianist for a new production of Gilbert and Sullivan's *The Pirates of Penzance*, to be directed by Wilford Leach, with orchestrations by Bill Elliott, and starring Linda Ronstadt, Rex Smith, and Kevin Kline.

Once the entire band was brought in, I played electronic keyboards and celesta alongside two fellow keyboard players. Bill's concept of orchestration turned out to rely greatly on improvisation. The band comprised a superb group of musicians, including brass, wind, and percussionists prominent in the new music world, who were capable of imaginatively embellishing Sullivan's original parts and turning the score into a zany, at times almost psychedelic portrait of itself.

Being in a theatre company was, as always, exhilarating. Like Bill, Wilford Leach created a warm and spontaneous atmosphere that encouraged the actors to invent their own characters and movements. The music was terrific, and the cast, designers, choreographer, director, and music director were brilliant. I met many wonderful new friends in the production.

The show opened at the Delacorte Theater in Central Park in the summer of 1980. It was a huge success, and it moved to Broadway's

Minskoff Theatre in the fall. In late August, inexcusably late, I handed in my resignation to the Mannes Preparatory Division. (I continued teaching at the Elizabeth Seeger School for another year.)

The Pirates of Penzance ran for two years, during which time we also made a cast album and recorded the soundtrack for a film version of the show. The financial stability this created was occasionally supplemented by studio sessions recording advertising jingles arranged for by the show's music contractor, where my stylistic versatility, good playing, and sight-reading skills came in handy. I was in touch with a world of high professionalism, where there was an actual connection between music and money. Apart from the fact that I suffered silently from the claustrophobic conditions of the recording studios, I had the qualifications necessary to be a good session musician. At one point, I was also approached about exploring a career in disco arranging. I also tried my hand at composing a few theme songs for television and radio that I did not have my heart in, and that mostly did not get used.

But I discovered something fundamental about myself in these experiences: I was miserable doing them. I did not know the word "agoraphobia" at the time. Its literal meaning is "fear of the marketplace." It would be convenient to simply say that I had an aversion to the marketplace, but it is more accurate to say that I lacked the ability to divide myself.

Two of my beloved uncles had been in the advertising business, and one of them probably truly enjoyed composing music to advertise Wrigley's gum. I lacked the gift, which my uncle Mike had, of being able to find meaning in an enjoyable professional task without thinking about its context. I had a hunger for meaning and understanding. For me, music was a refuge from the public world and from commerce. Even if it intersected with them, it needed to carve out its own independent space.

In the fall, I worked on two piano pieces during the day that were in the vein of *Jazz Suite*. They started with jazz-tinged themes but became streams of consciousness that evoked improvisation. The first became increasingly turbulent in the Ivesian vein of the first movement of *Nocturnes*. The much longer second was a kind of rondo that included a jazz waltz and counterpoint reminiscent of Keith Jarrett.

I performed these *Two Improvisations* at a recital I gave with Marilyn Dubow in which we also played Tobias Picker's Rhapsody, a work by David Macbride, and arrangements I made for violin and piano of music by Jelly Roll Morton. They were even reviewed by John Rockwell (who called them "appealing"). Although I put them back in my bureau, uncopied, their style was authentic, and led directly to two piano pieces that I felt were among my best so far.

Immediately after finishing the improvisations, I worked on *Four Jazz Preludes*, a closely argued group of four pieces that superficially resembled the *Improvisations* in their jazzy materials, but which were more carefully constructed and not "stream of consciousness" at all. Linked by a three-note melodic cell (a descending major second/minor third outlining a perfect fourth), they were concert portraits of jazz idioms. They teemed with influences: owing something to the hard-nosed Copland of *Four Piano Blues*, Ives's First Piano Sonata, the Gershwin Preludes, Jelly Roll Morton, Art Tatum, Scott Joplin, and to Bartók's use of folk idioms. Yet all the same, I felt that they were original.

After having an argument with J., I wrote the slow movement in a state of misery on the piano at the Seeger School. Many years before the issue of "appropriation" might have made me hesitate, I titled the third movement "Spiritual." The pieces were technically daunting to play (I had not worked with enough pianists to recognize that my large hand stretches were unusual) and aesthetically challenging too. Pianist Hadassah Sahr told me that even my own recording of the pieces did not fully capture what they contained.

Almost simultaneously, I worked on a chamber piece for flute, oboe, and harpsichord to be played at Merkin Concert Hall by Renée Siebert on flute, Humbert Lucarelli on oboe, and Judith Norell on harpsichord. I finished it just after the New Year in 1981—a busy period in which multiple projects overlapped.

It began with a "neoclassical" opening that turned into languorous, pastoral, lyrical music, leading to a short flute cadenza, a spirited sequence of jazzy passages, a climactic restatement of the lyrical music, and a recollection of the opening. Searching for a title for the twelve-minute work, I asked my father's advice, explaining to him that it seemed to me to be a "summer" piece. He suggested "Summer Pages," and the title stuck.

Perhaps influenced by Edward Rothstein's discouraging words about the piece in the *Times*, I thought that I had failed to truly integrate its stylistic materials or to achieve Boulanger's "long line." Today, I think I underestimated *Summer Pages*. It amalgamated the stream-of-consciousness writing of the *Improvisations* with the refinement needed in a chamber work.

I also composed a Second String Quartet for a group called the Cremona Quartet, which premiered in April 1981. The piece built on my first quartet but was more varied. It included a blues-inflected second movement that substituted for a scherzo.

My explorations of how I would earn a living included starting to try my hand at writing words, first by writing a few short humor pieces, and then with an article in the *Monthly* about music by Carter, Sessions, Wuorinen, Kim, Kirchner, Rzewski, Crumb, and Steve Reich. Praising their work gave me a chance to articulate what I valued in contemporary music, and to complain that so much of the best of it was performed in specialized concerts far from the general public:

> Orchestral conductors often settle for the comfortably reactionary piece, which may not displease the audience but arouses no great passion or respect in it either; or for the token avant-garde work... [However] in concerts at which only new music is played... a large body of music that would seem communicative and imaginative to any open-minded listener... is performed for a relatively small circle by a relatively small band of virtuosos.[2]

In this experimental phase of my life, I even did some illustrations for a prose poem by J. that was collected in a book of stories for children edited by Jonathan Cott. I was also still teaching at the Elizabeth Seeger School, but once *The Pirates of Penzance* reopened on Broadway after the first of the year, I began to think of leaving that position.

That same spring, I was already working on some music that Louis Malle had requested for my brother Wally's film, *My Dinner with André*. It was amazingly generous of Wally to recommend to Louis Malle that I be the composer for this project, which would prove to be a life-changing venture for him. I was entirely untried in this field.

The film had grown out of a script Wally had written based on two hundred hours of conversation that he had recorded between André Gregory and himself. André had directed several of Wally's

---

[2]   Allen Shawn, "Contemporary American Composers," *Atlantic Monthly*, April 1981, 115–18.

plays, starting with *Our Late Night.* Wally's plays were his center, and he had only recently become an actor.

The two men were playing versions of themselves, with much of what they said based on their actual words. Yet, they had also been molded by Wally into archetypes representing different approaches to life. They had memorized the carefully constructed text, and in preparation for the filming they performed it many times as a kind of play. I had been in the audience for some of these performances.

By the time I was brought in to create the music, the filming had been completed, and the restaurant scenes had included shots of a violinist, bassist, and pianist performing a waltz in the restaurant. As anyone who has seen *Elevator to the Gallows* with its Miles Davis score knows, Louis Malle had an amazing feeling for music and knowledge of jazz. He asked me to compose roughly twenty minutes of "source music" in the style of Stéphane Grappelli and Django Reinhardt that would appear to have been played live by these restaurant musicians during the beginning of André's and Wally's conversation, as well as one additional piece to accompany the final scene, in which Wally is by himself in a taxi, reflecting on what they discussed. Malle had been using Satie's familiar *Gymnopédie* no. 1 as a dummy track for this last scene and the credits that followed it.

The first track of my music was meant to start four and a half minutes into the film to accompany shots of Wally walking down the street towards the restaurant where he will meet André, putting on his tie, entering the restaurant, checking his coat, encountering the maître d' (who looks at him somewhat suspiciously), going to the bar to order a club soda (since André has yet to arrive) and being told, "I'm sorry sir, we only serve Source du Pavillon," which he accepts, after which he looks over at the musicians, and there is a shot of the violinist beginning to play.

There is an additional shot of the musicians a minute later, when he looks over at them again. André finally enters a moment later, and when they finally sit down at the table and begin their dialogue, a series of numbers at various tempi were to be heard in the background for another fifteen minutes, after which the music would vanish.

Using what I knew of the Grappelli/Reinhardt idiom as a springboard, I quickly wrote the music and hired a jazz violinist and bassist. (I would play the piano part myself.) I have no memory of composing it at all. Although every note was written down, the music evoked improvisation, drawing on my lighter, more spontaneous side.

For the first track, I composed a waltz, using a Moviola to replay the opening scene slowly, again and again, so that I could match what I wrote to the pianist's hands and the bowings of the string players. The other pieces continued in the same lighthearted, slightly decadent vein. For the "Taxi Music" at the end of the film, I wrote a poignant melody that I thought would capture the wistful mood created by the Satie.

My music was added to the film, and in May a screening was held in a theatre on the first floor of the production company. I remember how my stomach churned during this test of the film. Immediately afterwards, Louis Malle asked me to come upstairs with him, and told me with regret in his voice, "It does not work."

He went on to say that although he liked the music very much, it was his mistake to have thought that having it playing in the background would ease the viewer into André and Wally's conversation. It in fact delayed the point at which the audience would surrender itself completely to the intimacy of the film. The presence of music subliminally created the expectation that the camera would soon take us to the forest, to the desert, and to all of the other places André mentions, rather than remaining quietly with the protagonists at the dinner table.

In addition, he told me that he felt that the comforting familiarity of Satie's beautiful piece was the right accompaniment for the ending, rather than my "Taxi Music." And in place of the waltz I had written for the opening, he would substitute one of my other numbers, and work with the editor to place it so that the string bowings and pianist's hands would come close to matching.

Naturally, I was terribly sad that most of my music would not be used. But I also knew that in terms of the film itself, Louis Malle was right.

Those three and a half minutes are my only musical contribution to a feature film.

After the hectic rehearsal period was over, performing eight shows a week of *The Pirates of Penzance* became a way of life for almost two years, from January 1981 to November 1982, allowing me plenty of time to compose during the daytime, and forming a constant backdrop to other creative endeavors.

During this period I had the delightful experience of giving weekly piano lessons to Linda Ronstadt in her dressing room. Her charm, musicality, and the loveliness of her singing were central to the show's appeal. She was eager to become better at reading music and, despite her celebrity and accomplishments, was modest about not having had the classical vocal training that the other pirate "maidens" in the show all had. She said that putting her in the lead was "like asking a tap dancer to dance *Swan Lake*."

In her performance as Mabel in the show, she managed to seem to be the nineteenth-century female ingenue while somehow also communicating her own resilience, intelligence, and twentieth-century sass. Politically outspoken, she was dating California Governor Jerry Brown at the time. Once the two of us also did an informal recording of Schubert's *Ave Maria* at the legendary Hit Factory, as a gift for a friend of hers. Here and in the recording sessions for the movie and album, I got a glimpse of the work ethic and perfectionism in the studio that had contributed to her success.

Since I was now receiving a weekly Broadway paycheck, I had the means to hire my bandmates, additional musicians, conductor Jonathan McPhee, and a recording engineer, and to rent a recital hall in order to make a recording of *Nocturnes*, playing the solo piano part myself. (I paid each musician $20 for a three-hour session, so they were essentially donating their services.) It resulted in a tape that I could send to conductors, including Gunther Schuller.

He left me a long phone message that I listened to many times, telling me that it was an "impressive piece" that he hoped to perform someday. In a later phone call, he questioned whether the second movement was really all that jazzy, and made the excellent point that "sometimes one doesn't need transitions." Noting my strengths, he prophesized (correctly) about a currently neglected aspect of music: "Don't worry, harmony will come back!" Although a performance directed by Gunther never materialized, he stayed in touch, and eventually took four of my pieces into his publishing catalogue. He and I crossed paths several more times.

In November, rehearsals began for a full production of Lapine's *Twelve Dreams* at the New York Public Theater, and for this production I was able to expand my instrumentation to five players (a woodwind doubler playing flute, clarinet, and bass clarinet; a violin doubling on viola; double bass; piano; and percussion) and to considerably expand the music as well. Now the budget allowed me to rent an actual celesta to represent the music box belonging to the psychoanalyst's daughter, Emma. (I used a fully orchestrated version of my music box tune in the overture, the ballet music, the "Bird Dream," and the Entr'acte.) I found that being assigned moods to express was an invitation to experiment. I learned a lot about composing from taking the harmonically seductive 5/4 "waltz" of the overture and warping it into something dissonant during the dream sequences, or reducing it to a single line in the highest range of the violin for the "luminous ball" dream near the end of the play.

James had fascinating ideas about editing my music. I didn't always agree with them, but they sometimes upended my assumptions and made me see new ways of treating my materials; they taught me the value of letting go. The needs of theater encouraged me to experiment with the uses of pure sound, or with a kind of open-form writing (layering independent parts over one another without having them align) that I used in the "Bird Dream." The score served the play, but it also spoke for me. I identified with its exploration of childhood and psychological mystery, its humor, and its sadness.

Twelve Dreams ran for about six weeks at the Public Theater, and was later revived for an even more elaborate production at Lincoln Center Theater in 1995.

Thanks to Lapine's working relationship with Stephen Sondheim, J. and I spent a delightful day at the composer's home in Connecticut during the period they were developing *Sunday in the Park with George*. While J. toured his partner's extraordinary garden, "Steve" shared his take on current music and his enthusiasm for Ravel, Poulenc, and Stravinsky (particularly *Les Noces*, which he said he wished he had written himself). While expressing the highest regard for Milton Babbitt as his former teacher, he confessed that he disliked his music, by contrast saying that he was smitten with the work of Steve Reich, which he listened to every day. I had the pleasure of seeing the first half of *Sunday* when it was in workshop at Playwrights Horizons, and later learned the piano part and played a few nights of the show on Broadway as a substitute pianist.

Soon after *Twelve Dreams* closed, I started work on a Piano Sonata, beginning it at home in New York, and finishing it in March 1982 on an upright piano at my friend Tom Hayes's house in

Cambridge, Massachusetts, where I was able to stay while he was away.

It was quite different from anything I had ever written. The first of its four movements starts with what composer Robert Carl called a "low register, propulsive, bluesy shout." This generates what could almost pass for a long, wildly dissonant, virtuosic piano improvisation—a mash-up of Copland and Cecil Taylor. The second movement is a series of variations on a slow waltz in B flat that proceeds in a seamless and dreamlike manner, blurring the edges of its sections. The third emphasizes huge granitic, dissonant chords, ending with a long quiet processional over an ostinato in the bass that gradually reveals itself to be a slow iteration of the "shout" idea from the first movement.

Both the second and third movements are anticipated by passages in the first. The finale is a kind of revisiting of the Sonata as a whole, and it concludes with a complex coda that starts as an affirmation of the waltz's B flat major, and culminates in a powerful statement of the central harmony of the first movement. The chord is reiterated with its notes removed one by one, becoming quieter and quieter, until only the three opening notes of the Sonata are left, then two, and finally only a single quiet A natural. (It has always seemed to me that one could analyze the whole Sonata as a conflict between A and B flat, but I will leave the job of looking into that to someone else.)

Building on the principle I had found in composing *Cabaret Music*, I was able to "find" everything in the piece within its initial ideas, which in this case were not the opening at all, but were the granitic chords of the third movement. The chords were like suitcases that I unpacked, pulling the entire work out of them. It was a process I hadn't planned, and which I couldn't reconstruct later.

The piece had a grandeur, confidence and turbulence that I had not achieved before. But there was also a powerful cohesion; it was not a piece I could change or revise. Writing parts of it far from home, I was particularly aware of somehow channeling the inner storms I experienced when I traveled. I also can't help thinking that my friend Jonathan Schell's magnificent and terrifying book *The Fate of the Earth* had affected me. Although it wasn't my style explicitly to reflect global issues and politics in my music, somehow they got into it anyway.

I performed the Sonata in a concert at Fordham. The piece was so big and challenging that I didn't even have a chance to be nervous.

I was very happy when distinguished composer Erik Lundborg told me that it was "Beethovenian." I later documented the piece in a recording studio in the Village and edited the tape myself, something I had done previously when I had piano pieces I wanted to preserve. I shared it with some of my bandmates, and bassist Dennis Masuzzo said he listened to it every day for several weeks.

That summer, James Lapine asked me to compose the music for his production of *A Midsummer Night's Dream* at the Delacorte Theater in Central Park. The production featured William Hurt as Oberon, and my friend Deborah Rush as Hermia. James encouraged me to compose an extensive score for an ensemble of nine musicians that would include two solo songs and two choral numbers, including the fairies chorus, and the concluding "Roses, Their Sharp Spines Being Gone."

Playing *Pirates* every night had been a subliminal orchestration lesson, and it was wonderful applying what I learned to my *Midsummer* score. Although I felt somewhat ambivalent about my solo vocal writing, which seemed too operatic for this context, I was very pleased with the choruses. I only wished that they didn't need to be sung so fast to accommodate the staging.

The score was one of the most tuneful and tonal I composed, using key signatures in almost every number. The production had an extraordinary set by Heidi Landesman boasting real trees, grass, and a pond, which seemed to merge with the surrounding park. When the sky darkened and the moon and stars were out, and the fairies came out of the woods on the set, the effect was stunningly magical. Hearing the text was no less so, as close to music in its effect as any words I had ever heard. While I was downtown still playing *The Pirates of Penzance*, *Midsummer* was seen by two thousand people every night. The night my parents came, my father was as exhilarated by my involvement in a project as I had ever seen him.

I put a lot into the score, which included roughly forty-five minutes of colorful music for an ensemble of winds, strings, keyboard, and percussion, but I didn't have time to truly polish it. It might have been possible later to reassemble it as a complete musical work, to make sense of all of the cuts and patches made along the way, edit the music, and recopy the score, but with no prospect of a performance, I never got around to doing that. The production was filmed for television with only one or two microphones for the music, resulting in an unbalanced recording that did not capture the orchestration.

When Deborah Rush married actor John Bottoms later in the year, she asked me to arrange the "Roses" chorus for trumpet and organ for the occasion, which I did.

The experience was creatively thrilling, and led to further assignments in the theater, and even to finding a publisher. James Lapine's wife, author and filmmaker Sarah Kernochan, recommended me to her father, Jack Kernochan, a composer and law professor who was the president of Galaxy Music Corporation.

I visited the offices of Galaxy that fall and submitted many scores to Jack and the managing editor, Donald Waxman, two wonderful people whom I liked immediately. They readily accepted *Cabaret Music, Four Jazz Preludes*, and, to my surprise, *Summer Pages*, as well as *Nocturnes, Midsummer Night's Dream*, and *Twelve Dreams* for their orchestral rental catalogue, and they asked me to sign an agreement to give them right of first refusal for my future works.

I told them that I would only sign if they took my Piano Sonata, which was, in my opinion, my best piece so far. Donald told me that he actually hated the work, finding the harmony in the aggressive first movement "static." Jack somewhat agreed, adding, however, that "one couldn't change a note in it."

Nevertheless, they offered me a contract for it, and it was listed as available on the back of the other publications. (It actually remained unpublished until American Composers Alliance brought out all nine of my sonatas, in 2024.) We also discussed my Second String Quartet, but Donald said he found that the work did not "stick to the ribs." Adelaide Kernochan, Jack's wife, who worked at UNESCO as well as for Galaxy, designed a snazzy cover for *Four Jazz Preludes*.

In November, I was back inside the New York Public Theater composing music for *Hamlet*, directed by Joe Papp, using a delicate ensemble comprising oboe, recorders, lute, two trumpets, timpani, and snare drum, as well as writing a song for Ophelia, who was played by Pippa Pearthree. The production featured Diane Venora in the title role.

Being in this context required flexibility, and the ability to compose on the spot. For example, one day in the final week of previews, Joe asked me to add transitional music to be practiced within the hour and inserted in the show that night. I composed the transition and copied the parts right there in the theater seats. I was proud of this compact score, which suggested Elizabethan music in a quirky way. With no bass instrument in the ensemble, the timpani fulfilled that role, making the orchestration itself symbolic of Hamlet's fragile, ruminative nature.

I was not aware of it then, but one could easily draw a straight line from my teenage efforts—my love of Stravinsky's *Pulcinella, Oedipus,* and *The Rake's Progress*—to my *Midsummer* and *Hamlet* music, right through all of the many pieces in a somewhat tonal and "neoclassical" vein I wrote later (for example, my 1987 *Partita* for oboe and piano). All of this "old-fashioned" music had a validity I didn't accord it at the time, because of the current biases in the music world, and perhaps my own.

Late in 1980, I had been introduced to the great clarinetist Benny Goodman by Ved Mehta, the blind, Indian-born writer at *The New Yorker* who had become one of the regular members of my parents' small circle of friends. Goodman was seventy-two years old. We had lunch at the century club, after which I sent him a cassette tape of some of my pieces, including *Cabaret Music* and *Four Jazz Preludes.* He wrote back to say that he liked the pieces, and thought I used the clarinet very effectively in *Cabaret Music.*

In January 1981, on the same day that *Pirates* opened at the Uris Theatre on Broadway, he called to invite me to his apartment on East End Avenue to read through the Brahms Clarinet Sonatas and discuss a possible project. (The reader should bear in mind that, as an agoraphobic and claustrophobic, I anticipated all travel and elevator rides with dread. Goodman's apartment was on the twenty-fifth floor.)

His spacious living room overlooking the East River gave pride of place to a beautiful grand piano. The walls in the hallways were covered with framed photos of legendary people he had worked with. Benny played the Brahms with complete mastery and a smooth, beautiful tone.

The project he wanted to discuss turned out to be the commission of a double concerto for clarinet and cello that he could perform with cellist Nathaniel Rosen. He expressed his hope that they could perform it with the New Jersey Symphony. Naturally, I agreed immediately, and started having ideas for the piece almost as soon as I got home that day.

After our initial sonata session, I was invited back for lunch and read-throughs of the Brahms and Beethoven Trios with Benny and

Rosen, a genial man and formidable musician almost exactly my age, who put me instantly at ease. These sessions continued over the next two years as I made progress on my score, and continued to bring it to the two men to sight-read. Out of Goodman's list of previous commissions I had heard only Stravinsky's *Ebony Concerto*, the Copland Concerto, and the Bartók *Contrasts*, but they were helpful references showing me the level of difficulty he could manage. (I did not yet know the Milhaud, Malcolm Arnold, or Morton Gould works.)

Before playing, Benny would always start by laying a surprising number of reeds down on a table in front of him. He tested them out, and was in no hurry to choose which one he wanted to use. Likewise, there was a Zen-like calm behind his clarinet's amazing sprightliness. When I took the first movement at performance tempo to show him how it would eventually sound, he cautioned me that a good piece will sound just as good, or better, at a slow tempo. I was knocked out by Rosen's rich sound and virtuosity. Benny's agility, lyricism, and self-contained exuberance were perfect for my idiom. My piece was challenging, but he and Rosen were fantastic readers and sounded astoundingly good.

My Concerto eventually grew into an extensive three-movement piece, roughly twenty-five minutes in length, which, like so many of my post-Columbia pieces, merged elements of jazz (or "jazziness"), expressionism, chromatic harmony, and classical structure. Extroverted as much of it is, there are also moments of intimacy. I thought of the soloists as two friends sharing and exchanging classical and jazzy materials, both of them reflecting Benny's virtuosity, age, and history.

The first movement begins with an introduction in which the orchestra initiates the fast tempo of the principal section and is answered by quiet, slower interjections from the soloists. What follows is essentially a sonata-Allegro, with G as the tonal center. (I planned the Concerto tonally, with movements centered in G, A, and D.) As a second theme, I gave the cello solo the "Taxi Music" cut from *My Dinner with André*. I can still remember the moment when the transition I was writing started to suggest this theme, and my surprise realizing that it would fit perfectly there. Its simple texture contrasts nicely with the almost manic activity surrounding it.

In the recapitulation, the two themes are combined—I remember Rosen delightedly pointing this out to Benny—after which there is a wild coda. The tender second movement is called "Lullaby"; it seems to come from the lyrical world of the "Spiritual" in *Four Jazz Preludes*. In the third movement, a kind of rondo containing a multifaceted cadenza, the "Taxi Music" melody returns in several transformed guises—both slower and faster than the original. It reaches a paroxysm of joyful high spirits when it returns to the tonality of the opening movement and there is a restatement of the first theme in augmentation in the piccolo.

The look of some of the score suggests Stravinsky—for example, the opening is structured like the beginning of the *Symphony of Psalms*—but its sound is entirely different. I was proud of the fact that while it had its crowd-pleasing side, it was also reflective and honest, and honored Goodman as a serious musician.

At some point in our final reading session in 1982, Benny told me that he had decided not to play the piece. I don't know if Rosen already knew about this decision, but he almost immediately suggested that I make it a cello concerto. I couldn't imagine doing that. The entire character of the music had come from Benny's clarinet playing.

Some weeks into 1983, I called Benny to tell him that I had completed the orchestration, and that even if he wasn't going to perform the work, he should still pay me. I suggested a fee of $1,000, and he agreed.

I never knew if the music displeased him, if he felt that it had become too much to take on at that point in his life, if he found it impractical in some way, lost interest, or if declining health stood in his way. I believe that this was his final commission. Benny Goodman died on June 13, 1986.

Even though Galaxy Music accepted the work into its rental catalogue, and I continued to try to interest orchestras in performing it, I assumed that it just wasn't a good piece, and I put it in a drawer. I assumed that it had become overblown.

8

MORE THEATER AND PERSONAL MUSIC; VISIT TO BENNINGTON (1983-1985)

JOE PAPP HAD A long-standing commitment to Wally's plays, and in 1983 he commissioned the two of us to produce a music theatre work that could be presented at the New York Public Theater. In the end, it seemed he had not been prepared for a work that was as close to "modern opera" as the piece turned out to be.

I don't remember the precise moment when Wally brought me the libretto of *The Music Teacher*, but I remember my reaction. It was rather similar to my response to Stravinsky's death: I went to bed for several days.

The structure of the libretto was innovative. One third of it consisted of spoken monologue and dialogue; the other two thirds consisted of vocal music. In the piece an aging music teacher, Mr. Smith, and his former student, Jane, separately tell the audience about a time years ago when they were together at a rural high school, co-wrote an opera that was performed at the school, and had a brief affair in an unnamed city.

In the piece the opera—a bizarrely tragic and mythic love triangle set in ancient Greece—is performed in its entirety, and there are scattered musicalized scenes from real life before and after it. As in many of Wally's plays, the scenes from real life are strange, dream-like, and obscene.

The libretto was challenging on every level; the story both poignant and disturbing. The bulk of the music had to be in quotation marks—standing in for the work of the music teacher and Jane— but it also had to be sincere and passionate, drawing the audience into the story within the story, expressing the love of teacher and student for each other.

Because of deliberately awkward expressions in the "libretto-within-the-libretto," there would be moments when the music would convey an absurd humor simply by sincerely setting the lines that were there. The more "incidental" music needed to be in a different style, to read as more "realistic" and contemporary. However, there needed to be shared material between the two kinds of music so that the work would hang together as a whole.

The libretto showed Wally's extraordinary gift for storytelling. Like our old puppet shows, and like *My Dinner with André*, there was a theatrical frame around the entire work, but it also contained episodes within which the audience would become lost and forget the larger frame.

There were three kinds of sexuality in the piece: the repressed, desperate, and warped sexuality of Mr. Smith; the healthy sexuality of Jane; and the sexuality permeating American life, expressed by the airline stewardess on the plane that Mr. Smith takes to the city, and the lyrics of the song sung by the pianist in the restaurant Mr. Smith visits there.

Although Wally tactfully avoided asking me to set the more obscene passages to music—for example, Mr. Smith masturbating—the work as a whole was infused with them. And this is not to mention that, even then, thirty years before the "Me Too" movement, the story itself was provocative. It was a story that, like *Lulu* or *Lolita*, needed to be accepted as a complex exploration of human truths and viewed from more than one angle.

I don't know if Wally had my own operatic attempt *Desire* in mind when he conceived of the opera-within-the-opera. His text hints at the fairy tales he loved as a child, of *Pelléas*, and even of Wagnerian libretti.

Once I got over my initial reaction, I dove into composing the piece and was able to identify with all of its characters, and to relish composing for the human voice more than I ever had. I had never written anything so eclectic. Wally had shrewdly given me a chance to express my anxieties in composing music for the airplane scene, which I illustrated with a dissonant, wordless chorus. I enjoyed composing a mock "Rock Song" for two students to sing in their dorm, an Ivesian overlay of instruments being practiced, and a sleazy Cabaret song for the "pianist's song," which took the soprano up to a *Lulu*-esque high D. Meanwhile, the high school "opera" had its own language and structure, complete with its own entr'acte between its two sections, its idiom a mix of the neoclassical and the expressionistic, with suggestions of music theatre.

After I completed the short score of the piece, we found a cast to perform it for Joe Papp. The extraordinary tenor, Paul Sperry, was a brave and superb Mr. Smith, and a wonderful young soprano, Jean McClelland, played Jane. The pianist's song was sung by the virtuosic Penny Orloff, whom I had first heard singing Gershwin's "Slap That Bass" with four bassists at the Group for Contemporary Music, and with whom I later wrote a short children's opera.

Unfortunately, Joe felt that the work was essentially a "modern opera" and did not fit at the Public Theater. In our minds, it was more of a cross-genre, eclectic music theatre piece that would have been a challenge to place in an opera house.

Whether the focus on sex entered into his decision-making process, I never knew. The work was finally produced twenty-three years later in 2006.

Meanwhile, I worked on two piano pieces that I submitted to Galaxy Music but also had doubts about. The first was called *Three Latin American Dances* and was probably too indebted to Frederic Rzewski. Although the music was exciting and full of good ideas, it seemed a bit false, starting with the title. After all, I had never even been south of Pennsylvania.

The other was a set of nine short piano pieces I returned to many times, trying to create a convincing unity out of their disparate idioms. Although I never performed the set, I reused themes from some of the pieces in later works. When Galaxy Music was sold and works were returned to me, I found an envelope containing the *Nine Pieces* with a note pinned to it from one of their editors that read: "Must Run Soon—The Other Way!"

Performances during this time included concerts with violinist Marilyn Dubow, as well as an evening presenting Bartók's Sonata for two pianos and percussion, and Stravinsky's *Rite of Spring* (in its four-hand version), with my wonderful composer-pianist friend, Roberto Pace.

In March 1983, an article I had written about Nadia Boulanger appeared in the *Atlantic Monthly*. In early June, I went to hear John Adams's bravura, delightfully garish *Grand Pianola Music* at the New York Philharmonic and was able to greet him backstage afterwards, where he complimented me on the Boulanger article. It was astonishing to contemplate how much he had accomplished in the dozen years since I had last seen him.

Theatre work at the New York Shakespeare Festival beckoned again in the early summer, in the form of a job as rehearsal pianist and keyboard player in a production based on Donizetti's *Don Pasquale*, called *Non Pasquale*. It was to run in Central Park's Delacorte Theater, again with Bill Elliott as music director, and Wilford Leach as director. (A former "maiden" from *Pirates*, Nancy Heikin, had translated and rewritten the libretto.)

Only a few weeks into rehearsals, I received a call from the Bennington College Chamber Music Conference asking if I would be interested in spending a week there in August as a guest composer. The conference boasted a superb roster of faculty musicians who coached adult amateur musicians and performed two faculty concerts a week. My role would be to supervise a faculty performance of a piece of mine, and to compose something for an assigned group of adult participants. Alison Nowak had recommended me to her father, Lionel Nowak, who chose the composers for the festival.

I approached Bill Elliott about taking a leave from *Non Pasquale*, and he told me that a leave was out of the question. If I left for two weeks, I would miss out on being the keyboard player in the summer production and on the opportunity to follow the show to Broadway in the fall.

I told him that I was going to accept the Bennington invitation. When he tried to discourage me, I said, "But, Bill, they are inviting me to be a *composer!*"

The degree to which this small decision changed the course of my life is almost comical.

For several years, J. had been visiting Vermont regularly to house-sit for friends who were away so that she could write in seclusion. She felt less and less attached to New York, and she hoped we could move to a quiet, rural area. After all, she had grown up in Antigua, not a large urban center.

In the summers, we had started to spend some time together in our friend Jill Fox's guest house less than an hour from Bennington, and we planned to do so again that summer. I had still not learned to drive, so J. dropped me at the college for my week there. I brought a bicycle.

My experience at Bennington College that week gave me a renewed connection to Vermont. It felt almost like being back at Camp Kinhaven. I felt weirdly at home there, and, when I came into contact with some of its regular music faculty members— Lionel Nowak (who had extended the invitation), Jack Glick, Louis Calabro, Vivian Fine, Jeffrey Levine, and Maxine Neuman, whom I already knew—I felt weirdly at home with them as well. In the mornings, I bicycled down a dirt road half a mile from the campus to a delightfully rustic house belonging to a friend to work.

I had three days to compose a piece for the assigned participants group of clarinet, French horn, and bassoon, and I wrote a lively piece for them called *Jeté*. The faculty performers played *Cabaret Music* on one of their programs, and I ended up conducting *Jeté*, even though it was only a trio, just to provide security. My title ("Leap") seemed apt for this light, balletic piece, but also had a secret meaning: that any excursion from New York was difficult for me, and that this one had also involved bailing out of a professional opportunity. I obviously didn't know that I was about to leap into a new way of life.

Everyone seemed very enthusiastic about *Jeté*, and at the end of the concert Vivian Fine came up to me and said, "You wowed them." At the post-concert party I felt engulfed in good feelings and support.

In a novel or film, one could simply eliminate the next two years and proceed to the moment when I actually started teaching at Bennington. But in real life, there are no foregone conclusions. I didn't want to leave New York and all I was connected to there, including my parents, my brother and his girlfriend, our many friends, and the opportunities that possibly still awaited me there.

But J. wanted to move, and I wanted to be with her, and from the moment I visited Bennington I saw it as somewhere I could be— where we both could be. I told all of the faculty I had met that I felt that way, hoping that the college was such an eccentric place—as it appeared to be—that spreading this idea would bear fruit.

But at the end of that week, I returned to an uncertain present, looking for work to replace my lost position in the band of *Non Pasquale*, all the while telephoning conductors and orchestras, trying to interest them in *Nocturnes* and *Concerto for Clarinet, Cello, and Orchestra*. My datebook for the summer lists correspondence and calls with Schuller, Lukas Foss, John Harbison, and the Orchestra of St. Luke's. (Meanwhile, *Non Pasquale* did not continue on to Broadway.)

In November, I found work as rehearsal pianist and assistant conductor for *The Human Comedy* at the New York Public Theater, an ambitious oratorio-musical based on William Saroyan's novel, with music by Galt MacDermot, the versatile and skillful composer of *Hair*.

It was enough of a success to move briefly to Broadway in April of 1984. The band played onstage, and it was one of the few times I performed using a chord chart and improvising in a rock style, which I did by imitating Galt's own playing of the score. Working in the production, I met the formidable composer and conductor Tania León, who later won a Pulitzer Prize for her music.

Late winter and spring of 1984 was a very busy time. While performing in the show at the Public Theater, I worked on two pieces that had been generated by my trip to Bennington: a single movement work for violin and orchestra for Marilyn Dubow, and a short piece for piano-right hand for Lionel Nowak.

Lionel was a gifted composer and extraordinary pianist who lost the use of his left hand following a stroke. Since the majority of single-hand piano works are for left hand, many composer friends wrote right-hand pieces for him. My *Dialogue*, which I sent him right after the start of the year, was a conversation between two kinds of music—a lugubrious blues in the lower register and an animated banjo-like dance in the upper register.

Meanwhile, I was composing music for a play at NYU, *Night Music* by Clifford Odets, directed by Jack Gelber, author of *The Connection*. This was a tuneful score, recorded ahead of time, for woodwind doubler, trumpet, piano, bass, and drums, evoking the 1940s period of the play. I particularly liked a Dixieland-style tune in 5/4 + 4/4 time.

I had also brashly asked poet Derek Walcott if he would write the text of a short musical skit for me to use as a submission to Joe Papp, who was commissioning "ten-minute musicals." Derek, who was a friend of J.'s, was kind enough to agree (the fee was $200). In short order, he sent me a wild text written in a cabaret spirit, full of puns and topical references. "Adam" (Clayton Powell Jr.) and "Evita" (Perón) are in a post-apocalyptic garden of Eden; an ape ("Manny") is the devil, and God's voice issues from the sky. The title of the piece gives a sense of its tone: *Under the Bam, Under the Bomb, Under the Ban-the-Bomb Tree.*

The text brought out my spontaneous "puppet show" side, and I wrote the music very quickly. I particularly enjoyed composing the rather frightening music for God, an opportunity for characterization I had never had and haven't had since. I don't think that any of Joe's "ten-minute musical" submissions were ever performed.

I had two more plays to compose incidental music for that spring and early summer, both scores requiring recording ahead of time, as the music for *Night Music* had been. The first was Donald Margulies's play *Found a Peanut*, about children (performed by adult actors) playing in the backyard of their apartment house on the last day of summer. The second was music for *Henry V* directed by Wilford Leach at the Delacorte in Central Park.

For the Margulies, I wrote three Satie-esque pieces for two pianos that I overdubbed myself. For the Shakespeare score, Wilford asked me to compose for bagpipes, trumpets, French horns, and drums—a daunting combination, even just from the point of view of tuning. Composing contrapuntally for three bagpipes was fascinating.

Rehearsing with the players in a room at the Public Theater was a bit like having the group Queen come to perform "We Will Rock You" in your bathroom; it was the loudest indoor sound I have ever heard. And indeed, the curtain music from *Henry V*, with its trumpets and bagpipes over syncopated drums, actually did resemble rock music. For the "Battle of Agincourt" music, I came as close as I ever did to writing an electronic piece, by splicing together disparate-taped brass, bagpipe and drum fragments to create a disturbing soundscape.

In between all of these projects, I wrote two piano pieces that Galaxy immediately accepted for publication. One was an *Improvisation* no. 3 that was much more tightly coiled than the first two. Like the *Dialogue* I had written for Lionel Nowak, it alternated two themes, using explicitly jazzy materials that were handled motivically.

The second was a personal piece. In April, when *The Human Comedy* was in rehearsal at the Royale Theatre for what turned out to be its ten-day run on Broadway, J. called me backstage from Vermont, where she was writing, to tell me that she was pregnant. When I got home I realized that I had forgotten to give her a Valentine's day present, and I sat down at the piano and composed

Valentine for her, in one sitting. It is one of my most tonal and straight-forward pieces, with hints of Brahms and cradle song in it, essentially in D flat major, with an excursion into C major near the end and a transition back to D flat in which a phrase from the middle of the theme is used in inversion and then in canon.

Although technically not a Rag, I couldn't have written it without Bolcom's example.

The summer entailed performances of *Henry V* in Central Park, time spent in Vermont, driving lessons, and anticipation of a new child. In the fall, I renewed my acquaintance with Linda Ronstadt when I played keyboards in an English-language adaptation of *La Bohème* in which she played Mimì. (The actor-tenor David Carroll was an impressive, music theatre-style Rodolfo.)

In October, I returned to Bennington to conduct Marilyn Dubow in *Autumnal Song* for violin and orchestra with the Sage City Symphony. Although the performance was extremely ragged, it had its good moments, particularly the quiet opening and closing. Marilyn was extraordinary in the solo part. Vivian Fine approached me afterwards and said that the piece had a beautiful ending.

Our daughter Annie was born on November 13 at New York Hospital. What a gigantic change of life, a change in understanding everything, a burst of joy. There is no pretending that seeing a birth, caring for a small infant, and becoming a parent doesn't change one's identity. How such a momentous thing changes a person's art I'll leave to others to speculate. But having a child certainly pushed me to keep imagining a way of living in Vermont. Both J. and I pursued the possibility of teaching at Bennington.

Jack Kernochan had introduced me to the accomplished, Pulitzer prize-winning composer Robert Ward, who had in turn connected me with his son Tim, bassoonist and a member of the Aspen Wind Quintet. They arranged that I would compose a work for the group, which Galaxy would then publish.

It was an education to meet Robert Ward, a warm and generous person with an orator's resonant voice. He was an outspoken liberal Democrat, whose music fell squarely in the traditional tonal camp. I was as shocked by his view of Webern (about whom he said, "So what?") as I had been by Monod's view of Stravinsky. But it was a great lesson.

Ward's best-known work was his opera of *The Crucible*. One could feel that he was an independent, moral, and deeply humane person who truly loved composing and did it his own way. I learned once and for all that musical traditionalism could be associated with left-leaning convictions, even as a matter of principle, just as socially conservative or bigoted views could be held by creators of "modernist" art.

In the first months of 1985, I composed my wind quintet in the orange living room on Hudson Street, often with our little daughter asleep upstairs. Writing for the quintet medium took me back to the experience of playing clarinet in quintets at Kinhaven. With its transparency, clarity, and buoyant rhythms, this one allowed the neoclassical influence back in.

The first movement was laser-focused on a pithy three-note motive, maintaining its crisp 6/8 clip, balancing dissonance with a joyful lyricism. The quasi-Baroque slow movement began with an almost Bachian theme in the flute over dark clarinet accompaniment, flowering into five-part counterpoint. (Clarinetist David Krakauer, who was married to my recital partner, Marilyn Dubow, told me that in the opening, the clarinet was my sleeping daughter and I was the flute.)

In the Rondo-like last movement, there were witty digressions, including a sarcastic march, and moments when the ideas ranged outside the tonally oriented frame, even suggesting the idiom of *Pierrot Lunaire*.

I maintained my contacts with Bennington by attending a February performance by the American Composers Orchestra of Vivian Fine's *Poetic Fires* at Alice Tully Hall, with Vivian at the piano and Gunther Schuller conducting. Vivian looked formal and serious as she stepped out on stage; she had her hair done for the occasion. Like all of her works, the piece was rich, personal, and dramatic. The drama was earned. There was a system behind it, with her fingerprints on it. I felt a sense of kinship with her. It was exciting to go backstage afterwards, where I said hello to Gunther as well as Vivian. She asked me: "Did it speak to you?"

In April, I was working on another piece that was scheduled for the following year: a piece for two harpsichords for the Lucinda Childs Dance Company. Like so many connections formed through my having become a part of J.'s world, this one had a literary origin: I had met Lucinda through her companion Susan Sontag. The four of us often had dinner together, and I had given Lucinda tapes of my pieces, including the Piano Sonata. Susan was an avid follower of ballet, particularly the New York City Ballet.

Lucinda planned a full-evening's work danced to four pieces by four different composers, all employing Baroque instruments. The costumes and sets would be by Robert Mapplethorpe. Along with me, she asked for music from Michael Galasso, Elizabeth Swados, and Michael Nyman, each of us employing different instrumentation.

For Lucinda, dance was an exalted, meticulous, architectural craft. She created beautifully hand-drawn blueprints for her work, molding steps and group movement to music. To prepare for working with her, I watched her rehearse works choreographed to music by Philip Glass and my old classmate John Adams.

Assigned to compose for two harpsichords, I wrote an eighteen-minute single movement work in the mostly sunny, quasi-Baroque spirit of the Quintet I had just finished. While it is in no sense a minimalist piece, *Dance Music* contains more repeating patterns and ostinati than any of my other pieces. It includes plenty of dissonance, particularly accentuated in the crunchy two-harpsichord medium, but is unabashedly tonal, beginning and ending in C major, with a long lyrical middle section in A minor.

With the intention that the work would eventually be played by two performers, I recorded it for Lucinda so that she could choreograph it, overdubbing both harpsichord parts myself.

Perhaps there is nothing more poignant in retrospect than joy. Both the Quintet and *Dance Music for Two Harpsichords* so clearly reflect the happiness of having a baby daughter in the house and a sense of hopefulness about the future. Somehow, it is hard to listen to them now without feeling a sense of loss.

That summer, I was again involved in a New York Shakespeare Festival production, this time composing incidental music for *Measure for Measure*, directed by Mr. Papp, again at the Delacorte Theater in Central Park.

The most notable opportunity in the prerecorded score was that I could compose convent music for a women's choir. In theater music, I was doing my best to support the plays and the visions of the directors, but I was aware that there might be diminishing returns in my continuing to compose for one production after another. There was an ease about it. When I was asked for a particular snippet of music, it would just come to me; it was like plucking fruit from a tree. Sometimes the music might be cut or I would need to alter it, and my feelings might be momentarily hurt, but the fact that it was a shared project and a team effort was also a protection.

Composing an ambitious piece on my own was a different matter, and entailed far more risk. It was a lonelier process, requiring a more sustained kind of attention, and it made me feel that my life was at stake. When the results were good, there was an inner ecstasy and sense of peace, a feeling of having put something real down on the page that justified everything. It was a feeling of satisfaction far outstripping anything I could feel about composing a few short cues for a play. And soon I would feel a hunger to return to this demanding personal process and try to get better at it.

Composing for the theater didn't assuage this hunger. When I heard an ambitious, beautiful, complex, and expressive concert piece or opera, I was jealous of the composer for carrying out such a meaningful piece of work. When I heard even the most wonderful popular song or musical or piece of incidental music, I wasn't jealous.

In mid-June, I received a call from Bennington informing me that Vivian Fine had decided to teach half-time, and asking me if I would be willing to join the music program on a half-time basis. J. was offered a position in the Literature Division, and we both accepted.

Over the summer, we looked for a place to move to that was near the college. I composed a concise and carefully crafted Sonatina for piano in three movements. Though certainly better than the twelve-tone sonatina I had written ten years before, it seemed as transitional as the summer itself. For a while, I had started mentally assigning my pieces grades. The Sonatina was a solid "B." ("Piano Sonata", "Valentine", and my "Wind Quintet" each received an imaginary "A".)

Then I occupied myself with a project that I had had in the back of my mind for a year: I made a "Trio" version of my Concerto for Clarinet, Cello, and Orchestra. In doing this, I found that certain aspects of the structure could not work in a chamber version. I cut passages, placed the cadenza in a different spot, and created a lean piano part that at least approached being playable. Then I put the "Trio" back into my bureau next to the full score.

Our move to a little stone house on Main Street in North Bennington, Vermont, came at a transitional moment in my father's life too. *The New Yorker* had been sold to Samuel Irving ("S.I.") Newhouse in March, replacing the ownership of the Fleischmann family, who had never interfered in the editorial side of the magazine since they had founded it in 1925. My father, who was turning 78, was under the illusion that the new arrangement would be similar, and that Mr. Newhouse would let him determine his own successor. He would find out that he was wrong about this.

When we left the city, J. already had an enormous and richly deserved reputation as a writer. Although I had had some publications and opportunities as a composer, I had also had my share of setbacks, and I had frequently rejected my own music, leaving ambitious pieces uncopied and unperformed because I didn't think they were good enough. By and large, I had received better reviews and responses for my incidental theater music than for my "serious" compositions. Yet, it was clear in my mind that the latter category was where I wanted to put my energies.

There was no *New Yorker* for contemporary music, and I was beginning to think that perhaps there wasn't a place for it anywhere. Even among my intellectual friends, who avidly read modern literature and poetry and took in new films, theater, and art, there were not that many who eagerly followed new concert music. When I was at a party and was asked what I did, it was almost embarrassing to say that I was a composer.

For many years, I straddled the worlds of New York City and Vermont. There were still a few New York theater projects ahead of me, as well as many concerts and musical events in the city. But gradually there was a shift in my center of gravity, as college and teaching became my world.

At Bennington, I had the chance to burrow ever more deeply into composing, and to continue to learn about music alongside my students. In some ways, moving to Vermont and becoming a full-time teacher was the best thing that ever happened to me. But it also came at the cost of many relationships, and of a more public kind of life in New York.

9

BENNINGTON (1985–1988)

I HAD LEFT COLUMBIA ASSUMING I would never be a professor. Eight years later, I was one, although at a progressive college that doesn't use the term.

I used to say that I was "Half of Vivian," since she was now half-time and we taught in the same classroom. I also told her that I thought we had been "married in a previous life."

What was literally true was that my father remembered seeing her at the piano during the 1930s, when he had briefly composed for musical theatre and for the dance duo Gluck Sandor and Felicia Sorel. He and Vivian had both come from Chicago to New York, seeking a life in its artistic community. My father had even once brought some of his music to show to Aaron Copland, a mentor figure of Vivian's during the years she was a sought-after pianist, expert in new music.

While I felt a strong human connection to her, I was not yet able to entirely connect with her music; its language held me at arm's length. It was only many years later, when I taught classes about her music, that I began to fully appreciate what she had achieved and better understand her unique evolution. At this time, I identified most easily with Lionel's compositional world—rooted in his pianism, eccentric, personal, and temperamentally dark—and there was a kind of symbiotic connection between us.

I had not known him before his stroke. By some accounts, the man I encountered in the summer of 1983 and got to know so well after 1985 was warmer and more emotionally available than he had been earlier in life. I had a wonderful time talking with him and planning concerts with him, and he followed what I was up to with interest, giving me his candid feedback on my pieces, always saying things that I would have never expected.

Different as we may have been, I almost had the feeling that he saw aspects of himself in me, all the more so since he could no longer play as he once had. Every day as one entered Jennings Music Building, one could hear Lionel upstairs practicing études by Cramer, Czerny, Chopin and others with his right-hand. His piano playing had the clarity and ringing precision of Glenn Gould. I once told him that one heard the bones in his hand in the sound, as if a skeleton were playing. He loved hearing that.

If Vivian and Lionel were quasi-parental figures, Lou Calabro was like an inspiring uncle. A tremendously exciting percussionist and composer, with his burning eyes and extraordinary energy, he also seemed born to teach. He literally galvanized his students into productivity. Raised in an orphanage from an early age, he had enlisted in the Army as a demolitionist paratrooper during the Second World War, and then had been able to attend Juilliard on the GI Bill. A student of Vincent Persichetti, in many ways he reflected this lineage in his compositions, such as his irresistible Third Symphony.

Lou was my mentor and role model as a Bennington teacher and advisor. I can still remember his looking over at me with avuncular amusement in my very first day on the job, as students approached me hoping to sign up for tutorials to complete strange-sounding individual projects, or to see if I would be willing to help them to notate their scores properly, and as one of my student advisees came to me in tears with tales of registration woes that I barely understood.

Bennington was a wild and somewhat anarchic place in which the faculty were larger-than-life characters doing things their own way, with the small, often beleaguered administration acting as support. The various departments—"divisions," as they were called—were like small fiefdoms within a larger community, just barely held together through the teaching philosophy of active, student-centered learning and inquiry espoused by John Dewey at the turn of the century. The college had become coeducational in 1969.

I was extremely comfortable with this model since I had been raised in it at Dalton and Putney. One of the great innovations of Bennington when it was founded as a women's college the 1930s had been that the performing arts were deemed academically equal to the other humanities and the sciences, and that performing musicians were full faculty members, not adjuncts as at every other college in the country. This meant that my faculty colleagues included my friend from New York, cellist Maxine Neuman; violist Jacob Glick; flutist Sue Ann Kahn; bassist and composer Jeffrey Levine; tenor Frank Baker; clarinetist, composer, and instrument inventor Gunnar Schonbeck; and pianist Elizabeth Wright.

By 1985, when I arrived, electronic composer Joel Chadabe had built an electronic music studio and was also teaching electronic composition. In terms of music, I arrived at an important moment of transition when what had been a separate Black Music division for ten years—led by its creator, the trumpet player and composer Bill Dixon—was now being merged, by decision of the board of trustees, with the regular music division.

As a result, Bill Dixon, trumpet player-composer Arthur Brooks, and legendary free jazz drummer Milford Graves were combined into one division, with the group of colleagues listed above.

If I had to guess why it was that I was accepted so easily into the Bennington music department (after all, there was no true search for my position), I would say that it was partly because I could play the piano as well as compose, and partly because I had studied quite a bit, but most of all because I was independent, pursuing my work and finding my way without belonging to any particular compositional "school," and without being influenced by how my music was responded to in the press or even by audiences. It had never occurred to me that these last traits were virtues, just as it had never occurred to me that I might make so much of my living from playing the piano. But I had these qualities in common with my composer colleagues at the college.

J. stayed in her position on the faculty of Bennington for one year, eventually becoming a professor at Harvard. I am still there.

There was a precise instant when I wondered if this might in fact be my life's trajectory. It was when I visited Louis Calabro and his wife Christine at their home in Arlington, Vermont, in the summer before beginning my first term. Lou told me about his childhood, his period in the Army, his studies at Juilliard and arrival to teach at Bennington in 1955. Even though we were standing in a beautiful grove of fruit trees with his wife and two young children, and he was describing a journey to a wonderful job, creative fulfillment, usefulness to others, and what appeared to be stability, the thought that my life might be similar, and that thirty years or more stretched ahead of me in this same spot, left me deeply depressed.

If leaving Columbia marked the moment when I started to write my "mature music," coming to Bennington marked the beginning of my real evolution as a "serious" composer, and it gave me a connection to enough musicians to properly hear much of what I wrote.

For better or worse, it allowed me to pursue a more personal path, even as I remained deeply influenced by the training I had had in the theatre, which was akin to the journalistic training many fiction writers have had. This doesn't mean that suddenly everything I wrote was good, or that I didn't have many creative struggles ahead, more that I now had a context in which to fail: I was now a composer who taught, and who was continuously challenged by colleagues and students to keep trying things, learning, and, crucially, performing.

Given the fact that I was agoraphobic (a word and concept I hadn't yet encountered), there was also a risk that I would become quite isolated. That risk was partly mitigated by the connections I already had in New York, by the eventual advent of the internet, and by the surprising new path that opened up with my literary side.

There was an irony to my presence at Bennington, because its approach to teaching was profoundly different from the way I had been taught by Boulanger and Kirchner and others whom I admired. Students were encouraged to compose from the outset, and to learn notation, theory, instrumentation, history, and terminology alongside creating, and as an outgrowth of their own needs. Instead of being preordained, their choice of repertoire and their relationship to it varied according to their interests and to which faculty they were studying with.

The approach was radical, and reversed the traditional paradigm: Instead of a prescribed theory and history sequence, there were two essential music courses taken by all music students and taught collaboratively by all music faculty that put composition and improvisation and the learning of notation at the center, and in which all student work was performed and recorded.

Almost all Bennington faculty had in fact been trained in a different atmosphere and style than Bennington's. We could each find our own way to balance traditional training and student-led experimentation. The hidden and exciting secret about Bennington was that it was as highly intellectual and challenging as any college anywhere, and that the faculty were brilliant.

Although we were called by our first names, and the word "professor" was generally not used, some of us were teaching almost exactly as we would have in a traditional university.

It was a wild place, but in many ways the subjects taught were those of academia generally; only the teaching and learning style were different.

I was fighting my own internal battles between spontaneity and planning, notation and improvisation, knowledge and instinct, between stylization and confession. But teaching in the Bennington way made it possible for me to relive my own first exciting encounters with composing and to help guide students towards the skills they needed, without imposing myself and my sense of the present on them. I tried to give them what I most valued in my own education, and to avoid what I had found most unhelpful.

I could reconcile the inspiration and freedom I received from being taught by Miss Dillon and Emilie Harris with the foundational rigor, support, and global view of music I received from Boulanger. And when I played the piano, I could remember Leon Kirchner's and Boulanger's playing, and how much I learned from just listening to them, how revelatory it was.

While I was never enamored with the idea that students didn't need to know "the repertoire," and even found that notion maddening, I loved Bennington's wild, experimental spirit, and the fact that its students were looking for an alternative to traditional education. And I loved my colleagues, even those who were difficult.

Although it was not represented in any systematic manner, the repertoire was, of course, on display in the weekly faculty concerts and in the well-attended music workshops. But what was so remarkable about the Bennington music program in this era, the first nine years I was there, was that there was a complete openness to the world of new music, without any particular dogma or methodology being espoused.

This suited me very well, because I had a passionate interest in current music, without being a proponent of a method. The composers who taught—and had taught—at the college were wide-ranging in their interests and not easily categorized in terms of musical language. All of them had written tonal works, twelve-tone works, freely atonal works, and works using their own unique systems.

The ethos of the program was epitomized by two former faculty whose legacy could still very much be felt. The uncategorizable Otto

Luening, who had arrived in 1933 and put composition at the center of musical studies, had composed in every acoustic genre and been a pioneer in developing electronic music and in creating works for orchestra with electronics. Henry Brant became famous for his "spatial music," in which music of different kinds and in different instrumental combinations were played simultaneously in different spaces in the hall.

In fact, the building where we performed, Greenwall, was designed with Brant's work in mind, to provide balconies from which different instrumental groups could play back and forth, the way ensembles had played in Saint Mark's Basilica in Venice in the sixteenth century, and to be a gigantic acoustical shell in which they would resonate.

But Brant was also a fine pianist, steeped in Beethoven, an Ives expert, a great orchestrator, and in every way a versatile, practical performing musician-composer. (I personally was indebted to him because he was short like me and had built a platform on which he could stand to write at the blackboard, which I was able to use.)

The performing faculty—Jack, Maxine, Sue Ann, Liz, Jeff—were new music experts, ready to perform whatever students wrote. Because they were full time, they could leave their schedules open on Wednesdays to read student music from "Music I" or "Music II," in any combination of instruments. Because it was such a communal atmosphere, all of the composers wrote pieces for other faculty members and for each other.

The repertoire they left behind reflects this. For example, Vivian composed a great deal for violist Jack Glick, with whom she toured as a viola-piano duo, and she wrote a wonderful comic piece for Lionel Nowak, *L'École des Hautes Études*, in which eight études that he played for right hand alone were given inventive accompaniments to be played by clarinet, bass, and percussion.

It was a very temperamental group, and in music meetings, arguments were frequent. These greatly increased when Bill Dixon was present. But it was essentially a kind of fractious family. With the giant mansion that had once belonged to the prosperous Jennings family at the top of the hill overlooking the rest of the campus serving as the music building, and isolating it from the other divisions in the school, the music program was like a small, avant-garde conservatory.

Bill was a fascinating person, a talented painter, as well as a musician-composer, who had worked with Cecil Taylor, Sun Ra, and William Parker. He was cantankerous but never unengaged, a leader to his core, an intellectual who always looked spiffy in his velvet suits. For ten years, Bill had independently led his own mini-jazz conservatory with three to four faculty. This was mostly in another building, the Carriage Barn, which he had renamed the Paul Robeson House.

There had been vigorous debates at the college over the years about the worth and place of improvisation in contemporary music. There was even a heated panel discussion in which Cecil Taylor, with whom Bill had worked extensively, had quarreled over the matter with Lou Calabro and composer Hall Overton.

To the board of trustees, Bill had argued convincingly for an independent program for free jazz, steeped in a different repertoire and a different tradition of teaching and playing than what the rest of the music faculty were doing. He was an organizer by nature, having created festivals in New York and been a founder of the Jazz Composers Guild.

There were parallels between his story and that of Lou Calabro. Both attended conservatory as mature men on the GI Bill; both had first come to Bennington through the dance program; both found a refuge there, a place to flourish and develop their own work.

Very early in my Bennington experience, Lionel—always independent in his thinking—told me that he and Bill were friends and had a lot of mutual respect. I asked Bill to perform in a concert I organized in the fall of 1986 for Lionel's seventy-fifth birthday, which included pieces composed in his honor (Vivian's was a pizzicato fanfare for cello) as well as his wonderful Concert Piece for kettle drums and strings, with Lou Calabro playing kettle drums, which I conducted.

I also paid tribute to Lou by performing at his sixtieth birthday concert a few weeks later.

Bennington was not just a job. It was a full-time way of life. We were all working tremendously hard.

I had my own explosive encounter with Bill early on. I can remember the explosion, but not the cause. It happened in his office. In response to a remark from me, he suddenly turned on me, saying, "You are a racist." I flew off the handle, took his door and slammed it, and yelled, "Go fuck yourself!"

The reader will recall that a similar outburst from me resulted in my being fired by Joe Papp. But it had the opposite effect on Bill. His expression showed that he knew he had struck a nerve and he backed off. It created a kind of human connection between us; he understood what it was to lose one's temper.

He had also met J.—to whom he was at his most courtly—as well as our daughter. In later years, we had many good times together. As of today, I wish I could take back whatever clueless thing I must have said that provoked him, since I would guess that his reaction was justified. Whatever good instincts my parents and my teachers had, I had grown up in a society and in a musical education system that was racist in its very structure, and I was not separate from that, but a part of it.

A communal concert that left an indelible impression on me was the memorial for George Finckel in September 1987. It was the moment that I finally realized I had come to the right place, and even why it was right. I had recoiled from the commercial world, and I had also recoiled from the traditional academic world. In both cases, it seemed to me there was a danger of creating from confused motives: on the one hand, the need for money, and on the other hand, the need for respect and approval from mentors, the need to be academically respectable, the need to get an academic position or to acquire grants.

Here, composers wrote from inner need and out of a desire to communicate, not out of fealty to a theory or a mentor. The new music at the memorial was linked emotionally because of its purpose, but not stylistically. It also linked seamlessly with the three Chorale Preludes of J.S. Bach, arranged for four cellos, that began the program.

The college's tradition of music for cello quartet and multiple cello ensembles was started by George Finckel. This became a family affair when he was joined by his two cellist sons, Chris and Michael, and their cousin, David (later of the Emerson Quartet). George, Michael, Maxine, and others had contributed to a treasury of Bach and other arrangements for this medium.

The program included a new work from Jeff Levine, a mystical multiple-cello piece by Vivian, and a humorous work for cello quartet by Lou Calabro, illustrating moments in a poker game (poker being a weekly pastime he had shared with George).

Lou mentioned to me that he had originally written a lament for George in his Jennings studio but realized on the way home that he preferred to remember George with a tribute to the fun they had playing cards. He had turned his car around, driven back to Jennings, and written a new piece.

The best of Bennington was on display: a faith in the cello, in music as a way of life, and a cherishing of human beings.

Greenwall was packed. Lionel spoke from the heart, almost breaking down as he began, "To remember George is easy; to describe him is hard."

There was a genial character to the music I composed as I tried to make this transition, starting with the Sonatina, which I played for the opening faculty concert, followed by *Three Songs for Flute and Piano*, written for my spectacular flutist-colleague Sue Ann Kahn, which we played at the faculty concert in December that Vivian had urged me to give. My program consisted of the Alban Berg Piano Sonata, op. 1; Stockhausen's early Sonatine (1951) for violin and piano, played with Joseph Schorr; *Three Songs for Flute and Piano* ("Ballad," "Air," "Sea Chanty"); "2 x 4 x 7," a clangorous, atonal piece by Jeffrey Levine for seven pianists at two pianos; and a dance piece choreographed by Lynne Taylor-Corbett to my recorded score for *Night Music*.

If my Sonatina was a "B," what grade could I give *Three Songs for Flute and Piano*? Each movement was, in its way, an "A," but each was so distinct from the others. Did that mean that the piece as a whole deserved an "F"?

I was still trying to understand what kind of composer I was. I had so many musical affections and influences. I believed in being a Berg or a Webern, not in going from idiom to idiom from one piece to the next, or from one movement to the next. I didn't believe in being an "eclectic" and regretted that I was not more of a purist. But I had also learned the danger of censoring myself. I could only compose using the ideas I had.

At the same time, I wanted to be sure that I could at least be consistent in my language if I chose to be.

Earlier in the fall, when my two-harpsichord piece had been recorded by two players, Lucinda had found the tape unsatisfactory, and I had ended up making a professional quality overdub myself for the forthcoming performances at the Joyce Theater. My piece was to be the evening's finale. I was able to attend rehearsals in the New York studio, watching awestruck as the troupe in leotards zigzagged across the space in bewitching groupings and patterns, perfectly coordinated with the music, with Lucinda leading them like a goddess or the figurehead on the bow of a ship. It was thrilling.

At one of these rehearsals, I had the pleasure of meeting Philip Glass (a fellow Boulanger alumnus), after which we shared a cab. He appreciated my score and I liked him immediately.

I did not know at the time that Lucinda would almost be dressed as a ship herself, that Robert Mapplethorpe's costumes would engulf everyone in ballooning outfits (as elaborate as the ones in seventeenth-century French operas), obscuring their legs and foot-work, nor that this fourth work would be the finale of an evening in which the design elements, including the set, would go from spareness to complexity.

Once we were at the Joyce Theater, at the climax of the music, a cross-like shape ignited in flames at the back of the stage, a symbol as socially disturbing as it was dangerous-looking.

At the stage bows, I had the pleasure of meeting Liz Swados, a Bennington graduate, and Michael Nyman, who had just arrived on his flight from England in time to view the production and who was very kind about my music.

At the party after opening night, when I told Susan of my distress about having my music played while a burning cross on stage raised associations with the Ku Klux Klan, she begged me to tell Lucinda how I felt. I was a lowly composer, and Mapplethorpe was, of course, a great artist (his exquisite photographs of flowers were also used in the scenic design).

I approached Lucinda cautiously and expressed myself. She became indignant, saying that she would never dream of telling Robert Mapplethorpe what to do. I believe that we never spoke again.

As a whole, the ballet was negatively received in the press, although with nice mentions of the Swados and the Nyman pieces. I believe that I had unwittingly walked into the middle of a quarrel between Susan and Lucinda. I still cherish my memory of working with Lucinda Childs, and of seeing the original choreography.

In the spring, I got to hear my quintet wonderfully played by the Aspen Wind Quintet in Hartford, Connecticut, after which the piece was recorded and published by Galaxy.

In my first two years at Bennington, I felt released, as if I had been shot out of a cannon. I had boundless energy, and my music did too: it was dynamic and optimistic. I was developing my craft as best I could, taking advantage of my extraordinary good luck at having found a position as a teacher at a place that accepted my work and where I could share it and keep growing. I admired my fellow composer colleagues and learned from them.

I also learned from my students and sometimes collaborated with them. My advisee Claudia Friedlander was such an exceptional clarinetist that she could comfortably play the premiere of my new *Divertimento* for clarinet and piano with me at her senior recital. She was also a fine singer (leading to her eventual career path) and once performed both the clarinet and the solo soprano parts from Mahler's Fourth Symphony Finale, to the accompaniment of her own chamber orchestra arrangement of the piece. (This project typified for me what I loved about Bennington students.) I also was able to entrust an angular, rangy song cycle on poems by my friend Frederick Seidel to talented student soprano Susannah Waters, who likewise went on to a career as an opera singer.

In the spring of my second year at the college, my father's life was dramatically altered by his forced retirement from *The New Yorker*, where he was replaced as editor-in-chief by the Alfred A. Knopf editor Robert Gottlieb. He had often spoke of his regret at having abandoned writing, and he now found an office at the midtown Brill Building to work on a novella and do some freelance editing for Farrar, Straus and Giroux.

The New Yorker had given him a creative, social, and political outlet for the full range of his interests and abilities, and it had furnished him with a way to be sociable that perfectly suited him. An extraordinarily shy person, he had never been at ease in large gatherings, or addressing a group, and he had no habit of forming individual friendships. As editor of the magazine, he could focus on each person intently, but also separately and on his own schedule; he could end visits when he chose to; he could know multitudes of fascinating people, but on his own terms, and on his own turf.

Beginning a new lifestyle at age eighty must have been terribly painful for him, and the situation had also caused a conflict in our family, because his two daughters-in-law worked for the magazine. Our concerned and pragmatic mother, alarmed that Jonathan Schell and Lillian Ross had resigned in protest, privately cautioned both women to stay put and not harm their careers.

At the beginning of 1987, I wrote a Partita for Oboe and Piano for New York oboist John Ferrillo, soon to become principal oboist with the Boston Symphony. Rebellion can take many forms. In its way, the piece was a protest against all of the contemporary pieces I had sat through in which a kind of sonic saturation had taken over within a matter of seconds. How can it be that a Mozart, a Debussy, a Stravinsky, and even a Stockhausen can continually refresh the ear, while others only clutter it, with sound piled upon sound, eventually obscuring even the memory of how beautiful music can be?

Partita was a tonally grounded "suite in olden style" in seven movements, more or less based on Baroque models, including a short fugue, and ending with a chorale. It was such a pleasure to write, such fun to press just enough against its stylistic restrictions, once they were established, to feel that I was expressing myself and not producing an academic exercise. The Partita fulfilled my many efforts to create multi-movement pieces that had a unified style and reoccurring materials (as in the three related slow movements, or the "Gigue" that was a variation of the earlier "Toccata") and I suspected that no one would guess how personal and heartfelt (heartbreaking?) the piece really was. The epilogue, a poignant Chorale, had been an afterthought and changed the meaning of the work, I felt.

I drew courage not only from works of Stravinsky like *Pulcinella* and *Le Baiser de la Fée* in which (to me) something "backward" moved music itself forward, and from the vitality of Balanchine's stylized anachronisms, but also from the extraordinary realistic works of Picasso, like his 1938 pastel portrait of his daughter Maya, or his 1954 oil and charcoal portrait of his wife Jacqueline, that were done right along works of daring experimentation and grotesque distortion.

To me, these were life-giving lessons in the freedom of the artist to be traditional when it suited him, and to be "new" and "expressive" in whatever way gave him joy, even when "new" meant "old."

During this period, I also wrote two short piano pieces, *Humoresque* and a Tango that was played by a number of pianists in later years, and two simple sacred choruses (*Alleluia* and *Agnus Dei*) that almost picked up where my Harvard Senior Year "Gloria" had left off fifteen years earlier. When he heard them sung by the college chorus, Lou Calabro told me he thought I had an entire Mass in me.

Then I turned my attention to a huge project due the following fall. Jack Kernochan had arranged a commission for a symphony to be played by Greenwich Symphony Orchestra in Connecticut that would also serve as the score for a ballet to be performed by Atlanta Ballet Company in Atlanta, choreographed by Lynne Taylor-Corbett, with sets by Frances Barth.

I pictured the Symphony as shaped like two islands: one small (the lively first movement) and the second large (the slow second movement, connected without pause to a jazzy theme and variations finale). There would be an important solo role for the orchestral piano, a characteristic borrowed from my teenage Fantasy for Orchestra.

I planned the key relationships between the three movements (D–B-flat–D) and their timbral progression, featuring different orchestral choirs in each movement: 1) winds, 2) strings, and 3) brass. True to its dual purpose, the work became a symphonic-ballet score, visceral and outgoing.

Lynne Taylor Corbett listened to my piano tapes of the first movement as it evolved, always asking for greater compression. The movement went through multiple versions, each increasingly lean and focused. The slow movement contained three distinct dance episodes, arranged ABACA—A) Pas de Deux, (B) Waltz, and (C) Tango—with its quiet ending interrupted by a rambunctious piano solo leading into the theme and its variations. The latter unfolded increasingly frenetically, ending with a Gershwinesque flourish.

I learned a wonderful lesson from having begun the slow movement in a state of exhaustion. Far from simply lacking energy, what I wrote was beautiful and real, and just right for its place in the score. Fatigue had removed a barrier I hadn't even noticed was there.

While finishing the Symphony over the summer, I had a call from a colleague of John Ferrillo's in the Metropolitan Opera Orchestra, flutist Michael Parloff, asking if I would compose a piece for flute and strings for a concert of concertos he was performing in the fall at Alice Tully Hall. I wondered if I had the time to do it, but I said yes, and I was able to compose a fifteen-minute Concertino for this medium rather quickly. It was essentially a Concerto Grosso, leaning heavily in a neoclassical direction.

In the fall of 1987, Vivian Fine retired and, without an enormous amount of discussion, my position at Bennington was expanded to full time.

I took the train to Atlanta to see the ballet choreographed to my new Symphony and was put up at the Ritz-Carlton Hotel. I felt like a "real" composer. I have dealt with the tedious subject of my dread of travel elsewhere, so I will not go into the details of all of that here. But all anxiety vanished when I walked into the rehearsal room where the orchestra was in the middle of playing the transition into the final moments of the finale, the loudest and most dissonant moment in the Symphony. It was amazing to hear the piece come to life through the artistry and energy of seventy musicians, which is surely among the most addictive and memorable of all experiences. Apart from sex, I can think of nothing that so demands to be repeated.

The ballet was beautifully presented. I particularly loved the pas-de-deux second movement and Frances's hanging shapes, which reminded me of Miró and Noguchi. Then later in the fall, there was the orchestral premiere in Greenwich, with a much thicker orchestral sound and weightier brass in the slow movement. Jack Kernochan was there, as was Donald Waxman, in a large colorful tie that brought out his own composerly identity. Jack complimented the Symphony's "socko ending." Only a month later, I went to the flute and strings premiere at Alice Tully Hall.

Then, to my surprise, I crashed.

I can't reconstruct what pushed me over the edge. What I know is that after that first term working full time and the stress of my two premieres, I fell into a depression, got sick, lost my voice entirely, and felt that something had shifted in my relationship to composing. That the news of the change in my father's life had something to do with this I now see as likely, but I'll leave it to the psychoanalytically inclined to parse the connection.

For his part, my father's opinion—when I went to New York to consult doctors about my voiceless state—was that my problem was that I did not like teaching. It is true that it is not easy to combine teaching, practicing, composing, and raising a family. But no one's work life is easy, and mine suited me in a way that most people cannot say about theirs. I think that my condition had more to do with sorting out my identity as a composer than with a reaction to my job.

In the first three days of January, 1988, in a speechless state, I wrote a series of short pieces for Lionel, for piano right-hand, calling them *Six Miniatures*. There was no occasion for the piece, simply an impulse. There was something about writing for Lionel, with his courage, his limitation, and his particular pianism, that fit the moment. I was frightened that I had lost the ability to speak so inexplicably, and my problem did not feel just like laryngitis. The first of the miniatures, a Chorale in E flat major, unassuming as it seemed, was in fact my nonbeliever's prayer that my voice would return.

Or was I a "nonbeliever"? I find the concept of "belief" anthropocentric and absurd. Why would the universe be asking me if I "believe"? I also balk at the word "atheist," which seems to presuppose a norm of "theism."

I understand the impulse to bow down. I do not have a religion, but I can and do bow down, and I understand bowing down much better than not bowing down. For me, there is such a thing as a religious impulse, a need for faith and hope, unattached to specific beliefs, and it comes out in art. All music is connected with this religious impulse.

Something in me seemed to say that a certain phase of my composing had ended, that authentic as my work had been all these years, I had been straining to fulfill some intuited standard, that I had been carrying some mantle, that I hadn't been truly writing from within, as myself. I had been obliged to stay positive and rational, as if I were a normal person.

It had been ten years since my "breakthrough" with *Cabaret Music*, when I had begun deriving my theory and musical architecture from my own ideas and from the way my mind worked. But it had taken me until this moment to fully trust my own emotions. I now rejected the optimism of what I had been writing. It was as if a personal impulse had now become so overwhelming that it burned away the covering of other people's idioms and the pretense of rationality behind my music.

The period of depression and exhaustion left me changed. That winter, I listened to a lot of Mahler, Shostakovich, Sibelius, and Nielsen.

My friend Jean-Claude Comert, twenty-five years my senior, a great music enthusiast, had given me many Shostakovich recordings over the years, almost as if on a mission. M. and I had seen a great deal of him in Paris and later in New York, where he worked at Schlumberger.

Jean-Claude knew the worst of life. He had been in the Resistance, and at the age of twenty-two had been captured and interned as a prisoner of war for a year and a half in Mühlhausen, and at the Steyr Factory.

I had never allowed Shostakovich to get too close, but now I needed him. My next piece, *Two Night Pieces* for viola and piano, composed for Jack Glick, reflected the listening. It came from another place inside me, rejoining more completely with the lyric, sometimes sad strains of my childhood work.

The first movement begins like a motoric neoclassical piece but suddenly runs aground, and a dark-hued low register melody ensues in the viola. The second movement pursues this nocturnal moodiness more deeply, and there is even a kind of momentary "panic attack" halfway through it. The music is concentrated, with some moments that are reminiscent of Mahler and Berg, but not in an imitative way. It offers no particular comfort to the listener, only the potential balm of sharing itself.

The piece that followed this one was not another in a confessional mode, but a vacation from it, a piece for two pianos called *Eclogue*, which Elizabeth Wright and I performed at a faculty concert and later recorded. At the time, I didn't know what to make of it. Its two movements—the first almost fifteen minutes long, the second only five—seemed like a regression and rejection of what I had discovered, another work in the long line of my tonally rooted pieces with a classicized manner.

Now I hear it as a critic might, as a kind of apotheosis of—and farewell to—my "neoclassical" side, and as a celebration of pure sound. The first movement's serene sarabande uncannily evokes the bygone world of Germaine Tailleferre's 1918 two-piano *Jeux de Plein Air*, which I had not yet heard, juxtaposed with shards of a Toccata that comes uncomfortably close to Stravinsky's *Concerto for Two Pianos*, which I had.

Yet there is an increasing sense of distance from sources, and the elephantine minuet that begins the much shorter second movement, and the racy, almost taunting gigue that emerges from it in florid counterpoint, suggests a bursting out and moving away—a last salutation to the past. In retrospect, I can see that it fulfilled something in the two-piano segments I had composed for the play *Found a Peanut*, a short duo-piano fanfare I contributed to Lionel's birthday concert, and of course Partita.

But there had been a shift in perspective. I had come out from under the spell of early twentieth-century music and had started to exist in the present. Perhaps this was a case of "reculer pour mieux sauter" (to step back in order to jump further).

Eclogue was composed over the summer when J. was again pregnant, and finished on September first. Our son, Harold, was born on the twelfth.

Composing happened in counterpoint to teaching and to a busy family life that included all that the reader can imagine, the domestic chores, the worries about money, the nighttime bottle feedings I gave H., which allowed J. to sleep. There was a rocking chair in H.'s room, and those moments in the middle of the night in which I held and fed him and just sat in the dark in a quiet stupor with him were themselves in counterpoint to all of the horrors of the world and to all the lives that were declining and ending.

H., who one day would be a strong adult man a foot taller than me, leading his life and writing his own music, was just a tiny warm little fellow starting out, full of needs and wants. Once again witnessing a birth, once again becoming a father, helped me grow up, too, not so much healing the wound left by my sister, but helping me gain perspective on how having twins, one of whom was so troubled and damaged, must have affected my parents when they were my age.

In the fall, Maxine Neuman told me that she was a planning a CD with her cello quartet and asked if I could contribute to it. I had never had music recorded, and felt inspired. *Suite for Cello Quartet* proved to be an outgrowth of *Two Night Pieces*: a five-movement work which could be heard as a continuous narrative of slow music interrupted in movements two and four by fast music.

There was a potent sadness at the music's core. I wanted desperately to express myself and to be heard, and the intimacy of a recording provided the opportunity for direct communication. Yet in private, I found what I had written disgusting and alarming. Somehow it violated an unacknowledged need that I seem well. This was an "unwell" music. It was confident in expression but broken inside.

The third movement began with a "Bartók snap pizzicato," like the crack of a twig breaking, leaving behind a lonely held note. Even the waltz-like fourth movement had a moment of disintegrating into neurasthenic sighs. The work rounded itself out with a coda that recalled the first movement, resolving on a G flat major triad that was not so much a tonal center as simply a place to rest. I gave Maxine a chart showing the beginnings and endings of each movement, and how they led from one to another and created a through-line.

I had grown close to Maxine watching her rehearse my two multiple cello pieces, a Chorale for eight celli, and a Waltz in C for twelve, and had performed with her. (Somehow she had even convinced me to play the extraordinarily difficult Brahms F Major Sonata with her.)

I now knew her range of musical interests, everything from Medieval and Renaissance music, in which she was an expert, to Bach, to Shostakovich and Schnittke, to the pieces by Led Zeppelin, the Beatles, and Astor Piazzolla that she had transcribed. (She had worked with Piazzolla, and it was she who introduced me to his irresistible music.) I knew that she would be sympathetic to whatever I gave her.

Coming to her studio to hear the group play the Suite was a revelation. Instead of feeling repelled, a deep satisfaction flowed through me. All of the technical skill behind the piece was in service of a personal expression. Whatever limitations there may have been in what I wrote were less important than the truth of what I was saying, which I knew went all the way back to my first pieces, to my experiences playing Berg and listening to Bartók, and all the way back to the sorrows, mysteries, and wordless interchanges with Mary, and to the sides of her I carry within me.

And it was Maxine who had elicited this, because she had accepted me in a way that no other performer had, and that few people since Miss Dillon had. That is to say, she accepted—not uncritically, but unconditionally—whatever I might have to offer, whether it was my lightest, most humorous side or my most private and deepest.

Boulanger talked about Poulenc "always being himself" and about the lifelong continuity in the work of a composer like Jean Françaix. Even more telling was her account of writing regularly to Copland and not correcting her mistakes in English, "so that he would know the letter was from me."

Jonathan Schell used to tell me that my slow movements were where I emerged, where he knew it was me speaking: the slow movement of my String Quartet, of *Nocturnes*, of my Wind Quintet, of my *Symphony in Three Parts*, even the little slow movement in my youthful *Three Animals* in which he played at Harvard.

He was right. These were the moments where I couldn't help but be myself. Not what I should be, but what I am. It is not that with the *Suite for Cello Quartet* I discovered that my essential characteristic was sadness. But writing it showed me that in order to be a complete composer, I had to fully accept the sadness and not resist it when it came, just as I had not resisted my lassitude when I was composing the slow movement of the Symphony.

This was not the kind of lesson we discussed in our seminars at Columbia. It was in fact Earl Kim at Harvard who had told us: "Your weakness is your strength."

One had to be satisfied putting down only one note, if that was all one had. The energy would return. One needed to accept and be patient.

Not what I am supposed to be, but what I am.

10

DARKER MUSIC (1989–1992)

A LTHOUGH I HAD A tendency to follow one kind of composition with a very different kind, I immediately followed the Suite with a comparable piece for violin and piano, *Winter Sketchbook*, which was likewise in five movements and likewise steeped in a darker spirit. It was performed at the college by a wonderful violinist, Joanna Jenner.

In April of 1989, Claudia Friedlander, who had stayed on campus past her graduation to work in the administrative offices of the school, put together a program that would include the premiere of the Clarinet Trio, which she knew had a particular meaning for me.

In rehearsal, Maxine was reassuring that the Trio was not the musical failure I had assumed it to be. As always, I was very nervous performing, and the piano part to the Trio was ferociously difficult. But the clarinet and cello parts were no less so. Maxine owned her part, and Claudia's performance was simply stunning. I don't think I have ever had a more exuberant response from an audience than I had for that piece that night.

Only a month later, I performed the piano solo part in *Nocturnes* with the Vermont Symphony Orchestra, conducted by Efrain Guigui. I had a 103-degree fever. Astonishingly, this undercutting of confident self-expression by illness had persisted since childhood.

In May of 1989, Jack Kernochan called with the news that the Galaxy Music catalogue had been sold to E.C. Schirmer in Boston, and that he and Donald Waxman would no longer be dealing with submissions and publication.

It was a shock. Only two weeks earlier, Donald had written a long, detailed, and amazingly thoughtful letter about all of the recent pieces I had sent, offering reasons for rejecting the songs on poems by Frederick Seidel ("the only recent work of yours that presented, we thought, very real aesthetic problems"), accepting the Concertino into the rental catalogue, the Oboe Partita, *Eclogue*, and *Dance Music for Two Harpsichords* as facsimile editions, and the Sonatina, *Nine Pieces*, and *Three Songs for Flute and Piano* as regular publications.

Donald made careful distinctions in his comments: for example, saying which version of the group of *Nine Pieces* he preferred and why, and, of the Partita, that, "I'm not sure you were always that sympathetic to either the oboist's endurance or to the audience's for the continued stream of oboe playing. Particularly appealing were the nifty little fugue and the deft gigue, and I very much liked the innocent repose of the trio of the minuet." His views were wonderfully specific: "...in spite of its *semplice* opening, [the slow movement] rather quickly heats up with much articulation, and just maybe too many notes."

So often in life, one doesn't realize what one has until it's gone. While focusing on where I disagreed with Jack's and Donald's judgments, I had never fully appreciated or thanked them for what they had given me. Their support had helped me feel that my life as a composer made some kind of sense, and that despite evidence to the contrary, I was not deluded to keep at it.

Donald had done everything he could to help me become a professional, even giving a two-hour lesson in preparing the manuscripts so that they would be more legible. Galaxy had accorded me a kind of legitimacy. Donald and Jack had a shared point of view, and it was an astute and perceptive one. It accorded well with Boulanger's views and even, in a way, with the editorial traditions of *The New Yorker*.

I only realized this in retrospect, when I thought about which pieces they accepted and which they did not. They favored a language that was lucid and gave the listener a melodic and harmonic foothold. This at least gave me something to bounce off of. They articulated their judgments with specificity so that I could learn from their expertise, and they were idealistic. Galaxy had been losing money for many years.

But it seemed to me that I was trying for something in my Piano Sonata, Second String Quartet, and my Seidel songs and other pieces they didn't care for that I needed to keep pursuing. I thought of this as my "searching" side. Perhaps a certain clarity was missing in these works, but they were real, and possibly more meaningful than my more polished pieces.

Perhaps no one listener would like all of my sides. But I was not an exponent of any particular school, including the Boulanger School. I had my "Schoenberg" side too—by which I mean not that this side of my work sounded particularly like Schoenberg or that it used his methods, but more what Boulanger may have meant when she heard my little Theme and Variations, that it conveyed something more elusive and irrational.

As a listener, I have always gravitated towards music much more "far out" than my own. What mattered to me was whether a composer was genuinely doing their own thing. For example, I was very taken with a concert presented by Lucia Dlugoszewski in Greenwich Village in the early 1980s in which she played some of her captivating inside-the-piano works. Years later, I had the pleasure of sitting next to her at a concert at Jacob's Pillow and could tell her so, while we both commented on the beauties of a Ginastera String Quartet being performed.

Being complimented for being "accessible" or "melodic" was never a pleasure. If the music had those qualities, they were not the result of a position I was taking, but were simply what came from my own ear, mind, and heart.

I soon experienced the sting of no longer having my music being given careful consideration. My letters from the new publisher were focused entirely on whether my pieces were commercially viable, and in my visits to see them in Boston, I mainly had to listen to them extol the "approachable" music of others and the high sales figures they generated. I had to wait practically twenty years for them to again start accepting a few new scores from me, and my letters from them were not encouraging ("I'm sorry I must tell you that we cannot take on any of it..."). On top of this, they did not honor several contracts signed before the catalogue changed hands, including the Sonatina, Nine Pieces, Three Songs for Flute and Piano, and Divertimento for clarinet and piano, and eventually I forgot that these works even existed.

In the fall of 1990, I was eligible for a sabbatical, so J. and I took little A., now almost six years old, on the boat to Europe for three weeks, a trip fully funded by J.'s literary earnings and one I had planned with enormous care so that I could survive the stress. Sadly, we left H. behind, and even missed his second birthday.

On the boat, A. and I swam daily in the pool in the basement of the ship, where the sensation of swimming in a small body of water within the larger motions caused by the engulfing ocean was unforgettable; we gazed from the deck at night at the stars and the vastness; I played Joplin and Gershwin on the white piano in the lounge; we ate with strangers and tried to make small talk.

In London, we visited my friend Frederick Seidel on the set of a film he had written; in Paris we went to museums and visited Place Lili Boulanger (later renamed Place Lili-et-Nadia-Boulanger), and I was able to have lunch with Pierre Petit. It was a romantic and wonderful trip, and the last time I was in Europe, as of this writing. I took the long boat ride home, while J. and A. flew.

That fall, with the luxury of more free time, I wrote a Sextet for piano and winds, and a long Serenade in one movement for cello and piano for Maxine. Then I started to explore a world of vocal music I had neglected since *The Music Teacher* back in 1983.

Over the next two years, I completed a group of seven songs on poems by e.e. cummings (arranged in an arch form) and a short cummings choral setting, as well as a Cantata on ten poems by Robert Frost, settings of Robert Herrick, and a group of *vocalises* for children's chorus.

In between, I wrote some pieces for soprano saxophone and piano, and *Blues and Boogie* for cello and piano. When my student Amy Williams, a pianist and composer who has gone on to a significant career in the world of new music, had requested a piece to play with cellist Tom Calabro, son of Lou, I immediately pictured two pieces balancing each other—yin and yang. Sometimes one has a sense that a piece is "already there" to be written—the same sense that made Babe Ruth able to point his bat to where the ball would reach, or that makes a cat judge a leap to a ledge fifteen feet up.

The work is compressed and stylized, making use of jazzy materials, and it is hard to characterize as either light or serious. There are subliminal connections between the two movements, such as a row made from the second theme of the Blues which is planted into the exuberant "Boogie-Woogie."

I was proud of my Frost Cantata for chorus, soprano soloist, children's chorus, and piano, which set nine poems dealing with winter and solitude and ended with the optimistic "A Prayer in Spring." It emphasized the sense of isolation and darkness in Frost, whom I saw as a kind of poetic counterpart to painter Edward Hopper. I channeled my agoraphobia into "Good Hours":

I went till there were no cottages found.
I turned and repented, but coming back
I saw no window but that was black.

Frost had lived in Bennington and is buried outside Old First Church there. The performance by the community chorus in Bennington at the local high school was a moving occasion, and since I wasn't playing the piano part myself, I didn't have to be nervous.

I had entered my choral setting of e.e. cummings's "in time of daffodils" into a choral competition and travelled to Ithaca, New York, in February to attend it. To my astonishment, it won first prize in its category, and I had the thrill of walking up onstage, where Bruckner's thunderous *Te Deum* had just resounded, and receiving a small check amid applause. I was also able to meet the gifted composer Augusta Read Thomas.

The Ithaca prize came with a chance for the work to be published by Presser Music, but the firm told me that the piece was not commercial enough for them to take it.

With two growing children in the house, and only a modest income from teaching and intermittent income from my original music, I often felt that the choices I had made to be a composer needed defending. I wondered what I had expected a life as a composer to be like, and whether I had done something wrong. I would have loved to be paid large sums of money for my work, but it wasn't happening and probably never would. My extreme and debilitating phobias were no help. I had chosen to be in an esoteric field, and my problems were restricting my options even within that field.

I recognized the danger of becoming too isolated and therefore too precious about my work, and I saw the value of healthy interactions with audiences and with the public world, but I also saw the benefit of being independent from the marketplace and fashion.

I had a hunger to reach people and to share my music, but I also needed privacy in order to find my voice, and even saw this privacy as having a political meaning, as being in a sense subversive of a culture devoted to material things, and to whatever is public and publicized.

I felt that I had come to Bennington to compose an intimate music—not quiet or abstruse, necessarily, but on a human scale. It seemed to me that the world we lived in was one in which the freedom we all have within our own minds—the freedom to appreciate silence and solitude, to feel joy and to contemplate serious things, to be in contact with the deep mystery that we exist and with the unknowability of who we are—was at risk.

I felt that focusing on my own work was important, that it affirmed the worth of the individual, and that on some level, keeping a record of the inner life was a way of serving humanity generally. Not everything in life can be commodified. Not everything is physical and visible. There is an entire world within each person.

All the same, I was ambitious. I wanted my music played all over the planet, and I tried to make it durable and worthy of that.

I knew that I wasn't particularly modern. Writing about myself in the third person in a liner note I wrote about the Clarinet Trio, *Eclogue*, and *Winter Sketchbook*, I tried to locate myself in relation to the present:

> Although more obviously marked by earlier influences, his language still shows signs of having been formed during the 1960s and 1970s. While on the whole the ideas are tonal and traditional-sounding, there is always a push to take them in unexpected directions, into uncharted territory; there are moments of out-and-out atonality that poke through, almost like tonal references in a serial work; and there is a tendency towards a Carter-like independence of parts (as in sections of the Trio and the first movement of Winter Sketchbook) which one might not encounter in similar sounding music of the 1930s and 1940s.

In an *Atlantic Monthly* article, I made a related point:

> If the music of Varèse, Schoenberg, Ives, and Cowell is still very much with us, so are works that once seemed old-fashioned: pieces by Dmitri Shostakovich, Francis Poulenc, Samuel Barber, and Sergei Rachmaninoff. Can these works not also lay claim to being of their time and no other? As the years pass, one sees more clearly the ways in which these traditionalists were both inventive and original. If they had been true conservatives, we would not today so readily recognize the distinctive voice of each...[1]

Early in the fall of 1991, I had the unexpected pleasure of improvising with Bill Dixon at two pianos at a faculty concert. I don't remember how it came about, but I was certainly not known as an

---

[1]   Allen Shawn, "American Harvest," *Atlantic Monthly*, July, 1995, 83–86.

improviser. All I remember was that as we walked out onstage, Bill said, "I'll start." Otherwise, there had been no planning.

I was used to Bill's timbral explorations on the trumpet and flugelhorn, which often emphasized pedal tones and breathing effects with electronic delay, but unfamiliar with his piano playing. To my surprise, he started by laying down a carpet of lush harmonies over which I could extemporize in the upper registers, and our dialogue created something plaintive and tender. He later entitled it: *Collaborazione*. (Bill spent considerable time in Italy, performing and displaying his artwork there.)

In the period that I knew him, Lou Calabro was extraordinarily productive. Having begun by showing his affinity for Persichetti's idiom, he had passed through a twelve-tone phase, explored open-form writing, written a series of pieces using isorhythmic principles and exploring complex polyphony, and had composed countless works, large and small, for students to play or sing.

In all of these phases, his work was expert and sounded like him. In what proved to be his last period, he was at his most exuberant and rhythmically inventive in fast movements, and touchingly eloquent in slow, making productive use of the octatonic scale. The living composer he most identified at this stage was Ligeti.

In the early months of 1991, he started suffering from fatigue and a terrible cough and, although pressing on with his teaching and performing, was clearly ill. In the past, he had been a chain smoker and a heavy drinker, habits that had taken a toll on him.

We had scheduled a performance of Mozart's Concerto in E flat, K. 449, in which I would play solo, observing the two-hundredth anniversary of Mozart's death year. He managed to make it through the rehearsals and the performance of this lovely, underperformed work. Once again, I had the experience of being surrounded by Mozart's magical orchestration and playing his singing lines from memory at the keyboard, music of such apparent effortlessness that forces the performer, through its beauty, to bring their greatest concentration, tone, and care to it. It was moving working with Lou on this delicate piece, as he himself, someone of such passion and energy, was in delicate shape.

By the late summer, his lung cancer had advanced to the point that he could no longer teach or conduct, and I took his place leading the orchestra in the Shostakovich First Cello Concerto, with Maxine as the soloist.

I visited him several times in the hospital. As a young child, I had learned something essential about the fragility of what a human being is, about the mythology surrounding our sense of "self," but I had been spared the education in death some people have all too early. I was already forty-three years old, and perhaps this was the first time I understood the degree to which we are all on a conveyor belt moving forward to nothingness. It was also a lesson in courage.

Lou was emaciated, but, even in the delirium of morphine, very much himself. He had always been a person of such emotional directness. He talked about realizing how much energy it takes to compose—and that now he didn't have the strength even to write a simple canon: "And I am no shirker of canons." He said that the visits of friends and family had made him feel a bit better about himself. He was troubled when my words implied that he could still recover. "You are leading me down the wrong path," he said, then adding, "When I die, I don't want you to feel bad, or anything like that."

In our last visit, he recounted a dream. He said that he saw "a gigantic dominant seventh chord: D–F-sharp–A–C" before him. "And it came closer and closer. And soon it was just a D... And then I entered the D."

Jack Glick and Willie Finckel saw him the next day, the day he died. Afterwards, Jack called and asked me to compose a solo viola piece he could play in our friend's memory.

I struggled with the assignment, ending up with three different viola solos: an *Aria, Lament*, and *Scherzo*. The *Scherzo* was actually the closest of the three to being a portrait of Lou. At the memorial, Jack played the *Aria*.

But he soon surprised me with a recording he had made of all three pieces performed as a set. I felt that for all of its difficulties and faults, Bennington was a kind of heaven, and haven, for composers.

In the spring of 1992, I was working on a Piano Trio for Maxine, Joanna Jenner, and Elizabeth Wright when I received a call from my mother telling me that my father had come down with a flu-like illness that had left him confused and shaky on his feet.

This illness precipitated a long-delayed crisis in the family over our father's relationship with Lillian. He was now entirely under our mother's and a visiting nurse's care, and he begged Wally and me to intercede so that he could be allowed out to see the other woman in his life, along with her adopted son, Erik.

Up until this point, we had abided with the family rule that we could not reveal to our mother that we even knew of this relationship. In order to preserve her sanity, and to tolerate our father's dual life, she had kept her family unit intact and to all appearances inviolable, and our father had also maintained a compartmentalization between his two relationships. Our mother had never known that Wally and I had become aware of the situation, and that I had even spent some time with Lillian and Erik. Fearing that our father was gravely ill, Wally and I reluctantly intervened on his behalf. Our mother was devastated.

What ensued was a tortured several months, with our father exhibiting Parkinsonian symptoms in his shuffling gait, while our mother struggled to cope with his condition, with the pain and worry of his visits to see Lillian, and with the torment of knowing that her sons knew about the thirty-five-year relationship and had defended their father's right to see her.

On the night of our father's eighty-fifth birthday, our mother became seriously ill with bleeding colitis and was hospitalized for several days. Our father was brought to the hospital by the visiting nurse, tortured with remorse and worry about her.

During those days when they were apart, I had a chance to talk to each of them about what they had been through, and I started to keep a diary of what they said to better understand it all.

I sat with my mother for many hours in the hospital. Even though she was so clearly in physical discomfort, there was also a strange sense of relief between us, since a barrier of falsehood had been lifted. Our relationship was freed by it. As a child, I had complained to friends and to Wally that there was "something wrong" in the family, a sense of "falseness" in the air and in the way our mother spoke about our father. The falseness had stood in the way of her being her complete candid self with us, and had even dammed up the love I felt for her and could now express to her.

For his part, our father, now alone at the apartment for a few days, seemed suddenly able to tell me more about why things had played out as they had, about his love for both women, about why he needed them both and had agreed to stay in this compartmentalized life rather than leave either of them.

Keeping a journal helped me make sense of all of this and taught me that sometimes putting things into words is essential. In between conversations, I wrote to Jerry Salinger, knowing that he was close to Lillian and had at one time considered my father his best friend. So many doors had been shut in the family; perhaps this one could be opened a bit. Unfortunately, I didn't receive a response, and I don't even know if my letter was received.

I was going back and forth to New York during this period, while continuing to teach, compose, and perform in Bennington. I now hear the sadness of my father's decline in my *Three Reveries* for piano, written that summer. At the time, they seemed to merely constitute a kind of oasis of calm. Three slow pieces in a row was a first, and they had a new tone. The music had started to seem more current.

My former student Linda Catlin Smith and I had stayed close friends and were often in touch. She was now a successful composer, one I deeply admired, living in Toronto. She had mentioned the music of Morton Feldman as an inspiration. His setting of Beckett's *Neither* had made a strong impression when I heard it in New York. There is perhaps a touch of Feldman's gentle patience in *Three Reveries*.

The complexities of my parents' relationship were on my mind when I wrote a flute and piano piece for a good friend, the brilliant flutist-composer Su Lian Tan, a graduate of Bennington, Juilliard, and Princeton. In response to her request for a piece, I envisaged something evocative and nostalgic.

Taking her last name "Tan" as a starting point, I first wrote a tonal Tango and then dismantled it, using the disconnected fragments in a collage, introduced and interrupted by wistful, angular, atonal ideas. The intent was to suggest that the Tango was being remembered, like the romantic love between my parents that had become fractured, though not completely lost, over time. In employing this "collage" process, I was influenced by the way Mahler used his songs as material in his Symphonies.

Somehow during this period, I also completed an ebullient piece called *Terpsichord* for alto saxophone, clarinet, violin, cello, and piano for the Vermont Contemporary Music Ensemble.

Among the changes at Bennington was Lionel Nowak's retirement in 1992. This did not end our visits, but it meant that upon entering the music building in the morning, one did not hear his familiar nimble touch at the keyboard coming from his second-floor studio, as he worked his way through his own Practice Piece or a Czerny étude.

Fortunately, we had created a recording of his performances of works composed for him called *The Right Hand Path*, named for Otto Luening's contribution. I had tried to interest Galaxy and Gunther Schuller's Margun Music in publishing some of his works, but I had been unsuccessful. The gateways of sweet "Musick" are closely guarded.

I was not in New York on the morning my father died, December 8th, 1992. My mother called at eight a.m., and I drove to New York staring straight ahead and barely moving for four hours, then spent time by his silent side in their bedroom.

Then there was the funeral home. Coming straight from Massachusetts, J. met Wally, Debbie, my mother, and me at the crematorium. We each put a flower in the coffin, and we read a poem that had meant a lot to my parents when they were first together.

Everyone knows this experience from their own lives. Nothing was the same afterwards. It was strange what would make me cry thinking of him. It was the littlest things, like the fact that he would purchase oranges to put in our Christmas stockings.

Although I did not attempt to memorialize my father in a specific piece of music, later I often felt his presence when I was composing a given work or passage. But whether I was aware of him or not, he was always there in the notes, and the rest of the time.

11

UPHEAVALS (1993–1994)

M Y RELATIONSHIP TO THEATER had not entirely ended. Even though it meant using a round-trip airplane ticket, I accepted James Lapine's invitation to go to the San Diego playhouse in the summer of 1993 to compose and perform the piano score for his play *Luck, Pluck and Virtue*, based on the satirical novel by Nathanael West.

It was wonderful spending time with James and his wife Sarah in San Diego, and an additional delight seeing my old friends Harvey Sollberger and pianist Aleck Karis there.

What a temperate and consistent climate San Diego has. Although at first it was not easy for me to adjust to James's request to write a "Coplandesque" score—I was no longer accustomed to fulfilling a director's expectations—it soon became natural to improvise during rehearsals, come up with ideas, and withdraw to the desk in the lobby of the theater to polish and copy them.

A photo taken of me during that time shows someone I hardly recognize, a laid-back southern Californian, not the tightly wound East Coast neurotic I actually am. Perhaps this was a needed vacation from that other self. But it proved to be my last plane flight, at least as of this writing.

The play was revived at a small theater in New York in 1995, and not long after that, *Twelve Dreams* was remounted for a third time in a sumptuous production at Lincoln Center Theater, with a chance to do further work on that score.

Later that year, came *What Is the Beautiful?* for cello and piano, with a text by Kenneth Patchen, read by speaker Robert J. Lurtsema, who had chosen the poem. Although Prokofiev, Copland, Schoenberg, and Takemitsu handled this medium well, spoken narration and music can be a treacherous combination. Hearing the left-leaning sentiments of the poem spoken aloud alongside my music seemed to render them pompous and smug. Perhaps a more neutral sonic tapestry would have supported the text better. Political views and music are an uneasy mixture, at least for me.

In the fall, I worked on an impassioned, almost Brahmsian Piano Trio. The turbulent outer movements used processes of thematic transformation like those in nineteenth-century works such as the Liszt Piano Sonata. In between these, a tiny slow movement was contrastingly impassive, like a view of clouds drifting by.

I had asked for a leave of absence in the spring, which permitted fulfilling a number of requests for pieces and a few small commissions. But it also relieved the stress from the crisis brewing at the college. Although few foresaw its impact on my immediate colleagues, one couldn't help but feel the tremors.

I had also started to have ocular migraines, which started to occur with increasing frequency over the next several years, interrupting teaching or playing as if circuit breakers had been thrown in my brain, and leaving me drained for the rest of the day.

In the winter, I worked on a set of five piano preludes for Elizabeth Wright and a piece for flute, clarinet, and piano for Catherine and Helen Saunders, English twin sister wind-players. The five preludes were highly concentrated—perched on the border between the tonal and the non-tonal—containing some echoes of Prokofiev in the first and fifth movements and a somber seriousness in the second and fourth. A chord progression from the first measures haunted every movement. The piece was inspired by the depth and elegance of Liz's pianism and also by our shared enthusiasm for Kirchner's music.

Bill Dixon asked me to play the preludes at an otherwise improvised music festival he held at the college in October. His events always drew a huge audience, and it was very exciting playing in this context.

Although the set of three pieces for the twin sisters was performed the following year, it took another twenty to revise it satisfactorily. Contrapuntal and stylized, *Music for flute, clarinet, and piano* leaned in the direction of Poulenc to such a degree that it eventually seemed right to add the phrase *Hommage à Poulenc* to its title. It still hasn't been performed in its final form.

Photographer Mariana Cook asked if she could photograph A. and me for her book on fathers and daughters and had requested a written paragraph to accompany it.

Mariana was known mainly for her black and white photographs of people, but as befitted a former student and disciple of Ansel Adams, she was also an eloquent photographer of natural objects. She published an entire book devoted to photographs of stone walls that convey an uncanny timelessness and presence. In a way, her pictures of human beings also feel silent, still, and objectified, not as if they have been caught in mid-life, but as if time has stopped and they have been preserved exactly as they were when it did.

As my written contribution, I wrote a slow waltz for piano four hands that A. and I could play together. Since it had a "French" sound, the title "In the Tuileries Gardens" seemed apt, and it became the second piece in a *Suite Parisienne* of six pieces, representing six places A. and I had visited in the city.

Like most children, A. normally needed a lot of coaxing to practice, but in this instance she was doggedly committed to learning the music. Stravinsky's idea of making a "primo" part in which the hand positions remained fixed and the "secondo" part had all of the difficulties proved perfect for the situation, but with different meters and key signatures in each piece, the upper part was still challenging for a nine-year-old.

A. played them brilliantly, like a mature musician, and we performed them together publicly several times. Perhaps the most memorable rendition took place three years later at a benefit concert for the school that she and H. attended. The benefit included a reading by J., some solo pieces of mine, including a new one written for A., and two duets I wrote to play with H. during the brief period when he took piano lessons.

A. once again showed that when she was interested in a piece, she could prepare it beautifully.

Eight-year-old H., a restless piano student and, like A., an intermittent practicer at best, played his part in the duets with complete confidence and musicality, a harbinger of his future musicianship.

I then turned to writing a set of six movements called *Episodes* for cello and piano for a concert with Maxine. I experimented with being more deliberately eclectic, placing movements containing twelve-tone elements next to others that were highly tonal. With a somewhat sinister, sarcastic march framing the work as movements one and six, and a rather heart-rending "Song Without Words" as a penultimate movement, it is hard now not to associate *Episodes* with the disturbing college upheaval of that spring.

The origins of the situation went back decades, and were economic, social, and political as well as educational. Enrollment at Bennington had been declining, and for a college facing continual financial challenges, the situation had become dangerous.

There had been year-long discussions organized by the administration about strategies for the future, but many faculty members boycotted them and thought they were a sham. There were factions; there was faculty unrest; there was student unrest; there were personal animosities. There was disagreement about what was true, and what was actually happening. There was a stalemate.

In June, the board of trustees sent out a letter firing a third of the faculty due to fiscal exigency and fundamentally restructuring many departments, among them music. I received a call from Jack Glick saying, "I hope you enjoyed the letter the board has sent you for Father's Day." The decision was to eliminate faculty positions for instrumental musicians, retaining only a few composers and voice teachers.

I was left standing, along with Bill Dixon, Joel Chadabe, and a few others, but most of my friends and colleagues in music were out of a job, unless they chose to return as adjuncts. This included Peter Golub, Jeff, Sue Ann, Maxine, Jack, Elizabeth Wright, and others. None of my colleagues accepted the offer to return on a different footing, which, given their personal connections to the place, would have been like returning as servants to a place where they had once been in charge.

There were lawsuits, which proved unsuccessful. Many people called what happened a "purge." From everything I knew then and have learned since, the fiscal emergency was genuine. But the actual decisions seemed to combine arbitrary faculty cuts with those that deliberately targeted unwanted individuals and groups. From where I sat it looked as if elements of a purge were folded into an emergency action that had legitimate underlying causes. However, I thought that the cuts made in my own area—music—constituted collateral damage from this mess, with no political meaning whatsoever.

In the process of carrying out their faculty cuts, the college violated its own core principles and destroyed a special music community with ties to the summer chamber music conference and to musicians all over the country and the world. The school's lack of expression of concern for how students and alumni felt, their lack of apology and expressed gratitude to the eliminated faculty—some of whom had worked at the college for forty years—made the process resemble the most draconian corporate decision-making of the Reagan era.

To demand that a faculty member like Jack Glick, who was sixty-eight years old and had devoted his entire adult life to Bennington, clear out of his office in three days without giving him time to make proper preparations, and without publicly honoring him, was unforgiveable. There might be disagreement as to why it all happened, but the way the decisions were carried out was disgraceful.

The ruthlessness paralleled the way my father had been treated at *The New Yorker*. But, at least publicly, my father had not been disrespected, and the changes in *The New Yorker* had been billed as an inevitable transition. Bennington's public stance was that the cuts constituted a welcome improvement.

Over the summer, I sank into a depressed state. I had my own issues with seeing people "sent away." Although I had drawn the lucky straw, I wasn't sure I wanted to stay, and I sought the counsel of both Vivian and Lionel, each of whom advised me to remain and keep the old ways going, both for my family's sake and for the sake of the students.

Vivian said, "Of course you should stay." Lionel thought for a moment before saying, "There's always music. There are the students, who need you." When I asked him why he thought the music program had been among the hardest hit, he said, "When you vomit, you can't just say, 'I'll keep this part down.'"

Not everyone landed on their feet after this. Although she was in much demand and kept to an extraordinarily busy schedule of playing and teaching, Maxine could never replace this exceptional type of position, and it took her many years before the events of 1994 were not a part of our every conversation.

Fortunately, our friendship survived. She was and remained indispensable to me, and we still had many years of collaboration ahead. Likewise, my friendships with my other musical colleagues held.

12

A CHANGED CAMPUS; ECLECTIC PIECES; RUPTURE (1994-2001)

I RETURNED TO A VERY different campus in the fall of 1994. My original colleagues had been my musical family of origin at the college. Even those who were my own age had been my mentors, giving me a footing in a way of life that included composing, performing, and teaching.

Like me, many faculty felt set adrift by the administration in a situation in which we were simultaneously bereft and also singled out as fortunate, or worse, complicit, in something brutal.

I met with all of the music students. My classroom was packed, with at least seventy-five students crammed into the small space. No one had expressed any sympathy for their grief, their grievances, their feelings of having been betrayed, their concerns. It was astonishing.

For a while, I was like a pontoon bridge over which people walked as they established a new campsite across a ravine. I held the music program together on both ends, hanging onto the spirit and practices of the past while trying to facilitate the new. Some changes were for the good, others I resisted. Some of the changes I advocated for didn't happen. Some of my resistance I later regretted. Gradually, I just became one of many faculty members, and no longer a pontoon bridge.

It took many years for the music program to fully rebuild itself. When it did, it was on a new basis, suiting a new time. The radical make-up of the faculty structure initiated in the 1930s was never restored, and the old wounds never fully healed, but of course I developed new friendships among the new faculty and, as always, derived enormous pleasure from working with students, and continued learning from them and with them. They came to Bennington for the same reasons previous generations had, to learn and explore in an environment that was flexible, student-centered, and independent of traditional educational norms.

I had been able to persuade Tobias Picker and Yung Wha Son to come teach composition in that first year of change, and they were the first of many visiting composers, including Bun-Ching Lam, Kenji Bunch, Erik Lundborg, Amy Williams, Tamar Diesendruck, John Luther Adams, Su Lian Tan, and Stephen Siegel, a great composer and friend, who stayed for seven years. Eventually, composers Kitty Brazelton and Nicholas Brooke joined the faculty on extended contracts, both brilliant mavericks in the Bennington tradition.

After meeting with the newly appointed Dean, longtime faculty member Norm Derby, a kind, soft-spoken physicist with a passionate interest in music, I offered a hastily put-together course on Stravinsky in the fall of 1994, followed by one on Beethoven in the spring. Over the next many years, I taught more and more music history.

I quickly realized that many music students were unaware of what exciting music was still being composed for the concert hall. Far from trying to slavishly imitate Carter, Boulez, or Stockhausen, they had never heard of them.

For my part, I was mostly ignorant of the vibrant world of pop music in which they were often already expert and had little knowledge of music outside of "Western" music. But I felt a sense of mission about sharing what I did know, and I was unhappy thinking that such brilliant and artistic twenty-year-olds often viewed classical music as the slick expression of a stuffy elite, lacking in urgency and danger, formulaic and remote, without the authenticity and power of the great non-Western traditions, or of jazz and popular music. I felt that their society and educational system had failed them.

I eventually offered courses for entire terms on the music of J.S. Bach, Mozart, Beethoven, Stravinsky, and Schoenberg. I taught a one-credit listening course that met once a week to listen to a Symphony of Mahler, and have it introduced by a student. I taught a course on women composers three times, eventually retiring the designation, and simply adding Barbara Strozzi, Fanny Mendelssohn Hensel, and many other composers into my history offerings.

I particularly loved teaching "Music Since 1968," taking Berio's *Sinfonia* as my point of departure, while also going back a generation to set the stage. This course deepened my own knowledge of the music of Cage, Feldman, Schnittke, Gubaidulina, Ustvolskaya, Messiaen, Boulez, Stockhausen, Ligeti, Kurtág, Takemitsu, Saariaho, Andriessen, and many others, which in turn affected what I composed.

Eventually, I taught an entire course on Pierre Boulez, and one on the history of the music program at Bennington, in which I was able to honor my original colleagues and shed light on our program's past.

Ever since writing my Suite for Cello Quartet, it was as if some kind of spell had been broken. I carried my influences in my musical DNA but wrote simply as myself. During these years, the number of pieces I discarded as only half-baked decreased. Since I was commissioned only intermittently, I tried my best to interest players in performing pieces before they were written, regardless of whether there was an official commission involved. Knowing for whom I was composing was always a great inspiration.

But if I had assumed that there was one still point towards which my music would converge once I had the chance to truly commit myself to it, that still point eluded me. I was wary of eclecticism within a given work, even prided myself on being able to integrate whatever musical language each piece needed. But I found that more than one kind of language, more than one way of composing, was authentic to me.

I valued my austere, darker music most, but I had to face the fact that I also had an entertaining and outgoing side. If I tried to suppress one side of my musical personality in a given piece, it was sure to rear its head in the next one. Though I no longer worked in the theater, I still had the theater in me. I could choose to fully integrate my variety, or experiment with letting it show, but it was not up to me to choose whether or not my nature would ever become consistent.

There is an appetite to make a composition. Like any appetite, it follows its own laws. Sometimes it is stimulated by work. Sometimes it disappears. When it comes, one follows it. Some pieces grow from an immediate contact with sound, delight in sound itself. Others come from a more abstract place, a need to understand and find meaning in the world.

I felt it was not my responsibility to make sense of my work as a whole. Surely if it all comes from the same person, it will have a kind of unity. Just as a dancer must use her own body as her instrument and must appraise in the mirror whether her movements fulfill what her form is capable of, a composer's duty is to put an entire self on the page, using psyche and skills as instruments and reflecting not just some truth, but the whole truth, with all of its contradictions.

In the fall of 1994, oboist John Ferrillo had commissioned me again, this time to write a piece for oboe, bassoon, violin, and cello. I completed it in October and called it *Dreamscape*, because it seemed to proceed from moment to moment with a dreamlike logic. The strain of the past few months made its way into this intense piece, and the strain made its way into my health, too, since I once again came down with a fever and laryngitis.

While home for three days, sick and without a voice, I composed *Three Dance Portraits*, three up-tempo dances for piano four-hands. The second piece had a Latin feel I could never have achieved had I not written those abandoned *Latin American Dances* years earlier. I built the third dance on a rock rhythm and chord progression that I had played for fun for A. and H., adding a great deal of dissonance and fragments evoking Rachmaninoff and Stravinsky above them, as well as, at the climactic moment, the theme from the first movement.

I particularly enjoyed creating piano repeated notes in imitation of rock drum patterns. After all, I had once tried to be a drummer. Perhaps my most performed work, it suggests a composer in fine shape and buoyant mood.

But what it really illustrates is how independent the mind is from the body. It was the illness that allowed me to express joy, and it was a joy I didn't even know I had in me.

In the spring of 1995, I received a boost when my colleague Edward Hoagland nominated me for an award from the American Academy of Arts and Letters, and I went to New York to be presented with it. Awards can seem arbitrary and, in a way, meaningless, but I took heart from this message that a few people I deeply respected thought that my efforts had some value.

At the ceremony, I ran into several people I knew onstage, including David Del Tredici, who had jokingly asked me if I had brought the counterpoint assignments I still owed him from twenty-five years earlier. I met John Updike on the stairs as we headed into the auditorium, where he gave me a paternal reminder that the ceremony was exceedingly long and that we were passing the men's room: "Allen, this is the place, and now is the time."

(I received a second award from the Academy five years later, this time nominated by painter Ken Noland, who had been particularly struck by Elizabeth Wright's playing of my Five Preludes. Noland, a friend with a house in North Bennington, had a keen interest in jazz—particularly players such as Eric Dolphy and Chet Baker—and had an electronic keyboard at home on which he improvised. Like many painters, he listened to jazz while working, and it was jazz that he heard in my piano preludes.)

The challenge of writing long, unified one-movement pieces, like *Dreamscape*, continued to be fascinating, and in the next few years fueled *Letter to a Friend* for Piano, *Romances* for Violin and Piano, *Sleepless Night* for String Quartet, and *Elixir* for String Orchestra. These pieces probed cycles of moodiness, gloom, and recovery that had their origins in personal experiences. Frost settings, and a far-from-avuncular-and-cozy view of his poetry, returned in a cycle that was commissioned by Ida Faiella for her group L'Ensemble.

Sadly, having acquired only temporary rights to set the poems in this work and in the Cantata, I ran afoul of the Frost estate when I attempted to renew them. The estate had decided to reverse common practice by no longer renewing rights granted to composers on a temporary basis. My arguments over the years that, although legally permissible, their policy was unfair and destructive in a way that Frost himself would not have condoned were unsuccessful.

In 1995, came a "collage" piece for two pianos called *Essercizio*, using a Sonata in G major by Domenico Scarlatti as its basis. (The thirty single-movement Sonatas the composer published in his lifetime, of the five hundred and fifty-five he composed, were originally called *Essercizi*.)

Whatever motivated this experiment, it was related to Stravinsky's recompositions of works from the past, to more recent pieces in this vein by Schnittke, Berio, and others, and to my own *Song of the Tango Bird*. It was delightful to shed light on Scarlatti's astounding originality and inventiveness.

The approach was to use every note of the original, including repeats, but to interrupt it and accompany it with original music in a way that would obscure what was by Scarlatti and what was new. Some of the passages that sound like Scarlatti are not, and some of the modern-sounding modulations and juxtapositions are actually unaltered Scarlatti.

Next came a virtuosic short piano piece as a surprise present for former Bennington student Amy Williams, who had grown up with musician parents who were friends of Cage, Feldman, and Carter and had come to the college from a childhood in Buffalo steeped in new music.

Amy is a remarkable pianist who can handle anything thrown her way. Starting with a cascading figure in octaves, *Growl* consisted of a four-page explosion followed by a one-page coda of quietly drifting fall-out. Compressed, tempestuous, and jazzy, it lacked a tonal center and had an angularity that was new.

In spring of 1996, I prepared and conducted a performance of *Pierrot Lunaire* at the college. New colleague Ida Faiella was the expert and evocative soloist. It was performed on two nights, with translations of Albert Giraud's poems in "Rondeau" form projected onto a screen. The students were crazy about the piece, with some coming to hear both performances.

When I was teaching Schoenberg's music, students responded immediately and instinctively to his imagination and poetic sensibility. I felt that Schoenberg had been written about as if his music existed primarily on paper, and as if his early work, which is characterized by such a sumptuous sound, had nothing to do with his later music.

To introduce him to music lovers as the originator of "twelve-tone" music, rather than as an imaginative artist, did him a disservice. Showing his paintings, reading his writings—which are bursting with personality, humor, and integrity—and approaching his work first from a formal and sonic point of view made an understanding of how his twelve-tone approach had come about worth having, and made appreciating it possible.

It was J. who felt that I was capable of putting my way of presenting Schoenberg into the form of a book. The experience of walking into the office of Roger Straus at Farrar, Straus and Giroux and signing a contract was both exciting and bewildering.

Unproven as an author, I was well aware that my connection to my father and to J. herself had helped pave the way to this acceptance—but even so, how could my experience in this field be so different from my experience as a composer? I am almost embarrassed to admit that I burst into tears in the elevator leaving the office, not from gratitude, but from dismay that I had never had this degree of luck in music.

The more I studied Schoenberg, the more I felt that what I was writing was important. In 1912, the year of the premiere of *Pierrot* and the year *Le Sacre* was being completed, Stravinsky and Schoenberg had been friends and mutual admirers. But by the 1920s, the Schoenberg and Stravinsky camps had become polarized and saw each other as enemies. Boulanger had played a role in this, as an ardent advocate for Stravinsky's language and opponent of serialism.

For my generation, this opposition had become meaningless. Countless composers, including Stravinsky himself, had adopted aspects of serialism to their own uses, and literally *all* contemporary composers, including those I felt particularly close to, such as Harbison, Picker, and even John Adams, were equally indebted to both composers.

Yet, apart from his own writings and Dika Newlin's delightful diary from her years studying with him, all of the existing books about Schoenberg were theoretical studies. There was still no book for the non-expert that outlined his evolution and introduced his work as music to be appreciated and enjoyed.

Schoenberg himself was less doctrinaire than some of his disciples. In his writings there is ample support for the idea that musical intelligence has its own laws, and that there are times when composing is like sleepwalking.

For example, he did not recognize the formal logic in the tonal organization of *Verklärte Nacht* until after composing it or understand the formal processes behind *Five Pieces for Orchestra* until years had passed. He sometimes set poetry to music after only reading the first line, and then just proceeding by instinct. And after developing the twelve-tone system, he still sometimes felt the urge to compose tonal music, and he followed it.

Meanwhile, my article for *The Atlantic* about Robert Craft's latest series of recordings of Stravinsky appeared, in which I gave expression to my long interest in the conductor and his writings. He got in contact with me and offered to read my Schoenberg manuscript when it was completed.

The copy of the first draft is filled with his fascinating remarks, agreements, disagreements, and occasional corrections in the margins, scrawled in a cursive hand so tiny as to require a magnifying glass. We became friends without ever meeting in person, and eventually the friendship was extended to include his wonderful wife Alva and her son Ted. Craft expressed personal concern about me on several occasions, including at the very end of his life when he was extremely ill and in the hospital.

Schoenberg's way of thinking began to leave its mark on my music, without altering its general sound and personality. Although some of my previous music had been atonal, going back at least to the Piano Sonata, my approach became more systematic and conscious. I kept careful track of every pitch I used and often used rows, usually containing fewer than twelve tones, and rarely transposing them.

Another collage piece for two pianos followed *Essercizio*, using my own "Spiritual" movement from *Four Jazz Preludes* as its basis. I introduced, interrupted, and embellished the "Spiritual" as I had the Scarlatti. The piece was called *Remember?*

The collage approach had an impact on a Cello Concerto I was writing for Maxine Neuman as well. At first it seemed to lack an emotional center, but after I introduced the music of *Valentine* into it, putting the theme into different guises in all three movements, it became a highly dramatic work that had a very personal, sometimes turbulent quality.

Maxine had an uncanny feel for the moods of my music, projecting them as if from her own life experience, yet also straightforwardly and without artificiality. She brought formidable intelligence to the music's syntax and phrase structure, always grasping how one thing leads to the next and, if it was interrupted, why. She seemed to understand what place each note had in a given line.

If there was something she didn't understand or thought didn't work, she would tell me. Together, we modified any awkward cello writing. She questioned the quiet ending of the Concerto, suggesting an energetic coda, which I supplied.

When we performed the piece again some years later, she told me she had been wrong. But by that time, I had become attached to those extra ten measures, and kept them. It had come to seem right that instead of resolving itself, the music abruptly returned to the maelstrom of the rest of the work, like the hand that suddenly comes up from the earth at the end of the film *Carrie*.

Another piece of a personal nature emerged during the months that a book by Lillian Ross about her relationship with my father appeared in print. Naturally, Wally and I worried about the publication's effect on our mother. I wrote the intense three-movement piano piece *Recollections* during that time. Pianist Daniel Epstein, who played the work brilliantly, said that he saw a lot of Schoenberg on the page, even though he didn't hear it in the sounds. Robert Carl referred to the style of the frenetic last movement as "Broadway Noir."

Between 1994 and 1999, I wrote four pieces that touched on my Jewish heritage: a Hanukkah song in Hebrew for children's chorus; a clarinet solo called *Candles*, meant to evoke a meditation over Sabbath candles; a piece for three solo cellos and ensemble called *Ancestors*; and a Cantata of sacred fragments called *Hide Not Thy Face From Me*.

Raised in an atmosphere of indifference to religion, I only realized as an adult that this indifference had been dressed up in Christian traditions, and therefore in an atmosphere of denial. When A. was born, having become uncomfortable with celebrating Christian holidays, I resisted the idea of her being baptized, saying, "But I am a Jew."

This eventually led to J.'s own conversion to Judaism. While not a practicing Jew myself, I was a sympathetic onlooker as both of my children went through Hebrew studies and had their bar mitzvah and bat mitzvah.

Rabbi Howard Cohen encouraged me to give a talk at the local temple about why I did not attend. I did my best to trace my ancestry back to Lithuania and the Russian Empire, and to show how my parents' indifference and my own ambivalence stemmed from the persecution from which my great grandparents had fled.

Afterwards, the Rabbi asked me to give a second talk, on Schoenberg. It was moving to share musical excerpts—including Schoenberg's *Modern Psalm*, *Kol Nidre*, and passages from *Moses und Aron*—with the stained-glass Star of David and the Torah cabinet in view. Schoenberg's ecstatic dissonances and fervent prayers perfectly matched the setting.

Ancestors was commissioned by my old friend Judy Serkin, whose paternal line, like mine, goes back to Russian Jews. The colors of the ensemble were selected to create a sense of ceremony: along with the solo cellos, an entire cello and bass section (like forebears or elders to the soloists), plus two clarinets, solo violin, solo harp, and timpani.

The middle movement evoked klezmer music. The last movement was a long canon with some interruptions, in which the instruments finished one by one, fading out until only a single cello remained. The symbolism of links in a chain, and of voices being extinguished, seemed to express themselves naturally by being embedded in the musical structure.

Again, illness played a role in the gestation of the piece. I imagined and jotted down the theme for the canon while lying in a strange bed in the house, apart from J., when I was sick and shivering with fever. It was a scene worthy of a B movie about a nineteenth-century composer.

For his third commission from me, John Ferrillo specifically requested a sacred cantata. I complied by setting extracts from the psalms, phrases from William Blake, and a Hebrew prayer, all of which suggested a longing for faith rather than a settled sense of conviction. The singers in *Hide Not Thy Face From Me* were soprano and tenor (performed at the premiere by my colleagues Ida Faiella and Thomas Bogdan), and the accompanying ensemble consisted of oboe and strings.

My experiments with eclectic stylistic juxtapositions continued in this and other pieces from the time. The clashes between different idioms in the nine movements of *Hide Not* were extreme, with tonal music abutting angular twelve-tone writing.

They were also linguistic. The third movement was a setting of a psalm in Hebrew, and other movements intermingled Hebrew and English. In context, the fragments of Hebrew sound like memories. In hindsight, I wonder if the piece wouldn't be stronger without the William Blake setting and the two Stravinskian duets, which might have been simply crutches from the past.

In response to a commission from flutist Beth Anderson, I again composed three movements in diverse idioms, followed by a finale that attempted to reconcile them. After the first performances, this work was revised over an additional twenty years, eventually reaching completion with the title *Eclectic Suite*.

In 1996, I told Tobias Picker that I dreamed of composing a piano concerto, and he generously offered to call his close friend Ursula Oppens on my behalf to ask if she would be willing to be the soloist, if I wrote the work. Ursula had recorded my Sextet for Piano and Winds with the Aspen Wind Quintet back in 1990. Her agreement was a great inspiration to me, and it helped smooth the way to the work's performance and recording.

I sketched the work in one sustained month at Yaddo, the artist's colony. It followed the same four-movement plan as *Nocturnes*, with a brooding opening; a second movement that was tuneful, dance-like, and raucous (with accompaniment figures suggesting Piazzolla); a flowing, introspective, lyrical slow movement; and a kaleidoscopic finale, complete with cadenza.

Ursula felt the impress of Brahms's Second Concerto on the form and character of the work, but of course it was also an outgrowth of the Concerto that had been performed on two pianos in New York back in 1979 and discarded. This was a "mid-life" piece, with a roiling stew of influences that included Schoenberg, Prokofiev, and Gershwin, and Ursula was an astonishing interpreter, abetted expertly by David Alan Miller and the Albany Symphony Orchestra.

The night of the premiere was exhilarating. As an encore, David encouraged me to perform the "Can-Can!" from *Suite Parisienne* together with Ursula. What a happy memory!

Meanwhile, singer and writer Penny Orloff, who had performed in the 1983 reading of *The Music Teacher*, got in touch about composing a half-hour chamber opera for children based on Aesop's "The Ant and the Grasshopper." This proved to be a refreshing change of pace, a chance to complete a light, small-scale, dramatic piece whose idiom fell halfway between musical theatre and concert music.

My most eclectic piece of all from this period was *Five Pieces* for two pianos, which I had started back in 1995 with *Essercizio* and *Remember?*. When Amy Williams and her superb piano duo partner Helena Bugallo requested a work to perform together in 2000, I added three movements to these first two: a pianistic reworking of the second movement from *Episodes* for cello and piano called "Contrapuntal Waltz"; a solemn slow movement called "Bells"; and an eight-minute jazz piece in B flat called "Bluesdream," which is a perpetuum mobile.

In this case, I made no attempt to reconcile these utterly disparate pieces. The only connection between them was a linking device of a series of atonal chords that quietly interrupted the Scarlatti, introduced both *Remember?* and "Contrapuntal Waltz," and served as the main material in "Bells".

Wind Quintet no. 2 dated from the end of that year and was composed on commission from adult wind participants at the Bennington Conference.

A cheerful celebration of my songs and theater pieces came along at the college in the spring of 2001, organized by Ida Faiella and beautifully directed by Steven Bach. It included a belated one-time performance of *Under the Bam, Under the Bomb*, the e.e. cummings songs, additional songs once written for Wally's translation of Machiavelli's *The Mandrake*, excerpts from the (illegal) Frost Cantata, a few chamber pieces, and even *The Fisherman's Song*, to lyrics J. had written in New York, when we were contemplating creating an operatic piece called "Verna."

Drums, violin, and trumpet parts were added to the original piano score of the fourteen-minute Derek Walcott musical, and the chorus joined in on the refrain of *Under the Bam, Under the Bomb* at the end, which gave it a very touching effect. This was a festive infusion of support from colleagues and students which delightfully combined music of different kinds into a kind of Cabaret evening.

In 2000, J. and I received a joint commission for the first and only time. The goal was to produce a work for baritone and orchestra with a text that would honor the centennial of the birth of writer John Steinbeck in 2002 and be performed in Monterey, California, by the Monterey Symphony, conducted by Kate Tamarkin, with baritone Clayton Brainerd as soloist.

J. contributed a long, extraordinary prose poem, a kind of writer's meditation on words, love and identity that one could picture as a monodrama. (She had in fact taken a great interest in Schoenberg's *Erwartung*.) I worked intensely on the music over the winter of 2000 and the spring of 2001. When I was composing the piece, I had the impression that I was sailing on the waves of J.'s heroic and emotional writing, following the lead of the words with what felt like pure instinct.

The result was a sustained half-hour of romantic music with great forward momentum. Only the last five minutes seemed to need trimming. But, sadly, by the time this point was reached in the music, no such changes were possible, because J. and I were not speaking to each other.

We were in crisis. Our marriage was failing, and it dissolved irrevocably within a two-week period. During the second week, I had migraines six out of the seven days.

We had both planned to attend the performance the following year—even I had planned to, difficult as it would have been—but as things transpired, neither of us did, to the great disappointment of the presenters and the performers. Conductor Kate Tamarkin was in the unenviable position of leading a collaborative premiere unattended by its authors. I had worked with her when she had conducted the Vermont Symphony in *Elixir*, and it was one of the best performances I had ever had.

She and Clayton Brainerd did a magnificent job on this orphaned work, and they even brought it to Vermont for a second performance some months later, at which I could be present.

For the title, I had modified words from J.'s poem, calling the work, *And In The Air, These Sounds.*

PART III

13

NEW LIFE (2001–2007)

A DIVORCE, PARTICULARLY WHEN THERE are children involved, is a disaster. The pain of loss, and the pain of worrying about A. and H., were with me every day.

The String Quartet written that year for a local ensemble, Music from Salem, looked both forward and backward. As in the Bartók Sixth Quartet, all three movements start with the same sorrowful theme. The first movement is slow, hesitant, and lyrical. The second is full of intense energy and quotes from the waltz section of *And In The Air These Sounds*. As in the Bartók, the third movement is a lament based solely on the melody that had served as a recurring introduction.

I also had another piece in which to channel intense feelings. Steve Klimowski of the Vermont Contemporary Music Ensemble asked me to write a short piece for bass clarinet and piano in response to the massacre of September 11th. I felt unqualified to make a musical statement about something so tragic, and on such a scale, and I was also wary of being associated with the brand of Islamophobic patriotism that accompanied the invasion of Iraq.

In composing the piece, I focused my mind not on politics, but on the pain of one imagined individual who had lost someone. I called the piece *Dark Song*.

Much of what I wrote up until this point had been to a greater or lesser extent rooted in tonality. But with my greater immersion in the world of late twentieth-century music, I now relied increasingly on invented scales or collections of tones, and this gave my music a different orientation. I was making much clearer determinations about what compositional pallet I was using at a given time.

Although Maxine told me that what I wrote still sounded and felt similar, the angle from which I was writing had shifted. My music now occupied tonal areas or fields. Even while sketching the pieces,

I now wrote down the synthetic "scale" forms as they appeared in the piece, sometimes shifting from one to another group of pitches instinctively, sometimes planning out the changes in advance. At times I used all twelve pitches as my "scale."

It seemed to be my time to be more systematic, at least up to a point. The systems gave me strength; they were doorways leading to serious expression and deep pleasure.

My book on Schoenberg came out early in 2003, and to my astonishment it was reviewed favorably in *The New York Times* and elsewhere. I was shocked at the speed with which it circulated, and by the fact that many people read it who do not listen to contemporary music. Even though I did not consider myself a writer in the sense that J. or Wally and Deborah or my father were writers, it seemed that I had somehow reached people with my writing far more easily than I ever had with my music. Everyone reads.

I had written my Schoenberg book because his music thrilled and fascinated me. I tried to approach word-writing as if it too were music, singing my way through it, doing my best to touch the words, just as Takemitsu had urged his students to "touch the sound" of what they composed.

Shortly after the Schoenberg book appeared, I went down to Bard College to have a conversation with the president there, Leon Botstein. The music program at Bennington was becoming more stable, and I was wondering if it was time for me to go elsewhere. I hoped he might have some suggestions for me, or even that he might offer me a job.

To my surprise, our conversation ended up lasting two hours and involved my entire adult life, and, in particular, my phobias. Botstein's gravitas, articulateness, and empathy seemed to unlock something in me, and I unburdened myself to him about my failure to overcome the many internal, irrational obstacles I seemed to carry within me everywhere, despite years of treatments of various kinds.

I left nothing unsaid in my account, telling him about the terrible impact these phobias had had on my life and on my relationships, and that I had tried medications and hated them, since they neutralized my experience of life and put me at a distance from my emotions. But I also explained that my anxiety was such that it too altered my personality when I was in distress or anticipating distress, limiting my ability to take pleasure in what was happening or to behave normally when I was in circumstances that elicited my phobic responses. At the same time, I took enormous pleasure in my daily life.

Botstein listened with calm and steady attention and gave me advice that I did not expect. He told me to stop struggling and to live fully in the way I could, not in the way someone else could. I had tried to conquer these problems and had come to understand that they were intractable. I shouldn't waste any more energy trying to be something I was not.

"Kant barely left Königsberg, where he was born and died. Bach's entire life took place within a hundred-mile radius," he said. "I think you'll just need to accept that this is the way the world is configured for you." These remarks, which I am paraphrasing here, left a deep impression on me.

I was once again lucky in love. I started to get to know Yoshiko, a pianist who worked at the College, and a new relationship evolved. We would eventually marry in 2007, and have a son, Noa.

In summer 2002, I had written a collection of pieces for her called "Childhood Scenes," which explored my newly distilled musical vocabulary, and reflected her unique pianism.

Y. was born in Morioka, Japan, and had begun playing piano at the age of four. By the time she was twenty, she was entering competitions in Europe, including several Mozart Concerto competitions. Like me, she had spent years in Paris, and she had even studied at the École Normale de Musique, as I did, and knew Pierre Petit. She spoke French much better than I do, and with less of an accent.

From the first times I heard her, I felt that there was something truly special—stunningly beautiful and devoted—about her playing. No matter what the music, she brought a sense of occasion to it; nothing was ever casual. She had a very particular connection to Bach's *Goldberg Variations*; likewise to Scarlatti, Mozart and Beethoven. But she also played Chopin, Debussy, Ravel, Bartok, Stravinsky and Schoenberg with the same kind of effortless power and luminosity. The effect isn't easy to describe, because her manner was so natural and self-effacing.

Y. and I gave several concerts together as a four-hand and two-piano team. We eventually performed the Mozart Concerto for two pianos in E flat, k.365 with the Sage City Symphony.

Not too long after my meeting with Botstein, my friend Frederick Seidel suggested to me that I write a book about phobias. The idea stuck with me, even as I resisted it. Ultimately, it was the very fact that I had not been able to get over them that convinced me this was a writing project I should try. At least I could attempt to articulate the nature of these problems, and in so doing put them to constructive use. Perhaps even though I had failed to be cured, others would feel less ashamed as a result of my candor, would seek treatment, and it might work for them.

The book became part memoir, part research, and of course part apologia—to my friends and family, and to all those who had to put up with me and whom I had disappointed. The writing of it involved a painful airing of something both intimate and mostly hidden, surprising to almost everyone who knew me—surprising, at least in its pervasiveness, even to my own brother.

I had no difficulty in being motivated to undertake the research since I was desperate to better understand the underpinnings of a condition that had dominated so much of what had happened to me. Speaking to scientists like my colleagues Bruce Weber, Betsy Sherman, and Ron Cohen, and then following up by doing the readings they suggested, gave me an extraordinary education.

I did not mean the book to be an "exercise in self-regard" (to borrow a phrase from writer Daniel Menaker). The intent was to focus on an aspect of life that is universal. For this reason, I did not use names in the book. Although I took advantage of my father's own accomplishments and well-known history as a "phobic" to make important points, my hope was that anyone could find themselves in the subject.

When the book finally appeared, I was worried about its impact on my students and on their view of me. I gave a reading from it at the college, warmly supported by literature colleagues Marguerite Feitlowitz and April Bernard. It proved a moving occasion at which I felt once again all that being at Bennington had given me. The students listened with interest and identification, and understood that it was about them too.

Public responses to the book surprised me once again, as did the way that books can so quickly, if one is lucky, gain attention. The world of music is comparatively so much more fractured into pockets of audiences. Nothing stunned me more than Janet Malcolm's beautiful review linking my voice to that of my brother's and father's. I trembled reading what this most brilliant and masterly of wordsmiths had to say. I also received several supportive letters about my books from John Updike. I was pleased, but also, in a way, afraid. I had not experienced this kind of response to my music, and my sense of identity resided there.

I was surprised how important Mary became in my study of phobias, having never envisaged that the topic would sooner or later lead back to her, her distance from the family, and the issues surrounding our visits to see her. It began to seem almost inevitable that I would write a second book in which I would try to understand her better, and which would also motivate me to see more of her.

This undertaking proved once again to be a life-changing experience, deepening my understanding of Mary and reviving memories of a side of childhood that had never been easy to think about. Investigating the subject of autism and the decisions that led to her being institutionalized helped me reconnect with her, and to see my own strangeness in relation to hers. We are all on a spectrum.

The truthfulness in my writing also helped me be more and more candid in my music. But I have always been less outgoing and expressive than my music is. Music seems to come from a vast world beneath the ice on which we are skating, where fish are swimming and vegetation is blooming. I was once asked if my music didn't constitute a kind of "diary." I said it did, but then I needed to amplify:

> I think for composers, music is where we confide everything. Certainly in my own case, no matter how stylized and impersonal a piece might end up sounding, it always comes out of my life and out of my psychology. But perhaps the most important autobiographical aspect of music is what ends up being captured in it unselfconsciously, simply through the process and work of composition. Even though music is abstract and obeys its own laws, its meanings go way beyond anything we might have intended to put into it, revealing us in ways we could never plan, and probably can't even recognize. There is a quality of existing that music, alone of all the arts, seems to chronicle—the texture and quality of living, of time passing. Looking back on our work, we see that our music has charted our progress through life, mysteriously containing who we were and what we experienced along the way, whether we remember these experiences or not. Yet it is also nothing but an arrangement of notes, rhythms, and timbres.

This has turned out to be even truer than I realized when I said this. I now hear my naiveté, my maturing, my aging, my marital struggles, my pain and losses, even in pieces that I thought of as light or relatively impersonal when I wrote them. Furthermore, I now see to what degree all of my abandoned works were necessary sketches towards future accomplishments.

⅔ ⅔ ⅔

When my mother's mind had begun to deteriorate and she could no longer speak or sign her own checks, Wally and I had taken over her finances, and we had watched nervously as her account dwindled closer and closer to nothing. She died at the end of October 2005 in the apartment she had shared with our father and in which we had grown up.

There was a comfort in knowing that this is what she had wanted. Since they did not own the apartment, it was a miracle that she could stay there for thirteen years after our father had died. She had paid for it herself, without ever knowing it, since money she had secretly saved to leave to us had, along with the rules of rent control, made staying there possible.

The fact that her life gave out simultaneously with the funds she saved was almost enough to make one believe in a deity.

My brother and I were able to spend our mother's final hours with her.

As we were packing up her apartment and planning to vacate it, we were also preparing for a production of our 1983 opera *The Music Teacher* that would run for a month at the Minetta Lane, a small theater in Greenwich Village. It was a strange and oddly consoling convergence of events. Our mother had always been pragmatic and a realist. Yet her faith in the pursuit of serious art went in the opposite direction from practicality. The older she got, the prouder she seemed of the fact that her two sons were trying to be serious, adventurous artists and serious people. It was wondrous and comforting working in the same living room where Wally and I had once presented our puppet shows, surrounded by endless boxes and mementos from our parents' lives, orchestrating and attempting to improve my twenty-five-year-old score.

Like the production of *In the Dark* from 1976, rehearsing and performing this work with superb performers, conducted by the exceptional musician Timothy Long, was a thrilling experience. After the show closed came an additional pleasure: quite unexpectedly a benefactor stepped forward to pay for a recording of the work.

When I was back by myself in Vermont and was commissioned by two chamber groups to compose substantial works, I was overwhelmed by feelings about my mother, and I composed both pieces thinking of her. They were *In Memory Of* and *Three Nightscapes*.

Freud felt that as long as one's mother is alive, she acts as a barrier against death. Being without both parents doesn't just shift your perspective. It transforms the way you view all of life.

14

CONSOLIDATION AND GRATITUDE (2007–2019)

RECENT YEARS BROUGHT THEIR share of losses, among them the loss of close musician friends, including composers David Macbride and Stephen Siegel, my dear friends Maxine Neuman and Reinhard Humburg, my close childhood companion, Jay Hamburger. These losses have struck home in an entirely different way than the deaths from an earlier time, and they have magnified my sense of gratitude for having been allowed to live this long, and until recently with only minor health problems.

My migraines vanished as mysteriously as they had begun. Up until recently I escaped serious health issues, apart from two sobering reminders of life's finitude that had an impact on musical work: moderate hearing loss, limiting perception of upper frequencies and requiring hearing aids; and surgery on my left hand, contracting it, diminishing its mobility, and making it impossible to play many of the pieces that I used to navigate easily.

I have never tired of teaching composition, and I remain eager to see the students' work in progress, amazed by their inventiveness and imagination. I try to observe the Hippocratic Oath and "do no harm"; sometimes I can be helpful. I flatter myself that I may have absorbed some aspects of my father's editing skills.

I particularly enjoy exploring with students the old forms that Norwood taught us about, and I regularly offer a course with the electronic music faculty in composing music for acoustic instruments with electronics, despite having never worked this way myself.

Y. and I were married quietly in 2007, in the same month as the publication of *Twin*, during a blizzard, by justice of the peace Freida Sears of the Vermont National Bank, which had closed early due to the inclement weather, but which she kindly kept open for us. The one witness was our friend pianist Kanako Seki.

When my book *Twin* was published, I gave a reading at a local library that was attended by Bill Dixon. Y. came with me. Afterwards, Bill told me that he wished he had known about my sister earlier, saying that it made him see me differently. He related my twinship to the life I had led as an adult, saying that it helped explain why in my marriages I had "defied societal norms."

Our child Noa was born the following year and, as of this writing, is sixteen. Seemingly from the first day, he was outgoing, and infused our lives with his energy, laughter, and startling intelligence.

The period in which Y. was expecting was one of the most productive of my life. I returned to the ambitious and austere spirit of my 1982 Piano Sonata, and in less than two months had produced Sonatas no. 2 and no. 3 and three Piano Elegies. As if counterbalancing these serious pieces, there followed two lighter ones I called *Nostalgic Pieces*: a waltz and an exuberant "Boogie-Woogie."

While at work on these piano pieces, I received an email out of the blue from a German pianist, Julia Bartha, expressing an interest in my *Four Jazz Preludes* and other pieces from my first piano CD. This led to an extraordinary collaboration, giving rise to the three solo piano works I wrote for her (Sonatas no. 4 and 6, and *Five Pieces*), to a CD she devoted to my music, and to an ongoing friendship with her and her family. I later wrote for *Aria-Caprice* for Julia and her husband, bassist Holger Michalski.

During Y.'s pregnancy, I received an invitation to write a biography about Leonard Bernstein for the Jewish Lives series at Yale. I had grown up with Bernstein's Young People's Concerts, many of which I attended, and I had seen him conduct innumerable times, and of course had heard many of his recordings, but my education had steered me away from his music.

I accepted the assignment, not knowing how extraordinarily challenging it would be. Bernstein lived at least eight lifetimes in one. At a minimum, I needed to get to know his life history, his conducting, his music, his recorded performances, his politics, his relationship to Judaism and to Israel, his public and private writings, his public teaching—with the Philharmonic, on Omnibus, in the Norton Lectures—and his private teaching as a conducting mentor at Tanglewood and elsewhere.

I had assumed from the start that his life and personality would necessarily be a complete contrast to that of Schoenberg. I had even referred to the two composers jokingly as "Moses and Aaron." But the Bernstein I discovered was someone I admired more and more. I ended up focusing my biography on his music, arguing that the public rightly intuited his great intellect and creative authenticity, and that his charisma was rooted in his very real brilliance, musical gifts, and personal courage.

I rewatched many of the Young People's Concerts with Y. and infant N., sometimes helping N. conduct along with Bernstein.

The more I studied Bernstein's music, the more I related to it and regretted that I had never had a chance to show him my work when I was a teenager. Schuyler Chapin, who helped me meet Carter and Sessions when I failed to get into Juilliard, had written to my parents telling them that Mr. Bernstein had heard of my musical composi- tions from him and would be happy to meet me.

I didn't see the letter until I was looking through my parents' things after they were gone, so I don't know why this meeting never happened. Perhaps even my own hesitation was responsible. But studying his scores, particularly those of his often poorly regarded symphonic works, and of the music of his later years such as *A Quiet Place*, I was struck again and again by what a marvelous composer he was.

Even in works where the results were uneven, as I thought was the case with *Mass* or the *Kaddish* Symphony, there were always passages that were arrestingly beautiful, moving and genuine, and there was a natural craft. There would be something for any composer to learn from in the way Bernstein was able to recycle discarded theatrical materials in *Chichester Psalms*, adapt them to Hebrew texts, and weave them into a unified work.

I was perhaps most intrigued, as others clearly are not, by his more severe side, by places where he adapted twelve-tone proce- dures in his own way, as in the exciting "Din Torah" movement of the *Kaddish*, or the twelve-tone setting of *The Pennycandystore Beyond the El*. This led me to look into similar uses of twelve-tone procedures in the work of Britten, Shostakovich, and other mostly tonal composers. I felt that this mixture resembled my own recent work.

Most of all, I was struck by the way he composed as a part of his overall musicianship and out of his overflowing love of music. It made me think about the dryness of my college and graduate school studies, and about how in those years being thought to be "musical" was not necessarily even considered a compliment. We wished to be "interesting." Even Stravinsky, speaking derogatively of Gershwin, my early hero, said, "His music did not interest me." He also took a dim view of Bartók's "folkloric" tendencies. This seemed an expression of shame at his own "folkloric" side, which had engendered some of the greatest musical works of the twentieth century.

Isn't it the truth that folk music, the music that has simply been handed down over the centuries because people love to sing and play it, is the source of all other music? If, on some primal level, a concert work doesn't resonate with these ancient traditions, isn't it missing the essential thing?

The more I studied Bernstein, the more I lamented the absence of composers like him in the long-ago music curricula of colleges in the sixties and seventies. When I was finally studying music seriously, it was sad that no one had directed my attention to him, or to Shostakovich, Britten, Barber, Poulenc, and many others, who had their own integrity and plenty to offer a young composer as exemplary figures from their time. I might have identified. Instead, I had been encouraged to question my own musicality.

Among the many musical efforts of my next years were groups of songs, settings of words by John Cage, Lawrence Ferlinghetti, Georg Trakl (in German), Hagiwara Sakutarō (in Japanese), René Char (in French), and Anna Maria Hong. My chosen texts tended to be dark in tone. Since I don't speak Japanese, Y. recorded herself speaking each syllable of the Hagiwara Sakutarō poems very slowly for me, making an English transliteration for their pronunciation, complete with accent markings and a definition over each word.

Among the pieces making use of scales or collections of pitches, Piano Sonatas no. 4 and no. 5 experimented with modulating from one group of pitches to the next by changing one note at a time. In a group of twelve short movements for cello and piano called *Cello Notebook*, written for cellist Nathaniel Parke, and in an hour-long series of twenty-seven Études for piano, I assigned a different "scale" to each movement, planning the scales in an overall design that gave the works a formal unity. This sense of unity was inspired by Bach, and it wouldn't have come about had I not been teaching his work.

My Études began as a series of three, written in 2017 on a request from pianist Eunbi Kim. As soon as they were completed, I added six more, with a "recapitulation" of the opening scales in reverse order in Études seven, eight, and nine.

The second book introduced new scales and types of playing and was conceived as a kind of development section for the work as a whole. I dedicated it to Y., and she played it magnificently. Étude no. 16, "Hymne," was written in memory of Gordon Thorne.

In the third book, I brought together all of the scales and characters of the work, reached a point of emotional culmination, and ended with a quietly playful coda in the spirit and scale of Étude no. 1.

The whole work suggested a kind of cycle that could begin again, like the *Goldberg Variations*.

I also composed four more concertos: for violin, oboe, cello (Concerto no. 2), and contrabassoon.

In my musical output as a whole, I had always had at least three basic modes of operation: the "neoclassical," the more "confessional—chromatic" mode, and vocabulary instinctively derived from jazz, any one of which might be dominant in a given work, and any one of which might be dormant for a while, only to return at a later date.

If my work belonged to someone else, I might call the music composed between 2006 and 2019 "synthesis." Instead of bouncing back and forth between my various approaches and stylistic idioms, these works could not easily be described as either confessional, neoclassical, jazz-oriented, tonal, or atonal, but are a combination of all sides and they fulfilled my search for a consistent language, at least to the degree that I am capable of one.

In recent years, as has been the case throughout my life, the generosity of others has lifted me out of the doldrums and helped keep me on my path. I received commissions from Judy Serkin, Sarah Tenney, Nathaniel Parke, Londa Weisman, Maria Fisher, the Vermont Contemporary Music Ensemble, Sue Ann Kahn, the Bennington Chamber Music Conference, William Anderson, and others.

Maxine's husband, Reinhard Humburg, recorded chamber music and countless hours of my own playing for CDs, without accepting payment, making the recordings possible.

Out of the blue, in December 2014, musicologist Ralph Locke, an old Harvard classmate, recommended me as a composer contributor to Hungarian author Bálint András Varga when he was working on his book *The Courage of Composers and the Tyranny of Taste*.

Thus began a deep friendship in the form of email exchanges with Bálint, an extraordinary writer on contemporary music, that lasted the five years until his death on New Year's Eve, 2019. Exchanging thoughts with him regularly was one of the great honors of my life.

My dear friend Ron Fielding sponsored four performances of my music by the Rochester Philharmonic Orchestra, two of which were the commissioned Concertos for Violin and Oboe, played superbly by Juliana Athayde and Erik Behr.

Clarinetist Maureen Hurd Hause succeeded in arranging for the premiere performance of my 1983 Concerto for Clarinet, Cello, and Orchestra in September 2019. She and cellist Jonathan Spitz performed the work with the Rutgers Symphony, conducted by Tong Chen, a blissful validation after thirty-five years. Hearing the recording, Nathaniel Rosen wrote to me: "It was good then, and it is good now."

Then six months before the pandemic, in 2019, when I was turning seventy, a bassist whom I greatly admire, Michael Bisio, asked me to record an improvisational album with him, even though we had never played together and he had never heard me improvise.

At first, I declined, saying this was something I wasn't good at. But not long afterwards, when I was suffering from back pain and taking prednisone, which can create a mild sense of euphoria, I changed my mind and agreed to it.

The pandemic years proved experimental for almost everyone everywhere, requiring ad hoc solutions on the part of artists. The sessions with Bisio had opened up a new way of working for me.

Recording improvisations informally on my own, I sent them one at a time to my son H. in Los Angeles where he lives, hoping he might sample them or use them in his own composing. At first, they were simply a means of communication during a period of disconnection. Certainly, no conscious "method" was involved in inventing them, and it was a surprise to realize gradually that the pieces, as played, added up to an hour-long sequence that felt complete and coherent. Partly to test whether this was the case, I assembled them into a CD, released them, and dedicated the recording to H.

When I later transcribed the pieces, I began to notice all of the elements in them that related to music that had become part of my life. For example, at the loud apex of the piece "Cross Porpoises," the melody of "When the Saints Go Marching In" is clearly outlined in the right hand.

At parties in our New York apartment seventy years ago, my father used to save this rousing tune for last, joined by Wally on violin, writer Bruce Bliven on clarinet, and me, rather crudely, on whatever drums I had. Near the close of the final piece, "Epilogue," there is a reminiscence, again entirely unconscious, of the beautiful "Song of the Wood Dove" from Schoenberg's *Gurre-Lieder*.

Some of these improvisations later became the basis of songs in a music theatre piece Jean Randich, Sue Rees, Anna Maria Hong and I created out of *H and G*, Anna Maria's fragmented, poetic and impassioned feminist take on the Hansel and Gretel tale. We staged this at the college in 2021.

Somehow, an improvisatory spirit has made its way back into my notated music too.

In fact, all of the musical paths I have taken seem now to have gradually converged into one. Going back at least as far as the year 2000, I stopped needing to discard many pieces and stopped feeling the need to give them "grades." Naturally, there have been ups and downs, pieces that underwent considerable revision, and those about which I was ambivalent. But there has also been a consistency.

I memorialized George Floyd in my Piano Sonata No. 6, but did not feel that I was entitled to put his name on the score.

My Piano Sonata no. 7 was dedicated to the memory of Bálint András Varga.

I dedicated my Eighth Sonata to my dear friend Maxine Neuman.

Music may be intangible, but it is also real. It plunges us into the present. It banishes illness and non-being. It places in the foreground whatever characterizes it, from contemplation, to lamentation, to exultation. It refreshes our capacity to be amazed and surprised.

Nothing proved this to me more than that first 2019 recording session with bassist Michael Bisio. When we began to play, I felt like a fourteen-year-old, back in Emilie Harris's house in New Rochelle, sitting at the piano, playing what I felt like playing, with a breeze blowing through the open window, the tape recorder running, and her husband making milkshakes in the next room. Mike's ability to be attuned to whatever I offered up was contagious—I started to hear everything he played as if his ideas were my ideas, too.

There wasn't time to think in terms of "music theory." Some of the music was extremely tonal, and some was not, yet it hung together, informed by knowledge, almost as if an unseen presence were dictating it. We were making it up, but it had a life of its own.

APPENDIX: LIST OF WORKS BY ALLEN SHAWN

Books

Arnold Schoenberg's Journey. New York: Farrar, Straus and Giroux, 2002.
Wish I Could Be There: Notes from a Phobic Life. New York: Viking, 2007.
Twin: A Memoir. New York: Viking, 2011.
Leonard Bernstein: An American Musician. New Haven: Yale University Press, 2014.

Music

Orchestral Works

Nocturnes for piano and chamber orchestra (1978) (20'): Galaxy Music
Autumnal Song for violin and orchestra (1983) (15'): Galaxy Music
Concerto for clarinet, cello and orchestra (1983) (25): Galaxy Music
Symphony in Three Parts (1987). Galaxy Music (21'): Galaxy Music
Concertino for flute and strings (1987) (15'): Galaxy Music
Elixir for string orchestra (1996) (13')
Ancestors (1996) for 3 solo celli, 2 clarinets, violin, harp, timpani, celli and double basses (14')
Piano Concerto (1997–1999) (24'): E.C. Schirmer
Concerto for Cello and Orchestra (1999) (21'): E.C. Schirmer
Mosaic (Dec. 2002) for chamber orchestra (16') [fl. ob. cl. bsn. hrn. perc. hrp. Str.]
Five Orchestral Scenes (2005) (25'): E.C. Schirmer
Violin Concerto (2008–9) (28'): E.C. Schirmer
Vermont Fanfare (2014) (1')
Concerto for Oboe and Orchestra (2017) (23')
Concerto No. 2 for Cello and Orchestra (2018) (23')
Concertino for Contrabassoon and small orchestra (2022) for Will Safford (15')

Chamber Music

Six Pieces for violin and piano (1977) (8')
Cabaret Music for clarinet, violin, cello and piano (1978) (8'): Galaxy Music.
Movements for violin and piano (1979) (15')
String Quartet No. 2 (1981) (16')
Summer Pages for flute, oboe and harpsichord (1981) (13'): Galaxy Music
Trio for clarinet, cello and piano (1981–84) (22'): GunMar Music
Woodwind Quintet (No. 1) (1985) (14'): Galaxy Music
Three Songs for flute and piano (1985) (12')
Divertimento for clarinet and piano (1986) (12')
Partita for oboe and piano (1987) (17'): TrevCo Music Publishing
Two Night Pieces for viola and piano (1988) (7')
Suite for Cello Quartet (1989) (18'): GunMar Music
Winter Sketchbook for violin and piano (1989) (18')
Serenade for cello and piano (1990) (21')
Three Little Pieces for soprano saxophone and piano (1991) (7')
Waltz in C for ten celli (1991) (4')
Sextet for piano and winds (1991) (22')
Blues and Boogie for cello and piano (1991) (9'): GunMar Music
Lamento, Scherzo and Aria in memory of Lou viola solo (1992) (12')
Song of the Tango Bird for flute and piano (1992) (8'): GunMar Music
Terpsichord for clarinet, alto saxophone, violin, cello and piano (1992) (16')
Piano Trio (1993) (18')
Music for flute, clarinet and piano (1994) (16')
Dreamscape for oboe, bassoon, violin and cello (1994) (12'): TrevCo Music
   Publishing
Episodes for cello and piano (1994) (20')
Romances for violin and piano (1996) (14')
Sleepless Night (string quartet no. 3) (1996) (17')
Journal for flute, guitar and cello (1996) (12')
Lyric Pieces for flute and piano (1997) (14')
Candles clarinet solo (1997) (5')
For Lili Boulanger for twelve cellos (1998) (8')
Two Pieces for English horn, two bassoons, cello and double bass (2000)
   (7')
Birthday Music brass quintet (2000) (10')
Wind Quintet No. 2 (2001) (fl., ob., cl. in B flat, hn, bsn) (13'): TrevCo
   Music Publishing
Dark Song for bass clarinet and piano (2001) (5')
String Quartet No. 4 (2002) (17')
Music for Pat (2002) oboe solo (6'): TrevCo Music Publishing
Games for flute and clarinet (2003) (6')

Three Impressions (2003) (12') for piano and wind quintet
From the Sad Café (June, 2003) cello and guitar. 12' 30'
Four Bagatelles for bassoon and piano (2003) (7:30')
In Memory Of for clarinet, violin, cello, piano (2006) (24')
Three Nightscapes for flute, clarinet, piano (2006) (15')
A Chorale and Two Dances for trumpet and piano (2007) (13')
A Chorale and Two Dances for violin and piano (2008)
Five Miniatures for two cellos (2009)
Rhapsody for violin and piano (2010)
Waltz for two violins (2011)
Three Pieces for cello and piano (2012)
Elegy for violin and piano (Mvt. 3 from Violin Concerto) (arr. 2013): E.C.
     Schirmer
Pas de Deux for flute and double bass (2013)
Wind Quintet No. 3 (2013): TrevCo Music Publishing
Cello Notebook for cello and piano (2015) (25')
Two Poems for bass clarinet and piano (2015) (6')
Four Imaginary Folk-songs for cello and harp (2018)
Fantasia for cello solo (2018) (18')
Dialogue for piano and strings (2019) (8')
Summer Suite for trumpet and bassoon (2019) (10'): TrevCo Music
     Publishing
Two Fragments (contrabassoon and piano) (4'): TrevCo Music
Aria-Caprice for double bass and piano for Holger Michalski and Julia
     Bartha (2020) (17')
Piano Quintet (2022) for Doris Stevenson, Muneko Otani and the Cassatt
     String Quartet
Ein Lied für Reinhard for viola and piano, for Stefanie Taylor, in mem.
     Reinhard Humburg (2023) (13')

Works for Piano Solo

Four Jazz Preludes (1980) (14'): Galaxy Music
Piano Sonata No. 1 (1982) (25')
Lullaby Rag (1983) (4')
Dialogue for piano right hand (1984) (4')
Valentine (1984) (4'): Galaxy Music
Improvisation No. 3 (1984) (4'): Galaxy Music
Sonatina (1985) (10')
Six Miniatures for piano right hand (1988) (10')
Three Reveries (1992) 12'
Five Preludes (1994) (17')
Growl (1995) (3:30')

Letter to a Friend (1995) (14:10)
Three Pieces for Children [1. A Walk with Annie, 2. Dusk, 3. Spring Fever] (1997) (6')
Recollections (1998) piano solo (13')
A Dance Album (1999): Tango (1987)
Humoresque (1987)
Lonely Rag (1983/1999)
Pas de Deux (1993/1999)
Boogie Woogie (1983/1999): Oxford University Press (out of print)
Nocturne for Yoshiko (2001) (6')
Childhood Scenes (2002) piano solo (20')
Messages (2006) 10'
Piano Sonata No. 2 (2007) (19')
Piano Sonata No. 3 (2007) (13')
Three Elegies (2007) (14')
Nostalgic Pieces (2007) (8')
Piano Sonata No. 4 (2009) (20')
Five Piano Pieces (2013, rev. 2015) (12') [1. Fantasy Piece (insect dream), 2. Scherzo no. 1,
3. Blumenstück, 4. Scherzo no. 2, 5. Wiegenlied (Lullaby)]
Piano Sonata No. 5 (2015) (21')
Three Etudes (2015) (10')
Etudes (2017) (Etudes 1–3 and 4–9) (25'): E.C. Schirmer)
Piano Sonata no. 6 (2020) for Julia Bartha (13')
Piano Sonata No. 7 (in memory of Balint Andras Varga) (2020) (18')
Improvisation Diary 2020 (transcriptions) (2022) (55')
Sonata No. 8 (in memory of Maxine Neuman) (2023) (14')
Piano Sonata No. 9 (2024) (17') (for Linda Catlin Smith)

Works for Piano Four-Hands and Two Pianos

Eclogue for two pianos (1988) (17')
Four Studies for piano four-hands (1989) (7')
Suite Parisienne for piano four-hands (easy upper part) (1994) (8'): Galaxy Music
The Rainbow for two pianos eight-hands (1994) (5')
Three Dance Portraits for piano four-hands (1994) (8'): Galaxy Music/E.C. Schirmer
Five Pieces for Two Pianos (1995–2000). [1. Esercizio, 2. Remember?, 3. Contrapuntal Waltz, 4. Bells, 5. Bluesdream] (25')
Tango (1987) arranged for two pianos (2009)
Fantasy for piano four-hands (2011) (14')
Suite Parisienne (expanded version) for piano four-hands (2013) (15'): E.C. Schirmer

Works for Harpsichord or Organ

Dance Music for Two Harpsichords (1985) (16')
Passacaglia organ (10')

Vocal and Choral Works

Songs from the Mandrake, words by Machiavelli, trans. by Wallace Shawn (1981) (15')
The Fisherman's Song, words by Jamaica Kincaid (1983) (4')
Four Songs to poems by Frederick Seidel (1986) (25')
Seven Poems by e.e.cummings (1990) (17')
A Prayer In Spring for SATB, soprano solo, children's chorus, piano (1990) (27')
in time of daffodils for SATB and piano; text by E.E. Cummings (1990) (3') (1st perf. Bennington Children's Chorus)
Herrick Songs for baritone, violin, viola, cello and bass trombone (1991) (15')
Three Vocalises for children's chorus and piano (1991) (5')
What Is The Beautiful? for speaker, cello and piano; text by Kenneth Patchen (1993) (14')
Hanerot Halalu (These Holy Lights) for children's chorus, piano, Hannukah song in Hebrew (1994) (3'): E.C. Schirmer·
The Frozen Lake for soprano, violin and piano; poems by Robert Frost (1995) (20')
'The Grasshopper's Song' from *The Ant and the Grasshopper*; words by Penny Orloff [with violin – optional] (1998) (4')
Hide Not Thy Face From Me, Cantata for soprano, baritone, oboe and strings (1998–9) (19')
Songs from Nothing for mezzo-soprano and piano; words by John Cage (2004) (7')
I Would Marry You (2004); words by Perry Brass (4')
Five Poems of Georg Trakl for baritone and piano (2011)
Three Poems of Lawrence Ferlinghetti for soprano and piano (2014)
Three Poems by Hagiwara Sakutaro for soprano and flute/alto flute; oboe/ English Horn; violin; cello; guitar; guitar/mandolin (2014)
Donnerbach Mühle for voice and harp (2016) (7')
The Table and the Chair for soprano and marimba (2017) (5')
Three Songs for tenor and piano; poems by Anna Maria Hong (2020) (13')

Chamber Opera Works

In The Dark, for soprano, tenor, chamber ensemble – 7 players. Libretto by Wallace Shawn (1976) (35')

The Music Teacher, for two sopranos, tenor, baritone, chorus of four female
voices + additional choral parts, plus speaking roles; flute/piccolo/alto
flute; clarinet/bass clarinet; violin/viola; cello; contrabass; percussion;
two pianos. Libretto by Wallace Shawn (1983) (70')

The Ant and the Grasshopper, for SAT and chamber ensemble of nine
instruments – piano/vocal score available. Libretto by Penny Orloff
(1998) (25'): Boosey and Hawkes

H & G, Music Theatre work for voices and piano based on Anna Maria
Hong's novella *H & G*. Words by Anna Maria Hong and Jean Randich
(2022) (1 hr)

BIOGRAPHICAL GLOSSARY

THE FOLLOWING LIST INCLUDES all persons mentioned, except in passing. A brief description is given for all individuals except such figures of lasting world renown as Aesop, Beethoven, and Aaron Copland.

A. (see Shawn, Annie)
Adams, Ansel, photographer celebrated for his black and white photographs of the American West
Adams, John Luther, composer, visiting Bennington faculty member
Adolphe, Bruce, composer, author, music scholar, pianist
Aesop
Aks, Harold, choral conductor, educator
Alford, Emily, educator
Anderson, Beth, friend, flutist
Anderson, William, guitarist, composer, director of Cygnus Ensemble
Andriessen, Louis, composer
Arlen, Harold, American song writer
Arnold, Malcolm, British Symphonist and film music composer
Athayde, Juliana, violinist, concert master Rochester Philharmonic Orchestra
Austin, Lyn, theater producer, founder/director of the Music Theater Group

Babbitt, Milton, American composer, theorist, teacher, and writer about music
Babbitt, Sylvia, statistician, worker for charitable organizations, married to Milton
Bach, Johann Sebastian
Baker, Chet, jazz trumpeter, composer
Baker, Donna, German instructor, Harvard
Baker, Frank, tenor, Bennington College faculty 1955–95

Balanchine, George, Georgia-born American choreographer and founder of the New York City Ballet

de Balzac, Honoré, 19th-century French novelist, playwright

Barber, Samuel, American composer

Barth, Frances, painter, video artist, animator

Bartha, Julia, German pianist, friend

Barthelme, Donald, fiction writer, frequent *New Yorker* contributor

Bartók, Béla, Hungarian composer, pianist, ethnomusicologist

Basie, Count, American jazz pianist, bandleader

Beach Boys

Beardslee, Bethany, renowned singer of contemporary music

Beckett, Samuel, Irish novelist, playwright

Beeson, Jack, Columbia professor, and composer of *Lizzie Borden* and eight other operas

Beethoven, Ludwig van

Behr, Erik, principal oboe, Rochester Philharmonic Orchestra

Bellow, Saul, American novelist

Berg, Alban, Austrian composer

Berio, Luciano, Italian composer

Bernard, April, poet, Bennington College faculty

Bernstein, Leonard, American conductor, composer, teacher, writer

Birnbaum, Mark, composer, friend

Bisio, Michael, bassist, colleague at Bennington

Biss, Greg, pianist, composer, conductor

Blake, William, English poet, painter

Bliven, Bruce, prolific contributor of nonfiction pieces to *The New Yorker*

Bliven, Naomi, *New Yorker* staff writer, author of more than two hundred long book reviews and thousands of short ones, wife of Bruce

Bloch, Ernest, Swiss-American composer

Blow, John, English composer, organist

Bogdan, Thomas, singer, educator, Bennington faculty

Bolcom, William, celebrated composer of both tonal and atonal works in every genre, teacher

Borowicz, Jon, conductor, educator founder/musical director of the Vermont Philharmonic

Botstein, Leon, musicologist, conductor, President of Bard College

Bottoms, John, theater and film actor

Boulanger, Nadia, legendary music teacher considered one of the greatest in history, composer, conductor, organist, sister of composer Lili Boulanger

Boulez, Pierre, composer, conductor, writer

Brahms, Johannes

Brainerd, Clayton, baritone in opera and oratorio

Brant, Henry, iconoclastic composer known for spatial music, Bennington faculty

Brazelton, Kitty, composer, improvisor, band leader, singer-songwriter, flutist, Bennington College faculty

Brecht, Bertolt, playwright, poet, theatre practitioner

Britten, Benjamin, English composer, conductor

Brooke, Nicholas, composer, Bennington colleague

Brooks, Arthur, musician, composer

Brown, Jerry, politician, former governor of California, lawyer

Bruckner, Anton, Austrian composer, organist

Bugallo, Helena, pianist, music scholar expert on Nancarrow

Bunch, Kenji, composer, violist

Busoni, Ferruccio, Italian composer, pianist

Buttenwieser, Peter, educator, philanthropist, Democratic Party fundraiser

Byrd, William, English composer

Cage, John, American composer, writer, musical philosopher

Calabro, Louis, composer, percussionist, conductor Bennington College faculty 1955–91

Calabro, Tom, cellist, son of Louis

Captain Beefheart, American singer-songwriter

Carl, Robert, composer, teacher, writer about music

Carroll, David, Broadway and off-Broadway actor, singer

Carroll, Lewis, English author, poet, best known for *Alice's Adventures in Wonderland*

Carter, Elliott, distinguished American composer

Carter, Helen, sculptor, married to Elliott

Chabrier, Emmanuel, French composer, pianist

Chadabe, Joel, electronic composer, writer, Bennington College faculty

Chambers, Wendy, American composer

Chapin, Hank (Henry), friend, musician, teacher

Chapin, Schuyler, vice president of Columbia records, general manager of the Metropolitan Opera, cultural affairs commissioner for New York City, father of Hank

Char, René, French poet

Charles, Ray

Chen, Tong, conductor

Childs, Lucinda, dancer and choreographer who founded the company bearing her name

Chon, Myron, advertising composer, brother of William Shawn

Chopin, Frédéric

Cohen, Rabbi Howard, Rabbi of Congregation Beth El in Bennington, Vermont

Comert, Jean-Claude, journalist, resistance fighter, Schlumberger employee, friend

Cone, Edward, American composer, music theorist, editor of the periodical *Perspectives of New Music*

Cook, Mariana, photographer, friend

Cooke, Brian, friend, pianist

Cooke, Francis Judd, composer, organist, cellist, pianist, conductor, professor

Copland, Aaron

Cott, Jonathan, author, journalist, editor, friend

Cowell, Henry, composer, musical innovator

Craft, Alva, actress, wife of Robert

Craft, Robert, conductor, author, assistant to Igor Stravinsky

Cramer, Johann Baptist, pianist, prolific composer, a contemporary of Beethoven

Crawford Seeger, Ruth, American composer and scholar of folk music

Crumb, George, American composer

cummings, e.e., American poet, playwright, novelist, and essayist

Czerny, Carl, Austrian composer, pianist

Davies, Gwen, abstract expressionist painter, art teacher at the Dalton School

Davis, Miles

Davis, Peter G., music critic

DeVoto, Mark, composer, theorist, author

Debussy, Claude
Del Tredici, David, composer, pianist
Derby, Norm, physicist, professor
Dewey, John, American philosopher, psychologist, and educator
Diamond, David, American composer
Diesendruck, Tamar, American composer
Dietrich, Marlene, German-American actress
Dieudonné, Annette, composer, teacher, assistant to Nadia Bou-
    langer for nearly sixty years
Dillon, Frances, pianist, author, and teacher of pedagogy
Dixon, Bill, composer, musician, activist, and visual artist, Ben-
    nington faculty 1965–98
Dlugoszewski, Lucia, composer
Doinel, Antoine, character in *The 400 Blows* and films made by
    François Truffaut
Dolphy, Eric, versatile and innovative jazz and classical instrumen-
    talist, bandleader
Donizetti, Gaetano, Italian composer
Dubow, Marilyn, violinist
Dufallo, Richard, conductor
Dushkin, David, music teacher and co-founder of Kinhaven Music
    School
Dushkin, Dorothy, composer and co-founder of Kinhaven Music
    School
Dylan, Bob
D'Annunzio, Gabriele, Italian writer, politician, war hero

Eisenberg, Deborah, short story writer, playwright, essayist
El Greco
Ellington, Duke
Elliott, Bill, composer, arranger
Epstein, Bill, pianist, friend
Epstein, Daniel, pianist, teacher

Faiella, Ida, singer, teacher, founder of L'Ensemble, Bennington
    College colleague
Fast, Jonathan, author, social work teacher
Fauré, Gabriel, French composer, organist, teacher
Fay, Amy, 19th-century pianist and memoirist

Feitlowitz, Marguerite, writer, translator, professor

Feldman, Morton, American composer

Ferlinghetti, Lawrence, American poet

Ferrillo, John, principal oboe, Boston Symphony Orchestra

Fields, W. C., American actor and comedian

Finckel, George, cellist, professor

Finckel, Marianne ("Willie"), pianist, double bassist, member of
Bennington College faculty

Fine, Irving, American composer

Fine, Vivian, distinguished composer, pianist, member of Bennington College faculty

Fisher, Maria, friend, cellist

Flanner, Janet, Indianapolis-born *New Yorker* writer who lived in
France for 50 years, and wrote the Letter from Paris column
under the pen name Genêt

Flax, Laura, clarinetist

Fleischmann (family) included Raoul Fleischmann whose financial
backing made founding the magazine possible, and Peter
Fleischmann, who eventually took over as president of the
board and maintained the tradition of separation between
the business and editorial sides of the enterprise

Floyd, George, citizen murdered by police in May 2020, sparking
national outrage

Force, Monsieur and Madame, my Parisian landlords

Foreman, Richard, playwright, theater director

Foss, Lukas, German-American composer, pianist

Fox, Jill, painter, friend

Fra Angelico, Italian painter

Franklin, Aretha

Françaix, Jean, prolific composer, Boulanger student

Freud, Sigmund

Friedlander, Claudia, singer, teacher, vocal coach, author (and clarinetist as Bennington student)

Frost, Robert

Furtwängler, Wilhelm, German conductor, composer

Galasso, Michael, American composer, violinist, music director

Gelber, Jack, American playwright

Gentil, Jules, French pianist and teacher

Gershwin, George, American composer, pianist
Gesualdo, Carlo, Italian composer
Gibbons, Orlando, English composer
Gilbert, William Schwenck, English playwright, librettist
Gill, Brendan, film theater and architecture critic, author of fifteen
    books and more than a thousand articles for *The New Yorker*
    (where he was a staff writer for sixty years), family friend
Giraud, Albert, Belgian symbolist poet
Glass, Philip, American composer, pianist
Glick, Jacob, violist, Bennington College faculty member, champi-
    on of contemporary music
Godard, Jean-Luc, Swiss film director
Golub, Peter, concert, theater, film composer, Bennington College
    faculty member
Goodman, Benny, clarinetist and bandleader, active in both jazz
    and classical music
Gottlieb, Robert, editor, author
Gould, Glenn, Canadian pianist
Gould, Morton, American composer, pianist
Grappelli, Stéphane, French jazz violinist
Grateful Dead
Graves, Milford, legendary free-jazz drummer
Gribble, Greta, classmate, singer
Gubaidulina, Sofia, Russian composer
Guigui, Efrain, clarinetist and conductor of the Vermont Sympho-
    ny 1974–89

H. (see, Shawn, Harold)
Hamburger, Edith Iglauer, writer, frequent *New Yorker* contributor,
    mother of Jay
Hamburger, Jay, artistic director, writer, teacher, actor
Hamburger, Philip, *New Yorker* staff writer, family friend, father of
    Jay, husband of Edith
Handel, George Frideric, German-English composer
Harbison, John, American composer
Harris, Emilie, piano teacher
Haydn, Joseph
Hayes, Tom, writer, teacher, friend

Haywood, Charles, Belarus-born singer, musicologist, expert on
    Jewish and Latin American music as well as music written
    for Shakespeare, husband of Frances Dillon
Heikin, Nancy, film director, writer, singer, actress
Hendrix, Jimi
Hensel, Howard, opera singer
Herrick, Robert, English poet
Hindemith, Paul, German composer
Hinkle, Norwood, conductor, educator
Hitchcock, Alfred
Hoagland, Edward, prolific novelist, essayist, editor, teacher
Holst, Gustav, English composer, teacher
Holzman, David, pianist known for contemporary music
Hong, Anna Maria, poet, professor
Hopper, Edward, American realist painter
Hudson, Joe, composer
Humburg, Reinhard, attorney, recording engineer, married to
    Maxine Neuman
Hurd Hause, Maureen, clarinetist, educator, Benny Goodman
    scholar
Hurt, William, American actor

Ives, Charles, American composer

J. (see Kincaid, Jamaica)
Jackson, Isaiah, conductor
Jarrett, Keith, American jazz pianist, composer
Jefferson Airplane, American rock band
Jenner, Joanna, violinist
Johnson, Lyndon Baines
Joplin, Scott, American composer, pianist, known as the "king of
    ragtime"
Joyce, James, Irish novelist, poet
Jung, Carl

Kafka, Franz
Kahn, Joan, noted editor of mysteries, writer, artist, designer, sister
    of *New Yorker* writer E.J. ("Jack") Kahn, and of Olivia
Kahn, Olivia, painter, family friend, sister of Jack and Joan

Kahn, Sue Ann, flutist, chamber musician, Bennington colleague, friend
Karis, Aleck, pianist, teacher
Kennedy, President John F.
Kern, Jerome
Kernochan, Adelaide, author, educator, married to Jack
Kernochan, John (Jack), law professor, composer, music publisher
Kim, Earl, composer, Harvard professor
Kim, Eunbi, pianist
Kincaid, Jamaica (J.), novelist, essayist, professor, frequent *New Yorker* contributor, first wife
King, Carole, American singer-songwriter
Kirchner, Leon, composer, conductor, pianist, Harvard professor
Klemperer, Otto, German conductor
Kline, Kevin, American stage and film actor
Krakauer, David, clarinetist
Krupa, Gene, American jazz drummer
Kurtág, György, Hungarian composer

L., Lucille, girlfriend
La Barbara, Joan, innovative composer, singer
LaBrecque, Rebecca, pianist known for performances of new music
Lam, Bun-Ching, composer
Landesman, Heidi, set designer for theater
Landowska, Wanda, harpsichordist
Lapine, James, director, playwright, author
Lauth, James (Jim), composer, attorney, friend
Leach, Wilford, theater and film director, writer
Led Zeppelin
Lederer, Felix, Latin teacher, the Putney school
Lederer, Marissa Fazzini, Italian teacher, admissions director the Putney school, married to Felix
Lehrman, Leonard, prolific composer, music scholar, writer, conductor
Leoncavallo, Ruggero, Italian opera composer
Levi, Jonathan, doctor, childhood friend
Levin, Robert, music scholar, pianist, professor, composer
Levine, Jeffrey, composer, double bassist, teacher

Lewin, David, music theorist, composer, writer, teacher

León, Tania, Cuban-born American composer, conductor, winner of the Pulitzer Prize

Lieberson, Peter, American composer

Ligeti, György, renowned Hungarian composer

Liszt, Franz, Hungarian composer

Locke, Ralph, American musicologist, author, classical music critic, editor, professor

Long, Timothy, conductor, pianist

Losey, Carole, educator, founder of the Elizabeth Seeger School

Luening, Otto, composer, electronic music pioneer, conductor, flutist, author, teacher

Lundborg, Erik, composer

Lurtsema, Robert J., public radio classical music broadcaster, composer

Lutzke, Myron, cellist

M., Marina, French girlfriend

MacDermot, Galt, composer

Macbride, David, composer, teacher, friend

de Machaut, Guillaume, great 14th-century French composer

Machiavelli, Niccolo

Macomber, Curt, violinist, prominent in performance of new music

Mahler, Gustav, Austrian composer, conductor

Mailer, Norman, American novelist

Malcolm, Janet, Prague-born American journalist, staff writer for *The New Yorker*

Malle, Louis, French filmmaker

Mapplethorpe, Robert, American photographer

Margulies, Donald, American playwright

Marissa (see Lederer, Marissa)

Markevitch, Igor, Russian-born conductor and composer, studied with Boulanger

Martin, Barbara Ann, singer particularly known for her performances of contemporary music, teacher

Martin, Frank, Swiss composer

Martino, Donald, American composer

Marx Brothers, American comedy group

Masuzzo, Dennis, bassist

Mays, Willie, American baseball player

McClelland, Jean, singer, teacher, musical theater performer

McPhee, Jonathan, conductor

Mehta, Ved, blind Indian-born author of twenty-six books, many of which were serialized in *The New Yorker*

Mendelssohn Hensel, Fanny, composer, sister of Felix

Menken, Alan, composer

Menotti, Gian Carlo, composer

Merritt, Arthur Tillman, musicologist, Harvard professor, and expert on the Renaissance

Messiaen, Olivier, composer, organist

Michalski, Holger, German double bassist

Mike, Uncle (see Chon, Myron)

Milhaud, Darius, French composer

Miller, David Alan, music director of the Albany Symphony Orchestra

Miller, Robert, pianist known for his performances of new music, attorney

Mingus, Charles (Charlie), jazz composer, bassist, bandleader, author

Minoff, Edward (Ted), painter, educator, son of Alva Craft

Miró, Joan, Spanish painter, sculptor, ceramicist

Molière, French playwright

Monk, Thelonious, American jazz pianist, composer

Monod, Jacques-Louis, French-born composer, pianist, conductor

Monteverdi, Claudio, Italian composer

Morello, Joe, American drummer

Morley, Thomas, English composer, singer, theorist

Morris, Frank, instrument maker of violins, violas, and cellos, friend

Morton, Jelly Roll, American jazz composer

Mozart, Wolfgang Amadeus

Murray, Natalia Danesi, publisher, book editor, romantic partner of Janet Flanner

Mussorgsky, Modest, Russian composer

N., Noa (see Shawn, Noa Sato)

Neuman, Maxine, cellist, teacher, Bennington College faculty member

Newhouse, Samuel Irving Jr., chairman of Advance Publications
and of Condé Nast
Newlin, Dika, composer, musicologist, author, expert on Schoen-
berg, Mahler, and Bruckner, punk rocker
Nielsen, Carl, Danish composer
Noguchi, Isamu, American artist, sculptor, set designer, landscape
architect
Noland, Kenneth, American abstract painter
Norell, Judith, concert harpsichordist, baker, founder of Silver
Moon Bakery
Nowak, Alison, composer, violinist, teacher, friend
Nowak, Lionel, composer, pianist, Bennington College faculty
member
Nyman, Michael, English composer, pianist, musicologist

Odets, Clifford, American playwright
Olan, David, composer, clarinetist, music professor, friend
Oliver, Edith, *New Yorker* drama critic, staff writer, editor
Oppens, Ursula, eminent American pianist, known particularly for
contemporary music
Orloff, Penny, singer, actress, writer, producer
Ortega y Gasset, José, Spanish philosopher

Pace, Roberto, composer, pianist, music director, educator, friend
Papp, Joe, theater director, founder of the New York Shakespeare
Festival and the Public Theater
Parke, Nathaniel, cellist, Bennington College colleague
Parker, William, free jazz bassist, multi-instrumentalist, composer,
poet
Parloff, Michael, flutist, teacher, lecturer on music
Patchen, Kenneth, American poet, also known for combining po-
etry readings with jazz accompaniment
Pearthree, Pippa, stage, television, and film actress
Penderecki, Krzysztof, Polish composer
Perkins, John MacIvor, composer, pianist, teacher
Persichetti, Dorothy Flanagan, pianist, educator, composer, wife of
Vincent
Persichetti, Vincent, noted composer, pianist, teacher, author
Petit, Pierre, French composer, pianist, author, music critic, direc-
tor of the École normale de musique de Paris

Petrassi, Goffredo, Italian composer, conductor
Piazzolla, Astor, Argentine composer, bandoneon player
Picasso, Pablo
Picker, Tobias, American composer, known for operas, friend
Pine, Margaret, American music theater composer
Piston, Walter, American composer
Pompidou, Georges, President of France 1969–1974
Porter, Cole, American composer, lyricist, songwriter
Porter, Quincy, American composer
Poulenc, Francis, French composer
Powell Jr, Adam Clayton, American politician, minister
Presley, Elvis
des Prez, Josquin, Renaissance composer
Prokofiev, Sergei, Russian composer
Pugno, Raoul, French composer, organist, pianist, teacher
Purcell, Henry, English composer

Quan, Linda, American violinist

Rachmaninoff, Sergei, Russian pianist, composer
Randich, Jean, director, writer, librettist, Bennington College faculty
Ravel, Maurice, French composer
Redding, Otis, American singer-songwriter
Reger, Max, German composer
Reinhardt, Django, Romani-French jazz guitarist, composer
Rich, Buddy, jazz drummer, bandleader
Richter, Sviatoslav, Russian pianist
Rieser, Leonard, friend
Riesman, Michael, American composer, conductor, director of the
    Philip Glass Ensemble
Riley, Dennis, American composer, teacher
Robards, Jason, American actor
Robbins, Channing, cellist, teacher
Robbins, Rena, violinist
Robison, Paula, flutist
Rockwell, John, music critic, author
Rodgers, Richard, American composer, best known for musical
    theater work
Roeper, Karen, expert on body-mind wellness, founder of Essential
    Motion, friend

Ronstadt, Linda, singer, actress
Roosevelt, Franklin Delano
Rosen, Nathaniel, American cellist
Ross, Lillian, staff writer at *The New Yorker* for seventy years, romantic companion to my father, mother of adoptive son, Erik
Rothstein, Edward, musicologist, author, music critic
Ruggles, Carl, American composer
Rush, Deborah, stage, screen, and television actress
Ruth, Babe
Rzewski, Frederic, American composer, pianist
Saariaho, Kaija, Finnish composer

Sahr, Hadassah, pianist, teacher, professor, expert on American music
Sakutarō, Hagiwara, early 20th-century Japanese poet
Salinger, J.D. (Jerry), renowned author, family friend, frequent *New Yorker* contributor, whose book *Franny and Zooey* was dedicated to my father
Sandburg, Carl, American poet, writer
Sandor, Gluck, dancer, choreographer, actor, teacher
Saroyan, William, Armenian-American novelist, playwright
Sato, Yoshiko (Y.), pianist, teacher, wife
Saudek, Robert, television executive, producer
Saunders, Cathrine, English flutist, teacher, counsellor, sister of Helen
Saunders, Helen, English clarinetist, composer, sister of Cathrine
Scarlatti, Domenico, Italian composer
Schachter, Carl, American music theorist, author, teacher
Schell, Jonathan, American writer, journalist, staff writer for *The New Yorker* and principal Notes and Comments writer, author of books on the Vietnam War, the Nixon administration, and the nuclear threat, amateur oboist, family and personal friend
Schnittke, Alfred, late-20th-century composer
Schoenberg, Arnold, Austrian-American composer
Schonbeck, Gunnar, clarinetist, instrument inventor, composer, Bennington College colleague
Schorr, Joseph, violinist
Schubert, Peter, conductor, professor, theorist, author

Schuller, Gunther, composer, conductor, author, music historian, jazz musician, publisher, President of the New England Conservatory

Schuman, William, distinguished composer, president of The Juilliard School

Sears, Freida, personal banker, Justice of the Peace

Seeger, Charles, composer, theorist, folk music scholar, husband of Ruth Crawford and father of Pete

Seeger, Elizabeth, educator, author of children's books about China, India, and Russia, sister of Charles

Seeger, John, educator, principal of Fieldston School, nephew of Charles

Seeger, Pete, renowned folk singer, composer and activist

Seidel, Frederick, poet, friend

Seki, Kanako, pianist, friend

Sellars, Peter, opera director

Serkin, Judy (Judith), cellist, friend, daughter of Rudolf, sister of Peter

Shapiro, Leo, stage director

Shawn, Annie (A.), daughter

Shawn, Harold (H.), son

Shawn, Mary, sister

Shawn, Noa Sato (N.), son

Shawn, Wallace (Wally), playwright, essayist, actor, brother

Shawn, William, editor of *The New Yorker* magazine for thirty-five years, writer, father

Sherman, Betsy, biologist, educator

Sherry, Fred, cellist, particularly known as chamber musician and soloist, and for working with contemporary composers

Shostakovich, Dmitri, Russian composer

Sibelius, Jean, Finnish composer

Siebert, Renée, American flutist, teacher

Smiley, Pril, electronic music composer and former director of the Columbia-Princeton Electronic Music Center

Smith, Craig, conductor, pianist

Smith, Elizabeth H., longtime music department pianist, the Dalton school

Smith, Linda Catlin, American-born Canadian composer

Smith, Rex, American stage and television actor and singer

Sollberger, Harvey, composer, flutist, teacher
Son, Yung Wha, composer
Sontag, Susan, acclaimed writer, critic, intellectual
Sorel, Felicia, dancer, choreographer
Sosin, Donald, composer, pianist
Sperry, Paul, lyric tenor, teacher
Spitz, Jonathan, cellist, teacher
Stearns, Peter Pindar, composer, organist, educator
Steig, William, artist, cartoonist, writer, frequent *New Yorker* contributor
Steinbeck, John, American writer
Stockhausen, Karlheinz, German composer
Straus, Roger, co-founder and chairman of Farrar, Straus and Giroux publishers
Strauss, Richard, German composer, conductor
Stravinsky, Igor, Russian composer, conductor
Strozzi, Barbara, Italian composer, singer
Sullivan, Sir. Arthur, English composer
Sun Ra, experimental American jazz composer
Suskind, Joyce, composer, teacher
Swados, Elizabeth, American composer
Szell, George, Hungarian-American conductor

Tailleferre, Germaine, French composer
Takemitsu, Tōru, Japanese composer, celebrated for concert music and film scores
Tamarkin, Kate, American conductor, educator
Tan, Su Lian, composer, flutist, educator
Tatum, Art, jazz pianist
Taylor, Cecil, jazz pianist, composer
Taylor-Corbett, Lynne, choreographer, director, lyricist, composer
Tcherepnin, Ivan, composer, director of the Harvard Electronic Music Studio
Telson, Bob, American composer, song writer, pianist
The Beatles
Thomas, Ambroise, 19th-century French composer known for operas, teacher
Thomas, Augusta Read, American composer, professor
Thompson, Randall, American composer

Thorne, Francis, American composer, co-founder of the American Composers Orchestra

Thorne, Gordon, visual artist, promoter of community arts

Tovey, Donald, English musicologist, writer, composer, conductor, pianist

Tower, Joan, American composer

Trakl, Georg, Austrian expressionist poet

Trampler, Walter, German-born American violist and chamber musician

Troob, Danny, composer, orchestrator, arranger for stage and film

Trowbridge, Gus, educator, founder of Manhattan Day School

Truffaut, François, filmmaker, writer, actor, critic

de Unamuno, Miguel, novelist, playwright, philosopher, author of *The Tragic Sense of Life*

Updike, David, short story writer, novelist, teacher, friend

Updike, John, novelist, short story writer, critic, frequent *New Yorker* contributor

Ussachevsky, Vladimir, composer, well known for his work with electronic music

Ustvolskaya, Galina, Russian composer

Valéry, Paul, French poet, essayist, philosopher, playwright

Varga, Bálint András, author of ten books of penetrating interviews with contemporary composers, promotor of new music at Universal Editions

Varèse, Edgard, innovative French-born composer who lived in the United States

Vaughan Williams, Ralph, English composer

Venora, Diane, actress

de Victoria, Tomás Luis (Vittoria), Spanish Renaissance composer

Vitercik, Greg, musicologist, author, professor of music history, friend

Vosgerchian, Luise, pianist, music professor

Wagner, Richard

Walcott, Derek, Saint Lucia-born poet, playwright, winner of the Nobel Prize in Literature

Wald, George, biologist, professor, activist, winner of the Nobel Prize for his medical research

Ward, Robert, composer, winner of Pulitzer Prize for opera *The Crucible*

Waters, Susannah, British opera singer, writer, director

Waxman, Donald, composer, music editor

Weber, Bruce, evolutionary biologist, professor

Webern, Anton, Austrian composer

Weelkes, Thomas, early 17th-century English composer, organist

Weill, Kurt, composer best known for *The Threepenny Opera*

Wen-chung, Chou, Chinese-born composer, professor, chair of Columbia University music department, cultural ambassador

West, Nathanael, American novelist and screenwriter

White, E.B., American author, staff writer at *The New Yorker* for sixty years, whose writing some say epitomized its stylistic ideal

White, Robert, American psychologist, author, Harvard professor

Wilbye, John, English composer

Wilder, Alec, composer, writer, scholar of American popular song, who lived at the Algonquin Hotel

Williams, Amy, composer, pianist, professor

Wilson, Robert, writer, director of theatre and opera

Wolpe, Stefan, composer, teacher

Wright, Elizabeth, pianist, teacher, Bennington College colleague, friend

Wuorinen, Charles, composer, teacher, winner of the Pulitzer Prize for *Time's Encomium*

Xenakis, Iannis, composer, architect

Y. (see Sato)

Zappa, Frank, composer of both rock and concert music, bandleader

INDEX

Adams, Ansel, 150

Adams, John, 33, 36, 37, 44, 115; *Grand Pianola Music*, 108-9

Adams, John Luther, 154

Adolphe, Bruce, 54

Aks, Harold, 14

Albany Symphony Orchestra, 163

Alford, Emily ("Alfie"), 14, 62, 85

American Composers Orchestra, 63, 114

Anderson, Beth, 162

Anderson, William, 180

Antheil, George: "Jazz Symphony," 73

Arlen, Harold, 5

Arnold, Malcolm, 104

Aspen Wind Quintet, 113, 127, 162

Athayde, Juliana, 181

Atlanta Ballet Company, 130

Atlantic Monthly: author's writing for, 95

Austin, Lyn, 73

Babbitt, Milton, 61, 62, 64, 71, 73, 99

Babbitt, Sylvia, 64

Bach, Johann Sebastian, 171; Chorale Preludes, 8, 125; *Christmas Oratorio*, 18; Concerto in D Minor, 9; *Goldberg Variations*, 171, 180; Mass in B Minor, 18, 19, 51; *The Musical Offering*, 8-9; *St Matthew Passion*, 18

Bach, Steven, 164

Bach Society Orchestra, 31, 32, 36, 91

Baker, Chet, 157

Baker, Donna, 38

Baker, Frank, 120

Balanchine, George, 129

Barber, Samuel, 89, 142; Piano Concerto, 11

Bard College, 170

Barth, Frances, 130, 131

Bartha, Julia, 177

Barthelme, Donald, 67

Bartók, Bela, 7, 63; *Bluebeard's Castle*, 34; Concerto for Orchestra, 22; *Contrasts*, 104; *Divertimento* for String Orchestra, 3; Sixth String Quartet, 3-4, 169; Stravinsky on, 179; String Quartets, 63, 82; Three *Rondos*, 8

Basie, Count, 76

Beardslee, Bethany, 39, 71

Beckett, Samuel: *Endgame*, 13; *Neither*, 146

Beeson, Jack, 66, 69, 70-71; *Captain Jinks of the Horse Marines*, 73

Beethoven, Ludwig van, 71; Eighth Symphony, 18; Fifth Symphony, 26; First Piano Concerto, 31; *Missa solemnis*, 51; Overture to "Egmont," 22; Sonata in C Major, op. 2, no. 3, 55; Sonata, op. 111, 38; *Sonata Pathétique*, 8; Third Symphony (*Eroica*), 19

Behr, Erik, 181

Bellow, Saul: *Henderson the Rain King*, 43, 75

Bennington Chamber Music Conference, 180

Bennington College Chamber Music Conference: author as guest composer at, 109-10

Bennington College: author as
    teacher at, xi, 110, 116-17,
    154-55; and author's evolution
    as a composer, 121, 128-30;
    approach to teaching at, 121-24;
    colleagues at, 120; performing
    arts as important at, 119-20;
    unrest and upheaval at, 151-52,
    153-54; as a way of life, 124-25
Berg, Alban, 11, 15; *Lulu*, 24, 35, 38;
    Lyric Suite, 64; Piano Sonata,
    op. 1, 9-10, 92, 126; *Vier Stücke*,
    69; *Wozzeck*, 16, 34-35, 36
Berio, Luciano, 71, 157; *Sinfonia*, 155
Bernard, April, 172
Bernstein, Leonard, 65; author's
    biography about, 177; author's
    reflections on, 177-79;
    Chichester Psalms, 178; as
    composer, 178-79; Norwood
    Hinkle on, 19; *Kaddish*
    Symphony, 178; *First* Symphony
    (*Jeremiah*), 64; *Mass*, 178; *The
    Pennycandystore Beyond the
    El*, 178; *A Quiet Place*, 178; *and*
    recording of Ives's Second
    Symphony, 17; Roger Sessions
    on, 64
Birnbaum, Mark, 68, 73
Bisio, Michael, 181, 182
Biss, Greg, 31
Blake, William, 162
Bliven, Bruce, 12, 182
Bliven, Naomi, 12
Bloch, Ernest, 10; Concerto Grosso,
    18
Blow, John, 67
Bogdan, Thomas, 162
Bolcom, William, 73-74, 91, 113;
    Graceful Ghost Rag, 74, 86
Borowicz, Jon, 25
Botstein, Leon, 170-71
Bottoms, John, 87, 102
Boulanger, Nadia, x, 46, 77, 91, 138;
    author's article about, 108-9;
    author's studies with, 46,
    47-57, 69, 122; her approach

to teaching, 50-52, 70; on
    composers and composing, 135;
    romantic life of, 56-57; tastes
    and preferences in music, 55-56
Boulez, Pierre, 56, 62, 71; college
    course on, 155; *Éclat*, 35; master
    class taught by, 72; Piano
    Sonatas, 72
Brahms, Johannes: Clarinet Sonatas,
    103; German Requiem, 19;
    Horn Trio, 22; *Liebeslieder-
    Walzer*, 19; *Schicksalied*, 19;
    Second Piano Concerto, 163;
    Sonata in F Major, 135
Brainerd, Clayton, 164, 165
Brant, Henry, 123
Brazelton, Kitty, 154
Britten, Benjamin: *Peter Grimes*, 76
Brooke, Nicholas, 154
Brooks, Arthur, 120
Brown, Jerry, 98
Bruckner, Anton: *Te Deum*, 141
Bugallo, Helena, 163
Bunch, Kenji, 154
Busoni, Ferruccio, 8
Buttenwieser, Peter, 14
Byrd, William, 19, 78

Cage, John, 15, 41, 44, 179; *Six
    Melodies for Violin and Piano*,
    89
Calabro, Christine, 120
Calabro, Louis, 110, 125-26, 130;
    background of, 120, 124;
    compositions by, 143; death
    of, 144; illness of, 143-44; as
    mentor to author, 119, 120;
    Third Symphony, 119
Calabro, Tom, 140
Caldwell, Sarah, 35
Carl, Robert, 100, 161
Carroll, David, 113
Carroll, Lewis, 44
Carter, Elliott, 95; author's meetings
    with, 60-61, 64, 178; *Elegy
    for String Orchestra*, 11; First
    String Quartet, 11; Lincoln

Center exhibit focusing on, 63; Piano Concerto, 41; Variations for Orchestra, 63
Carter, Helen, 64, 69, 71
Cavell, Stanley, 38
Chabrier, Emmanuel, 57
Chadabe, Joel, 120, 151
Chambers, Wendy: *Ten Grand*, 74
Chapin, Hank (Henry), 15, 64
Chapin, Schuyler, 64, 178; on serialism, 15
Char, René, 179
Charles, Ray: "Let the Good Times Roll," 16
Chen, Tong, 181
Childs, Lucinda, 114-15, 126-27
Chopin, Frédéric, 16; Études, 55; Prelude in B Minor, 9
Chon, Myron (Uncle Mike), 15, 93
Cohen, Howard, 161
Cohen, Ron, 172
Columbia University: author as composition student at, 66-78; author's master's thesis at, 73; author's sense of alienation at, 69-73; theory of creativity at, 69-70
Comert, Jean-Claude, 132-33
Composers Ensemble, 69, 81
composers: training and attributes of, 65-66
composing/composition: approaches to, 65-66, 69-74; as aspirational, ix, 4; experience of, 83, 115-16
contemporary music: divergent views regarding, 41-43; as part of the curriculum at Bennington, 154, 155; the university's role in, 42-43; and the Vietnam War, 43-44. *See also names of individual composers*
Cook, Mariana: and photography of author and Annie, 150
Cooke, Brian, 34
Cooke, Francis Judd, 34, 35, 38, 89

Cooke, Nym, 35
Copland, Aaron, 65, 72, 118; Concerto, 104; *An Outdoor Adventure*, 20; *Four Piano Blues*, 94
Cott, Jonathan, 95
Cowell, Henry, 15, 142
Craft, Alva, 160
Craft, Robert, 35, 159-60; *Themes and Episodes* (with Stravinsky), 34
Cramer, Johann Baptist, 119
Cremona Quartet, 95
Crumb, George, 67, 95
cummings, e. e.: author's songs inspired by, 140, 141; "in time of daffodils," 141
Czerny, Carl, 119, 147

Dalton School: author's music classes at, 8; author's music performances at, 13-14; teachers at, 14
D'Annunzio, Gabriele, 57
Davenport, LaNoue, 14
Davies, Gwen, 14
Davis, Miles, 96
Davis, Peter G., 83
Debussy, Claude, 51, 53; *Estampes*, 55
Del Tredici, David, 33, 82, 91, 156; musical settings of poems by James Joyce, 44; *Syzygy*, 44
Delacorte Theater, 92, 101, 109, 115
Derby, Norm, 154
DeVoto, Mark: *Three Little Pieces*, 31
Dewey, John, 119
Diamond, David, 21, 61
Diesendruck, Tamar, 154
Dieudonné, Annette, 52, 53, 55, 57
Dillon, Frances: as author's music teacher, 7-10, 11, 16, 37-38, 69, 122; death of, 37
Dixon, Bill, 120, 123-24, 149, 151, 177; improvising with, 142-43; and tensions with author, 124-25
Dlugoszewski, Lucia, 139

Dolphy, Eric, 157
Donizetti, Gaetano: *Don Pasquale*, 109
Dubow, Marilyn, 89-90, 93-94, 108, 111, 113, 114
Dufallo, Richard, 58
Dushkin, David, 21, 22, 54
Dushkin, Dorothy, 21-22, 54
Dushkin, Samuel, 22, 54
Dydo, Stephen, 66

École Normale de Musique, 54, 55, 171
Eisenberg, Deborah, 75, 147
electronic music, 70-71
Elevator to the Gallows (film), 96
Elizabeth Seeger School: author as teacher at, 62, 85, 93, 95
Ellington, Duke, 16, 71, 73, 76, 78
Elliott, William (Bill), 92, 109
Emmanuel Music, 38
Epstein, Bill, 44-45
Epstein, Daniel, 161

Faiella, Ida, 157, 158, 162, 164
Farrar, Straus and Giroux, 128
Fast, Jonathan: *Variations on a Hexachord*, 22
Fauré, Gabriel: Requiem, 48
Fay, Amy, 9, 11, 37
Feitlowitz, Marguerite, 172
Feldman, Morton, 146
Ferlinghetti, Lawrence, 179
Ferrillo, John, 129, 130, 156, 162
Fielding, Ron, 181
Finckel, Chris, 125
Finckel, George: memorial for, 125-26
Finckel, Michael, 125
Finckel, Willie, 144
Fine, Irving, 22
Fine, Vivian, x, 110, 113, 118, 123, 124, 125, 126, 131, 152; *L'École des Hautes Études*, 123; *Poetic Fires*, 114; *Suite for Voice and Piano*, 27

Fisher, Maria, 180
Flanner, Janet, 12, 40
Flax, Laura, 90
Fleischmann family: as owners of *The New Yorker*, 116-17
Floyd, George, 182
Foreman, Richard, 67; *Dr. Selavy's Magic Theatre*, 61-62
Foss, Lukas, 111
400 Blows, The (film), 45
Fox, Jill, 109
Françaix, Jean, 135
Friedlander, Claudia, 128, 137
Friends Seminary School, 18
Frost, Robert: author's Cantata on poems by, 140-41; "Good Hours," 140-41; "A Prayer in Spring," 140
"Full Fathom Five," 15
Furtwängler, Wilhelm, 21

Galasso, Michael, 115
Galaxy Music Corporation, 102, 105, 108, 112, 113, 127; sale of, to Schirmer, 137-38
Gelber, Jack: *The Connection*, 111
Gentil, Jules, 55
Gershwin, George, 5, 90; Preludes, 94; *Rhapsody in Blue*, 5; "Slap That Bass," 108
Gesualdo, Carlo, 56
Gibbons, Orlando: "The Silver Swan," 19
Gil Evans Orchestra, 63
Gilbert, W. S., 92
Gilbert and Sullivan: *The Pirates of Penzance*, 92-93, 95, 97
Gill, Brendan, 58
Ginastera, Alberto, 139
Giraud, Albert, 158
Glass, Philip, 33, 115, 127; *Einstein on the Beach*, 75
Glick, Jack (Jacob), 110, 120, 123, 133, 144, 151, 152
Godard, Jean-Luc, 71
Golub, Peter, 151

Goodman, Benny, x; author's
    collaboration with, 103-5; death
    of, 105
Gottlieb, Robert, 128
Gould, Glenn, 119
Grappelli, Stéphane, 96
Graves, Milford, 120
Greenwich House Music School, 92
Greenwich Symphony Orchestra,
    130
Gregory, André: and My Dinner
    with André, 95-97
Gribble, Greta, 40
Group for Contemporary Music, 90,
    91, 108
Guigui, Efrain, 137

Hamburger, Edith, 12
Hamburger, Jay, 14, 176
Hamburger, Philip, 12
Harbison, John, 31, 91, 111; Piano
    Concerto, 73
Harris, Emilie, 13, 26, 37-38, 58, 59,
    122, 182
Harvard University: author
    as student at, 32-45;
    competitiveness at, 33-34;
    Wally as student at, 30
Haydn, Franz Joseph: D Major
    Concerto, 9; Symphony no. 104
    ("The Clock"), 18
Hayes, Tom, 99-100
Haywood, Charles, 37
Heikin, Nancy, 109
Hendrix, Jimi, 41
Henry V (Shakespeare, 112, 113
Hensel, Howard, 74
Hindemith, Paul, 10, 20, 41; In
    Praise of Music, 22
Hinkle, Norwood, 18, 19, 21
Hinkle, Steve, 21
Hitchcock, Alfred, 83
Hoagland, Edward, 156
Holst, Gustav, 20
Holzman, David, 74
Hong, Anna Maria, 182
Hopper, Edward, 140

Horace: Odes
Hudson, Joe, 68
Human Comedy, The: author's
    involvement with, 111, 112
Humburg, Reinhard, 176, 180
Hurd Hause, Maureen, 181
Hurt, William, 101

Ives, Charles, 5, 15, 58; First Piano
    Sonata, 94; Fourth Sonata, 89;
    Largo, 69; On the Antipodes, 58;
    Robert Browning Overture, 11;
    Second Sonata, 89-90; Second
    Symphony, 17; Sonata no. 2
    (Concord), 26

Jackson, Isaiah, 31
Jarrett, Keith, 93
jazz: author's interest in, 16; as
    source of tension at home, 16
Jenner, Joanna, 137, 144
Johnson, Lyndon, 75
Joplin, Scott, 86, 94
Josquin des Prez, 67; Pange Lingua,
    51
Joyce, James, 44
Juilliard School: author's admission
    interviews at, 60-61, 64
Jung, Carl, 88

Kafka, Franz: The Visitation, 34
Kahn, Joan, 12
Kahn, Olivia, 12
Kahn, Sue Ann, 120, 123, 126, 180
Kant, Immanuel, 171
Karis, Aleck, 74, 148
Kennedy, John F.: assassination of,
    20
Kern, Jerome, 5
Kernochan, Adelaide, 102
Kernochan, Jack, 102, 113, 130, 131,
    137, 138
Kernochan, Sarah, 102
Kim, Earl, x, 45, 95; as author's
    composition teacher, 32, 39-40,
    136; Exercises en Route, 39;
    political views of, 39-40

Kim, Eunbi, 179-80
Kincaid, Jamaica (J.), 147; author's divorce from, 169; author's marriage to, 84, 85-86, 164-65; background of, 83-84; and conversion to Judaism, 161; and joint commission with author, 164-65; pregnancies of, 112, 134; as teacher at Bennington, 116, 120; in Vermont, 109
Kinhaven Music Camp, 16-17, 21-23
Kinhaven Wind Counsellors, 24
Kirchner, Leon, ix, 61, 95; as author's composition teacher, 32, 41-43, 122; as conductor of Stravinsky's music, 36; on contemporary music, 41-42; *The Forbidden*, 76; *Lily*, 75; *Little Suite*, 30; *Music for Cello and Orchestra*, 76; *Music for Orchestra*, 41, 75; *Music for Orchestra II*, 76; *Music for Twelve*, 76; and negative review of *Lily*, 75-76; *Of Things Exactly as They Are*, 76; Piano Concerto, 30; Second Piano Concerto, 43; and Stravinsky's advice to composers, 42, 69; String Quartet no. 3, 43
Klimowski, Steve, 169
Kline, Kevin, 92
Krakauer, David, 114
Krupa, Gene, 6

La Barbara, Joan, 62
La Bohème (Leoncavallo), 113
LaBrecque, Rebecca, 92
Lam, Bun-Ching, 154
Landesman, Heidi, 101
Landowska, Wanda, 24
Lapine, James, 101; *Luck, Pluck and Virtue*, 148; *Twelve Dreams*, 88, 98-99, 148
Lapine, Sarah, 148
Lauth, James, 68, 73, 90
Leach, Wilford, 92, 109, 112
Lederer, Felix, 21, 45

Lederer, Marissa, 21
Lehrman, Leonard, 32, 43
Lenox Arts Center, 67, 73; author as pianist at, 58, 61, 66; *In the Dark* presented at, 74, 174
León, Tania, 111
Leoncavallo, Ruggero, 56
L'Ensemble, 157
Levi, Jonathan, 14
Levin, Robert, 32-33
Levine, Jeffrey, 110, 120, 123, 125; "2 x 5 x 7," 126, 151
Leviticus, Book of, 50
Lewin, David, 32
Lieberson, Peter, 66, 69
Lincoln Center, 30
Lipkin, Seymour, 30
Liszt, Franz, 9; Piano Sonata, 30, 51
Locke, Ralph, 180
Long, Timothy, 174
Losey, Carole, 62
Lucarelli, Humbert, 94
Lucinda Childs Dance Company, 114-15
Luening, Otto, 76, 122-23, 147
Lundborg, Erik, 66, 101, 154
Lurtsema, Robert J., 148
Lutzke, Myron, 82, 90

Macbride, David, 68, 94, 176
MacDermot, Galt, 111
Machaut, Guillaume de, 67
Machiavelli, Niccolo: *The Mandrake*, 164
Macomber, Curt, 82, 90
Mahler, Gustav, 71; Fourth Symphony, 128
Mailer, Norman, 43
Malcolm, Janet, 172
Malle, Louis x; and *My Dinner with André*, 95-97
Mannes School of Music, 7, 16, 90; author as teacher at, 58
Mapplethorpe, Robert, 115, 127
Margulies, Donald: *Found a Peanut*, 112
Markevitch, Igor, 53

Marnie (Hitchcock film), 83
Martin, Barbara Ann, 74
Martin, Frank: *Le Mystère de la Nativité*, 31
Martino, Donald: Trio, 68
Masuzzo, Dennis, 101
Mays, Willie, 17
McClelland, Jean, 108
McPhee, Jonathan, 98
Mehta, Ved, 12, 103
Melville, Herman: *Moby Dick*, 19
Menaker, Daniel, 172
Mendelssohn, Fanny, 154
Mendelssohn, Felix, 30
Menken, Alan, 59
Menotti, Gian Carlo, 56
Merkin Concert Hall, 94
Merritt, Arthur Tillman, 65
Messiaen, Olivier: *Hymne*, 53; *Le Merle Noir*, 30
Michalski, Holger, 177
Milhaud, Darius, 41, 61; *La Cheminée du Roi René*, 22
Miller, David Alan, 163
Miller, Robert, 91
Milton, John: *Paradise Lost*, 13
Mingus, Charlie, 16
Minskoff Theatre, 93
Molière: *The Misanthrope*, 86-87
Monk, Thelonious, 16, 26
Monod, Jacques-Louis, x, 52, 71, 77, 86; *Cantus Contra Cantum*, 71
Monteverdi, Claudio, 55; *The Coronation of Poppea*, 38
Morello, Joe, 6
Morley, Thomas, 19
Morris, Frank, 21
Morton, Jelly Roll, 92, 94
Moussorgsky, Modest, 51
Mozart, Wolfgang Amadeus, 71; Concerto for two pianos (K. 365), 171; *The Marriage of Figaro*, 33; Piano Concerto in A Major, 32; Piano Concerto in C Minor (K. 491), 20-21; Piano Concerto in E flat (K. 449), 143; Piano Sonata in B flat major,

20; Requiem, 19; Symphony No. 40, 18, 22
Murray, Natalia, 40
Music from Salem, 169
Music Teacher, The: opera commissioned by Papp, 106-8, 174; sexuality in, 107
My Dinner with André (film), 95-97; author as composer for, 95, 96-97, 104

Neuman, Maxine, 110, 169, 176, 182; as cellist, 90, 120, 123, 125, 134-35, 137, 140, 143, 144, 150, 151, 160
New Calliope Singers, 86
New York Shakespeare Festival, 109, 115
New Yorker, The: under S. I. Newhouse, 116-17; William Shawn as editor-in-chief of, 4, 117
Newhouse, S. I.: and purchase of *The New Yorker*, 116-17
Newlin, Dika, 159
"Nobody Knows the Trouble I've Seen," 9
Noland, Ken, 157
Norell, Judith, 94
Nowak, Alison, 66, 67, 68-69, 73, 77, 109
Nowak, Lionel, 109, 110, 111, 118, 123, 132, 152; author's connection with, 118-19; and memorial for George Finckel, 126; as pianist, 119; retirement of, 146-47; seventy-fifth birthday celebration for, 124; works composed for him (*The Right Hand Path*), 147
Nyman, Michael, 115, 127

Odets, Clifford: *Night Music*, 111, 112
Olan, David, 66, 67, 68-69, 73, 77, 82
Oliver, Edith, 12
Oppens, Ursula, 31, 74, 91, 92, 162-63

Orloff, Penny, 108, 163
Overton, Hall, 124

Pace, Roberto, 108
Papp, Joseph: and commission to produce a music theatre work, 106, 108; as director of *Hamlet*, 102-3; as director of *Measure for Measure*, 115; "ten-minute musicals" commissioned by, 111-12; and tensions with author, 87, 125
Paris, France: author's studies and experiences in, 47-57
Parke, Nathaniel, 179, 180
Parker, William, 124
Parloff, Michael, 130
Patchen, Kenneth, 148
Pearthree, Pippa, 102
Penderecki, Krzysztof, 56; Capriccio for Violin and Orchestra, 41
Perkins, John MacIvor, 32
Perón, Evita, 111
Persichetti, Dorothy Flanagan, 29
Persichetti, Vincent, 10, 22, 61, 64, 119, 143; as influence on author's music, 29
Petit, Pierre, 140, 171; as author's teacher in Paris, x, 54-56, 57, 77
Petrassi, Goffredo, 46
Piazzolla, Astor, 135
Picasso, Jacqueline, 129
Picasso, Maya, 129
Picasso, Pablo, 129
Picker, Tobias, 154, 162; Rhapsody, 90, 93-94
Pine, Margaret, 86-87, 90
Pirates of Penzance (Gilbert and Sullivan): author's involvement with, 92-93, 95, 97
Piston, Walter, 10, 19, 34; Fourth Symphony, 11
Place Lili Boulanger, 140
Pompidou, Georges, 62
Porter, Cole, 5
Porter, Quincy, 64

Poulenc, Francis, 49, 65, 73, 135, 142
Powell, Adam Clayton, Jr., 111
Presley, Elvis: "Blue Suede Shoes," 6-7; "You Ain't Nothin' But a Hound Dog," 7
Prokofiev, Sergei, 11; Piano Concerto no. 3, 15; Sonata no. 2 in D Minor, 9
Psalm 100, 78
Public Theater (New York): and author and Wally's commission for, 106-108; *Twelve Dreams* at, 98-99
Pugno, Raoul: as Nadia Boulanger's romantic interest, 56-57; *La Ville Morte*, 57
Purcell, Henry: "In These Delightful Pleasant Groves," 19
Putney School: author as student at, 16, 18-21

Quan, Linda, 91

Rachmaninoff, Sergei, 142
Randich, Jean, 182
Ravel, Maurice: *Le Tombeau de Couperin*, 55
Rees, Sue, 182
Reich, Steve, 95, 99
Reinhardt, Django, 96
Rich, Buddy, 6
Richter, Sviatoslav, 11
Rieser, Leonard, 26
Riesman, Michael, 33
Riley, Dennis, 67-68; String Trio, 68
Robbins, Channing, 14, 15, 16
Robbins, Rena, 14
Robison, Paula, 62
Rochester Philharmonic Orchestra, 181
Rockwell, John, 94
Rodgers, Richard, 5, 7
Roeper, Karen, 21
Ronstadt, Linda, 92, 98, 113
Rosen, Nathaniel, 103-5, 181

Ross, Erik, 145

Ross, Lillian, 28, 129; and book about her relationship with William Shawn, 160; William Shawn's relationship with, 12, 144-46

Rothstein, Edward, 94

Ruggles, Carl: *Angels*, 59; *Evocations*, 59; *Men and Mountains*, 59; *Portals*, 59

Rush, Deborah, 87, 101, 102

Rutgers Symphony, 181

Rzewski, Frederic, 95, 108; *The People United Will Never Be Defeated!*, 91

Sage City Symphony, 3, 113, 171

Sahr, Hadassah, 26, 94

Sakutarō, Hagiwara, 179

Salinger, Claire, 27

Salinger, J. D. (Jerry), 69; author's visits to the home of, 26-27; film library of, 26; as friend of the Shawn family, x, 23-24, 74-75, 146; "Hapworth 16, 1924," 23; *Seymour: An Introduction*, 23, 24

Salinger, Matthew, 27

Salinger, Peggy, 27

Sandburg, Carl, 27

Sandor, Gluck, 118

Saroyan, William: *The Human Comedy*, 111

Satie, Erik: *Gymnopédie* no. 1, 96, 97

Saudek, Robert, 11

Saunders, Catherine, 149

Saunders, Helen, 149

Scarlatti, Domenico, 157-58

Schachter, Carl, 37, 52, 59, 63, 66-67

Schell, Jonathan, 36, 37, 128-29, 135-36; *The Fate of the Earth*, 100; *The Village of Ben Suc*, 43

Schirmer, E. C. (music publisher), 137

Schnittke, Alfred, 157

Schoenberg, Arnold, 39, 42, 56, 65, 142; *Accompaniment to a Film Scene*, 22; author's book about, 159-60, 170; *Erwartung*, 164; *Five Pieces for Orchestra*, 159; *Gurre-Lieder*, 182; as influence on author's music, 160, 182; *Kol Nidre*, 161; *Modern Psalm*, 161; *Moses und Aron*, 35, 161; Phantasy, 89; *Pierrot Lunaire*, 114, 158; *Sechs Kleine Klavierstücke*, op. 19, 8-9, 10, 92; and Stravinsky, 159; Suite, op. 29, 41; *Verklärte Nacht*, 159; *Von Heute auf Morgen*, 74

Schonbeck, Gunnar, 120

Schorr, Joseph, 126

Schubert, Franz: *Ave Maria*, 98; *Wanderer Fantasy*, 51

Schubert, Peter, 86

Schuller, Gunther, 98, 111, 147; as conductor, 35, 114; *The Visitation*, 34

Schuman, William, 10, 63, 72

Schumann, Robert: A Minor Concerto, 9; Fantasie, 51

Sears, Freida, 176

Seeger, Charles, 14, 62

Seeger, Elizabeth, 62;

Seeger, John, 14

Seeger, Pete, 14, 62

Seeger, Ruth Crawford, 14, 27, 62

Seidel, Frederick, 128, 140, 171; songs on poems by, 137, 138

Seki, Kanako, 177

Sellars, Peter, 38

Serkin, Judy, 161, 180

Sessions, Roger, 39, 43, 95, 178; on Leonard Bernstein, 64

Shakespeare, William: *Hamlet*, 102; *Henry V*, 112; *Measure for Measure*, 115; *A Midsummer Night's Dream*, 101-2; *The Tempest* 14

Shapiro, Leo, 87

Shawn, Allen: as actor, 61-62; in Atlanta to attend performance of his work, 131; as author of book about phobias, 171-73; baseball as interest of, 17; books by, xi, 159-60, 170, 171-73; at Bennington College, 110, 116-17, 151-52, 153-55; and the borderline between tonal and non-tonal, 8-9; and Nadia Boulanger, 47-57; childhood of, x; as clarinet player, 18; and collaboration with Wally, 74, 106-8; commissions received by, 180; on composing, ix, 4, 25, 65-66, 69-74, 115-16, 126, 128-30, 155-56, 169-70, 173-75, 180, 182; as composition teacher, 62-63; at Dalton School, 14-15; depression experienced by, 131-32; and divergent views on contemporary music, 41-42; and diverse sides as manifested in compositions, 138-39; and divorce as painful experience, 169; early compositions by, 4, 5-6, 10, 13-14, 15-16, 27-28; early influences on, 8-11, 29-30, 103; early interest in music, 6-7; early performances of pieces by, 23; on folk music as the source of all other music, 179; health issues experienced by, 176; height of, 85; and his father's relationship with Lillian Ross, 145-46, 161; honors and awards given to, 59, 141, 156-57; Jewish heritage as inspiration for compositions by, 161-62; later influences on, 94, 155, 159, 160, 163; on the loss of close friends, 176; and loss of his voice, 131-32; at the march on Washington (1969), 43-44; with Marina in Paris, 49; and marriage to Jamaica Kincaid,

84, 85-86, 164-65; and marriage to Yoshiko, 171, 176-77; and Mary's absence, x, 6, 84-85; on music and spoken narration, 148-49; on music as self-expression, 173-74; his parents' encouragement regarding his compositions, 16; in Paris, 47-57; phobias as experienced by, xi, 50, 53, 86, 93, 121, 141, 170-71; popular music enjoyed by, 24; publication of works by, 102, 112; and puppet shows with Wally, 12-13, 40; reflection and introspection by, 141-42; reviews of works by, 25, 74, 83; on sabbatical in Europe, 139-40; Stravinsky as influence on, 34-36, 37, 40, 88, 103; as student at Harvard, 32-45; as teacher, 58, 62-63, 116-17; *Twin*, xi, xii, 176-77; *Wish I Could Be There*, xi, xii. *See also* Bennington College

Shawn, Allen, compositions by: *Agnus Dei*, 129-30; *Alleluia*, 129-30; *Ancestors*, 161-62; *And In The Air, These Sounds*, 163, 169; *Autumnal Song*, 113; *Bells*, 55, 163; *Blues and Boogie*, 140; *Bluesdream*, 163; *Cabaret Music*, 81-83, 89, 90, 91, 100, 102, 103, 110, 132; *Candles*, 161; *Cello Notebook*, 179; *Childhood Scenes*, 171; Clarinet Trio, 137, 142; Concertino for flute and strings, 130, 137, 138; *Concerto for Clarinet and Cello*, 103-5, 110; *Concerto for Clarinet, Cello, and Orchestra*, 116; Concertos for Violin and Oboe, 181; "Contrapuntal Waltz," 163; "Cross Porpoises," 181-82; *Dance Music for Two Harpsichords*, 115, 138; *Dark Song*, 169; *Desire*, 59-60, 68;

Dialogue, 111, 112; Divertimento for clarinet and piano, 128, 139; *Dreamscape*, 156, 157; *The Dying Accordion Player*, 4; *Eclogue*, 133, 134, 138, 142; *Elixir*, 157, 165; *Episodes*, 150-51, 163; Essay for Orchestra, 22, 28; *Essercizio*, 157, 160; Études, 179-80; *Evening Songs*, 24, 34; Fantasy for Flute and Piano, 76, 90; Fantasy for Orchestra, 22, 25, 28, 130; *The Fisherman's Song*, 164; *Five A.M. Blues*, 55; *Five Pieces* for two pianos, 163, 177; Five Preludes, 157; *Found a Peanut*, 134; *Four Jazz Preludes*, 94, 102, 103, 105, 160, 177; Frost Cantata, 140-41, 157, 164; "Gloria," 45; *Growl*, 158; *H and G*, 182; Hide Not Thy Face from Me, 161, 162; *Humoresque*, 129; *Improvisation* no. 3, 112; improvisations, 181-82; *In Memory Of*, 175; *In the Dark*, 74, 174; "In the Tuileries Gardens," 150; *Jazz Suite*, 76-77, 84, 90, 91, 93; *Jeté*, 110; *The Kiss Refused*, 42, 83; *Letter to a Friend*, 157; *Marsch*, 36, 37; *Measure for Measure*, 115; *A Midsummer Night's* Dream, 101-2; *Movements for Violin and Piano*, 90, 91; *Music for flute, clarinet, and piano*, 149; *The Music Teacher*, 74, 140, 163, 174; *Music, When Soft Voices Die*, 86; *Night Music*, 126; *Nine Pieces*, 108, 138, 139; *Nocturnes*, 89, 93, 98, 102, 110, 136, 137; *Non Pasquale*, 109, 110, 111; *Nostalgic Pieces*, 177; *Older Brother*, 15, 16, 89; *Overture to a Ball Game*, 17, 22, 24; Partita for Oboe and Piano, 103, 129, 134, 138; Piano Concerto, 92; Piano Elegies, 177; Piano Sonata No. 1, 99-101, 116, 138;

Piano Sonata No. 2, 177; Piano Sonata No. 3, 177; Piano Sonata No. 4, 177, 179; Piano Sonata No. 5, 179; Piano Sonata No. 6, 177, 182; Piano Sonata No. 7, 182; Piano Sonata No. 8, 182; Piano Sonatina, 73, 116, 126, 138, 139; Piano Trio, 144, 149; "Piece for Miss Dillon," 10; *Prelude*, 54, 55; *Recollections*, 161; *Remember?*, 160, 163; *Romances* for Violin and Piano, 157; Rondo for Orchestra, 22; Sextet for Piano and Winds, 24, 140, 162; *Six Miniatures*, 132; *Sleepless Night*, 157; *Song of the Tango Bird*, 157; *Spring Breeze*, 55; String Quartet No. 2, 63-64, 66, 68, 95, 102, 136, 138; String Quartet No. 4, 169; *Suite for Cello Quartet*, 134-35, 136, 155; *Suite Parisienne*, 150, 163; *Summer Pages*, 94-95, 102; Symphony in Three Parts, 130, 131, 136; *Tango*, 129, 146; *Terpsichord*, 146; Theme and Variations, 59; *Three Animals*, 37, 136; *Three Dance Portraits*, 156; *Three Latin American Dances*, 108, 156; *Three Nightscapes*, 175; *Three Reveries*, 146; *Three Pieces in Memory of Louis Calabro*, 144; *Three Songs for Flute and Piano*, 126, 138, 139; *Twelve Dreams*, 88, 98-99, 102; *Two Improvisations*, 93-94; *Two Night Pieces*, 133, 134; *Valentine*, 112-13, 116, 160; Wind Quintet, 114, 127, 136; Wind Quintet no. 2, 164; *Winter Sketchbook*, 137, 142
Shawn, Annie, 139; birth of, 113
Shawn, Cecille Lyon, x; death of, 174; illness of, 145, 174; and William Shawn's relationship with Lillian Ross, 144-45
Shawn, Harold: birth of, 134

Shawn, Mary, xi, 29; as author's twin, 6, 84-85, 173; as intellectually disabled, x, 6; as the subject of *Twin*, x, xii

Shawn, Noa, 171, 177

Shawn, Wallace (Wally), x, 6; and collaboration with author, 74, 106-8; *In the Dark*, 74, 174; and his father's relationship with Lillian Ross, 145-46; "Loping Dogs and the Tiles of Time," 10; *The Music Teacher*, 74, 140, 163, 174; and *My Dinner with André*, 95-97; *Our Late Night*, 96; and puppet shows with author, 12-13, 31; Salinger's comment on plays by, 75; as student at Harvard, 30; as violinist, 25, 31, 182; as writer, 75, 84

Shawn, William, 39; as composer, 118; death of, 147; and departure from *The New Yorker*, 128-29; as editor-in-chief of *The New Yorker*, 4; heart attack suffered by, 53; illness of, 144-46; as jazz pianist, x, 4-5; and his relationship with Lillian Ross, 12, 144-46; in *Wish I Could Be There*, xii

Shelley, Percy Bysshe, 86

Sherman, Betsy, 172

Sherry, Fred, 62

Shostakovich, Dmitri, 45, 71, 133, 142; First Cello Concerto, 143

Siebert, Renée, 94

Siegel, Stephen, 154, 176

Silverman, Stanley, 61, 62, 89

Smiley, Pril, 88

Smith, Craig, 38

Smith, Elizabeth, 7

Smith, Linda Catlin, 62-63, 68, 146

Smith, Rex, 92

Sollberger, Harvey, 67, 76, 90-91, 148

Son, Yung Wha, 154

Sondheim, Stephen: author's visit with, 99; *Sunday in the Park with George*, 88, 99

Sontag, Susan, 114-15, 127

Sorel, Felicia, 118

Sosin, Donald, 68, 73

Sperry, Paul, 108

Spitz, Jonathan, 181

Starting Over (film): Wally's role in, 77

Stearns, Peter Pindar, 59, 63

Steig, William, 23

Steinbeck, John, 164

Stockhausen, Karlheinz, 71, 78; *Mantra*, 70; Sonatine, 126

Straus, Roger: and author's book on Schoenberg, 158-60

Stravinsky, Igor, 7, 15, 62, 150, 179; *Agon*, 36; *Apollo*, 30, 53; on composing, 91; Concerto for Piano and Winds, 24, 30; *Concerto for Two Pianos*, 133; Concerto in E flat (*Dumbarton Oaks*), 34, 37; *Danses Concertantes*, 36; death of, 53; *Duo Concertant*, 22, 74; "Easy Pieces," 22; *Ebony Concerto*, 104; *The Flood*, 30; Huxley Variations, 35; as influence on author's music, 35-36, 37, 40, 88, 103; *Jeu de Cartes*, 36; *Le Baiser de la Fée*, 129; *Le Rossignol*, 35; *Le Sacre du printemps*, 4, 11, 22, 108; *L'Histoire du Soldat*, 68; Mass, 36, 51; Monod on, 71; *Movements*, 36; *Oedipus Rex*, 35, 103; *Orpheus*, 36; *The Owl and the Pussycat*, 35; *Petrushka*, 7; *Pulcinella*, 36, 103, 129; *Ragtime for Eleven Instruments*, 30; *The Rake's Progress*, 34, 36, 40, 42, 60, 103; *Requiem Canticles*, 35, 48; and Schoenberg, 159; Symphonies of Wind Instruments, 53; Symphony in Three Movements, 30, 36; Symphony of Psalms, 30, 105; *Themes and Episodes*, 34; Violin Concerto in D, 22

Street, Tison, 33

Strenger, Sandy, 74
Strozzi, Barbara, 154
Sullivan, Arthur, 92
Sun Ra, 124
Suskind, Joyce, 81
Swados, Elizabeth, 115, 127

Tailleferre, Germaine: *Jeux de Plein Air*, 133
Takemitsu, Tōru, 65, 170
Tamarkin, Kate, 164, 165
Tan, Su Lian, 146
Tatum, Art, 16, 94
Taylor, Cecil, 124
Taylor-Corbett, Lynne, 126, 130
Tchaikovsky, Pyotr Ilyich: *Swan Lake*, 7
Tcherepnin, Ivan, 33
Telson, Bob, 32
Tempest, The (Shakespeare): author as Ariel in, 14
Tenney, Sarah, 180
Theatre of the Open Eye, 88
Thomas, Ambroise, 53
Thomas, Augusta Read, 141
Thompson, Randall, 19
Thorne, Francis, 73
Thorne, Gordon, 180
Tovey, Donald, 18
Tower, Joan, 91
Trakl, Georg, 179
Trampler, Walter, 62
Troob, Danny, 32
Trowbridge, Gus, 14
Trulove, Anne, 40
twelve-tone method: author's interest in, 22, 35, 36; as applied in author's compositions, 73, 76, 150; as applied by Schoenberg, 158, 159; Bernstein's use of, 178; and Lou Calabro's pieces, 143; and Kirchner's compositions, 43

Updike, David, 39
Updike, John, x, 156-57, 173; author's friendship with, 38-39

Ussachevsky, Vladimir, 76-77

Valéry, Paul, 69; *Mon Faust*, 53
Varèse, Edgard, 15, 69, 70, 142; *Ionisation*, 71
Varga, Bálint András, 182; *The Courage of Composers and the Tyranny of Taste*, 180-81
Vaughan Williams, Ralph, 18
Venora, Diane, 102
Vermont Contemporary Music Ensemble, 146, 169, 180
Vermont Philharmonic, 25
Vermont Symphony Orchestra, 137, 165
Vietnam War: music inspired by the social upheaval relating to, 43-44
Vitercik, Greg, 56
Vittoria, Tomás Luis de, 19
Vosgerchian, Luise, 32, 36, 40, 43, 46

Wagner, Richard: *Götterdämmerung*, 64
Walcott, Derek, 164; *Under the Bam, Under the Bomb, Under the Ban-the-Bomb Tree*, 111-12, 164
Wald, George, 38
Ward, Robert: *The Crucible* (opera), 113-14
Ward, Tim, 113
Waters, Susannah, 128
Waxman, Donald, 102, 131; on author's compositions, 137-38
Weber, Bruce, 172
Webern, Anton, 15, 35, 39; *Six Bagatelles*, 20
Weelkes, Thomas, 19
Weill, Kurt, 74
Weisman, Londa, 180
Wen-chung, Chou, 69
West, Nathanael, 148
White, E. B., 28, 69
White, Robert, 38
Wilbye, John: "Adieu, Sweet Amaryllis," 19

Wilder, Alec, 34; advice to author on composing, 28-29
Williams, Amy, 140, 154, 158, 163
Wilson, Robert, 75
Wolpe, Stefan, 74
Wright, Elizabeth, 120, 123, 133, 144, 149, 151, 157
Wuorinen, Charles, 69, 95; *Arabia Felix*, 66-67; Flute Variations, 67; *Glogauer Liederbuch*, 67

Xenakis, Iannis, 56

Yoshiko (Y.): author's meeting and marriage to, 171, 176-77; as pianist, 171
Young People's Concerts: as conducted by Bernstein, 178

Zen Buddhism: Salinger's interest in, 26, 27